CYBER MERCENARIES

Cyber Mercenaries explores the secretive relationships between states and hackers. As cyberspace has emerged as the new frontier for geopolitics, states have become entrepreneurial in their sponsorship, deployment, and exploitation of hackers as proxies to project power. Such modern-day mercenaries and privateers can impose significant harm undermining global security, stability, and human rights. These state-hacker relationships therefore raise important questions about the control, authority, and use of offensive cyber capabilities. While different countries pursue different models for their proxy relationships, they face the common challenge of balancing the benefits of these relationships with their costs and the potential risks of escalation. This book examines case studies in the United States, Iran, Syria, Russia, and China for the purpose of establishing a framework to better understand and manage the impact and risks of cyber proxies on global politics.

Tim Maurer co-directs the Cyber Policy Initiative at the Carnegie Endowment for International Peace. He is a member of several US track 1.5 cyber dialogues and the Freedom Online Coalition's cybersecurity working group. He co-chaired the Advisory Board of the 2015 Global Conference on CyberSpace, participated in the Global Commission on Internet Governance, and supported the confidence-building work of the OSCE. His work has been published by *Foreign Policy*, *The Washington Post*, *TIME*, *Jane's Intelligence Review*, *CNN*, *Slate*, *Lawfare*, and other academic and media venues. He holds a Master's in Public Policy from the Harvard Kennedy School.

Cyber Mercenaries

THE STATE, HACKERS, AND POWER

TIM MAURER

Carnegie Endowment for International Peace

CAMBRIDGE
UNIVERSITY PRESS

University Printing House, Cambridge CB2 8BS, United Kingdom

One Liberty Plaza, 20th Floor, New York, NY 10006, USA

477 Williamstown Road, Port Melbourne, VIC 3207, Australia

314-321, 3rd Floor, Plot 3, Splendor Forum, Jasola District Centre, New Delhi - 110025, India

79 Anson Road, #06-04/06, Singapore 079906

Cambridge University Press is part of the University of Cambridge.

It furthers the University's mission by disseminating knowledge in the pursuit of education, learning and research at the highest international levels of excellence.

www.cambridge.org
Information on this title: www.cambridge.org/9781107566866
DOI: 10.1017/9781316422724

First published 2018

A catalogue record for this publication is available from the British Library

ISBN 978-1-107-12760-9 Hardback
ISBN 978-1-107-56686-6 Paperback

Contents

Figures

Preface

At first glance, Kiev in the summer of 2015 seemed like an odd place to investigate the relationship between hackers and the state. It was a beautiful July weekend and people were out on the streets and in the parks. You could hardly tell that the country was at war. Not the old kind of war, the one with a declaration of war and soldiers in uniform. This was a war of the twenty-first century, where "little green men," as the locals called the unmarked foreign agents, had appeared in the country to exploit local tensions and to escalate them into a bigger conflict.[1] Over a year had passed since the eastern part of Ukraine had fallen into the hands of pro-Russian fighters, but the capital was relatively peaceful except for occasional violence, such as the deadly clashes in front of parliament that occurred in between my two research trips to Kiev.[2] Nevertheless, the situation felt a bit surreal when I arrived at what looked like an old industrial complex a few miles south of the center of town to meet Eugene Dokukin, the self-declared commander of the Ukrainian Cyber Forces, one of Ukraine's most prominent hacktivist groups.[3] In contrast to the pro-Russian fighters in eastern Ukraine, who were an old kind of proxy, Dokukin and his cadre of followers were a new kind of proxy, adding a new dimension to an already intricate conflict.

Originally, my plan was to meet Mr Dokukin at a café near my hotel in central Kiev. However, a few days prior to our planned meeting, he changed his mind. He said that he had been planning to go to a classical concert and suggested we meet there instead. Based on our previous exchanges online, it seemed probable that he would cancel if I did not accept his change of plans, so I ventured to the location he provided. What looked like an old industrial complex turned out to be the historical Dovzhenko Film Studios, created in 1928 and named after one of the most important Ukrainian filmmakers, Alexander Dovzhenko.[4] Once I had found my way through the maze of old buildings, I eventually got to an amphitheater of sorts where some

I thank the Cooperative Cyber Defence Centre of Excellence for granting permission to include material in this section from Tim Maurer, "Cyber Proxies and the Crisis in Ukraine," in *Cyber War in Perspective: Russian Aggression against Ukraine*, ed. Kenneth Geers, (Tallinn: NATO CCD COE Publications, 2015), available at https://ccdcoe.org/multimedia/cyber-war-perspective-russian-aggression-against-ukraine.html.

200 people, mostly families, had gathered to listen to classical music in the afternoon sun. After watching this scene at the birthplace of Ukrainian cinema for several minutes, I noticed a man making a movie of a more modern sort – standing with his back turned to the orchestra, he held an iPod in his hand, recording me on video as he passed by. A text message a few minutes later confirmed my suspicion that it was Dokukin. We spent the next hour walking in circles around the concert site with the classical music playing in the background, while Dokukin explained why he decided to form the Ukrainian Cyber Forces a year earlier, how they were structured, and his relationship with the government.

The 32-year-old Dokukin shared with me how he had used social media to start recruiting a group of (unpaid) volunteers angered by the Kremlin's aggressive actions. Over the previous months, their number had fluctuated from several dozens to a few hundred, and primarily included ordinary people without a technical background. They were based not only in Ukraine but also abroad – for example in Germany and the UK, highlighting the transnational character of many of these hacktivist groups.[5] Together, they carried out a series of activities, ranging from the unauthorized monitoring of CCTV cameras and troop movements in eastern Ukraine, to reporting separatist activities to Web companies such as PayPal in an effort to shut down the separatists' accounts, to launching distributed denial of service (DDoS) attacks against websites and leaking sensitive documents from the Russian Ministry of the Interior that revealed details about separatists in eastern Ukraine being paid by Russian authorities.[6]

Dokukin shared information about the group's actions with the media and the government, but there was no evidence that the government coordinated with or supported him financially or otherwise.[7] Dokukin told another interviewer that the Ukrainian Cyber Forces work independently, unlike Russian hackers with ties to the Russian FSB (the Russian Federal Security Service, the successor organization to the KGB).[8] The Ukrainian security services were certainly aware of the group's activities given Dokukin's media interviews.[9] And while the government could interfere and stop Dokukin's and the group's activities, it was turning a blind eye instead.

Why did I become interested in proxy actors in the first place? When I started working on this book in 2013, the debate over whether there could be a cyber war was in full swing.[10] But there was something puzzling: the debate was state-centric, while the media was full of reports about the significant role non-state actors play in this field, including private companies such as Gamma International and Vupen, hacktivist groups from Anonymous to the Syrian Electronic Army, and cyber criminals operating with impunity from different hotspots around the world.[11] These reports were telling a different story in the shadow of the debate about whether cyber war will or will not take place, a story in which non-state actors have become increasingly active in cyberspace. States are only one subset of a larger group of actors with significant offensive cyber capabilities.[12] In fact, the US Secret

Service agent Ari Baranoff stated in 2014 that "Many of the [non-state] actors that we look at on a daily and weekly basis have capabilities that actually exceed the capabilities of most nation-states."[3]

I became particularly interested in the capabilities of these actors and the dynamic relationship between them and the state in peacetime, in wartime, and in the increasingly blurry space in between. How have these new global coercive cyber capabilities become organized?[14] How do states use actors detached from the state to project power? And how do states that aspire to a monopoly over the legitimate use of force pursue these efforts in the context of offensive cyber operations? Looking back, my conversation with Dokukin was more than a bit surreal. Yet it was similar to other stories I experienced during the three-year research for this book, which took me to more than a dozen countries around the world, including China, South Korea, Mongolia, India, Israel, France, and the United States.

Between the origin of this book and its release, a lot has changed. The last twelve months alone have been full of noteworthy events that have raised greater awareness of this dynamic field generally and of proxies specifically. In March 2016, the US government unsealed two indictments against seven Iranian hackers and three members of the Syrian Electronic Army with details about their relationship to the Iranian and Syrian governments respectively.[15] A year later, another indictment shed light on the relationship between the FSB and hackers in Russia.[16] Meanwhile, in May 2016, US Cyber Command awarded a contract of USD 460 million to six private security companies that included assisting with offensive cyber operations.[17] In China, the government has been actively supporting cyber militias at universities and companies during the past several years.[18] A member of Russia's State Duma has openly acknowledged that the Nashi youth movement was mobilized to support the DDoS attack that flooded and crashed the websites of the Estonian government in 2007.[19] A hacker in a Colombian prison boasted in an interview with *Bloomberg Businessweek* that he had been hired by political campaigns in various Latin American countries,[20] and the hack of the Italy-based company Hacking Team shed light on a globalized market of cyber capabilities.[21]

These examples not only illustrate how states outsource certain functions to non-state agents but also shed light on the much murkier reality in which states cultivate loose relationships with actors that are not formally part of the state, yet work to its benefit. This is an under-appreciated phenomenon. To capture this reality and to compare states' behavior globally, the concept of proxy relationships is useful. I define *cyber proxies* as intermediaries that conduct or directly contribute to an offensive cyber action that is enabled knowingly, whether actively or passively, by a beneficiary. This broad definition covers the phenomenon of states committing to support specific proxies as well as states omitting to take certain actions and turning a blind eye to a non-state actor's malicious actions.[22] Most states will use a variety of proxies with differing relationships, so the focus of this book is rather on a state's broader *modus operandi* and the organization of proxy relationships generally.

I argue that projecting coercive power through cyberspace is not only a state-centric affair but often a dynamic interplay between the state and actors detached from the state. This raises important questions over control, authority, and the legitimacy of the use of cyber capabilities. For example, states use these proxies for a wide variety of purposes not limited to projecting power abroad; in both Russia and Iran, reports about government-supported hackers targeting dissidents predate reports about such proxies hitting targets abroad. Moreover, states' proxy relationships range across a spectrum: from delegation to orchestration and sanctioning. *Delegation* describes proxies held on a tight state leash and under the state's effective control. *Orchestration* applies to proxies on a looser leash with the state but usually sharing strong ideational bonds with the state and receiving funding or tools. And the concept of *sanctioning* (approving or permitting) builds on the concept of "passive support" developed by counterterrorism scholars to describe situations where a state is aware of the activity of a non-state actor but turns a blind eye towards it and indirectly benefits from its actions. Nevertheless, while countries pursue different models for proxy relationships and have different doctrines for the use of coercive cyber power, they also face a common challenge and have an interest in balancing the benefits of proxy relationships with the cost and increased risk of escalation.

What I learned in Ukraine was also remarkable for another reason. My questions focused on offensive cyber operations and their role in the conflict in Ukraine, namely those targeting critical infrastructure. Yet, in most interviews, the conversation would quickly turn away from these type of actions; interviewees seemed less concerned about the impact of cyber operations on the military outcome and much more concerned about the impact of information operations on the broader political outcome. In view of the Russian operation targeting the 2016 US presidential election, the Ukrainians were clearly ahead of their time. I left Ukraine with answers to some of my original research questions but also with new questions and an increasingly gnawing concern. What if the focus on the military dimension of offensive cyber operations and the long discussion about cyber war obscured other potential ways in which international stability can be and is being undermined through offensive cyber operations? Why focus on the use of offensive cyber operations during a military conflict if cyber capabilities can be used to help empower politicians that would make such an escalation less likely? This implies that the relevance of proxies lies not only in their ability to cause harm but also in their ability to wield power more broadly.

Some of my conversations with experts helped crystallize the multiple dimensions of cyber capabilities. In May 2016, a Google employee and I discussed the changing media landscape, how some governments actively plant false information, and what this means for companies like Google. When I mentioned my research and what I had learned about Dokukin and his volunteers, the Google employee's immediate reaction was that these were "the kind of grass roots actors that are needed to counter government-sponsored information operations."[23] Through his lens, Dokukin was essentially an important guardian for the media and of the effort to present a verifiable truth in the face of intentionally spread false information and rumors. Others, including Dokukin himself, saw the Ukrainian cyber forces through more of a militaristic lens. It is reminiscent of the famous story of the group of blind men touching an elephant to understand what it is but each only touching a single part.

These different perspectives are an important reminder of how much terminology matters in this field. Activities funded through the US State Department's "Internet Freedom" program are labeled "cyber terrorism" by Iran's communications minister. What Russia and China view as information "threats" are considered content and a protected human right in many other countries. This explains why international cybersecurity negotiations are indirectly also a battle over human rights. Or, to use a historical analogy, whereas the negotiations for the landmark 1975 Helsinki Accords had a track focusing on security and one focusing on human rights,[24] today's cybersecurity negotiations essentially combine these two baskets, and some states are unwilling to separate them.[25] These different perspectives shape which actors are perceived as proxies and also pose conceptual challenges and special escalatory risks. Since, analytically, I strive to incorporate global perspectives, my discussion of proxies' activities and their political effects is broader in scope than that of other scholars[26] and not limited to proxy actors causing disruptive and destructive effects. At the same time, I reject some governments' implied moral equivalency that leads them, for example, to equate expressing public support for a peaceful protest in another country with using an aggressive influence operation against that state.

This book stands on the shoulders of giants in numerous different fields; the literature ranges from international relations to international law, communications studies, and the still-nascent cybersecurity scholarship spread across different academic disciplines. I also reviewed reports from nontraditional sources, including reports by cybersecurity companies and nonprofit organizations such as the Citizen Lab. Corporate reports come with obvious additional risks regarding quality, bias, and verifiability. Their inclusion therefore depended on technical details, considerations of possible alternative explanations, and vetting by other experts. Some new data is included based on qualitative, semi-structured expert interviews. Given significant data limitations, I rely on historical narrative and an illustrative case study approach. In my view, there is simply not enough data publicly available to date to allow for robust, comparative quantitative analyses testing hypotheses across countries. The phenomenon of cyber proxies is still relatively new, usually hidden behind a shroud of secrecy, and information is often shared only off the record. I therefore focus on developing a framework for analyzing cyber proxies that will inform future empirical research and allow for the study of changes over time. When analyses of the same incident contradict each other, as in the case of the Georgian-Russian war in 2008, I present what I consider to be the most accurate account based on my analysis of the literature and interviews. In light of the pace at which this field is changing and new literature published, it is also worth mentioning that I only include publications available as of November 2016, when the manuscript was submitted for review (with the exception, in light of their importance, of the indictment of the Russian nationals by the US government and the information about Guccifer 2.0 that became available between the submission and publication).

I hope this book will reach several audiences. There is a growing demand from academia, with a proliferating number of courses, and even degree programs, now dedicated to the Internet and cybersecurity. There also remains a significant gap in the international relations context between traditional concepts and the study of cyberspace. Professors and students alike will ideally find this publication a useful contribution to their scholarship, syllabi, and thinking. Working at the Carnegie Endowment for International Peace, a global think tank dedicated to informing policy through quality research, I also hope that policymakers will find value in the analysis presented here. The proposed frameworks present tools that may help them think through and structure the world of cyber proxies, its implications, and how to manage it. Last but not least, cybersecurity is no longer an obscure topic that requires alarmist books to raise attention. By Christmas 2014, the geopolitics of cybersecurity had entered people's living rooms when the US president went in front of television cameras to accuse North Korea of hacking Sony and to reassure the American people that there were no secret North Korean sleeper cells waiting to attack moviegoers. So, this book is also written for a general audience that does not follow cybersecurity news on a daily basis but is generally curious.

The first part of this book focuses on the main argument that it is important to focus on proxies as well as states and that proxies are capable of causing significant harm. Chapter 1 explores cyber proxies' power and what their capabilities are likely used for, as well as the implications of the attribution problem, the challenge of attributing a malicious cyber action to its source. The second chapter outlines the analytical frameworks helpful in the study of cyber proxies, including a review of the various manifestations of proxy relationships throughout history, ranging from privateers to Italy's condottieri, satellite states, militias, and spies for hire. It also draws on insights from organizational and institutional theory to discuss the under-lying conditions that allow proxy relationships to exist in the first place. Chapter 3 provides an overview of the geopolitics of cyber power and the different perspectives of Russia, China, Iran, and the United States. These countries are also the focus of case studies in the second part of the book (Chapters 4–7), which describe in detail the different types of proxy relationships. This part underscores the second main argument of the book that how states use cyber proxies is not very different from how states have used conventional proxies. What is new, and is the third main take-away from this book, is the diffusion of reach, which allows state and non-state actors to cause effects remotely across vast distances through offensive cyber operations.

The implications of cyber proxies and how to effectively manage them is the focus of the third and final part of the book. Chapter 8 reviews the utility of international

law and its nuanced distinctions for taking action against malicious activity by
a cyber proxy. Chapter 9 discusses the different approaches for managing proxies
held on a tighter leash as well as those on a loose leash. This is of interest not only for
academic scholarship but also for practitioners and policymakers. Recent arrests of
members of the hacktivist group Anonymous in the United States and Europe, as
well as China's arrests of hackers as part of the government's overall anti-corruption
campaign,[27] illustrate efforts to punish those whose malicious activity is not considered legitimate in the eyes of the state. The US government's recent unsealing of
indictments represents another attempt to create a deterrent effect by exposing and
shaming foreign nations who keep proxies on a looser leash. Finally, Chapter 10
summarizes the findings and conclusions and outlines some suggestions for future
research.

Acknowledgments

Writing a book takes a long time, sometimes longer than the author's time with a single institution. I am therefore particularly grateful to the Carnegie Endowment for International Peace, which I joined in the autumn of 2015, for giving me the time to finish writing it. I still remember the first conversation with my new colleague, Ariel "Eli" Levite, over breakfast and his comment about studying cyberspace not for the sake of studying cyberspace but for what cyberspace can tell us about the changing world writ large, a perspective that's particularly influenced my writing in the final stages of this book. I thank George Perkovich for his support in words and in action that was crucial to get me across the finish line and for inspiring me along the way. A particular gem I have come to treasure at the Carnegie Endowment is its in-house library and its staff, who were tremendously helpful and whose research assistance I have greatly appreciated.

This book would not exist without Peter Bergen, Vice President at New America and Director of its International Security Program. It was his early encouragement at the beginning of 2013 that led me to embark on this adventure. Thank you. I also owe gratitude to New America and its inspiring leader Anne-Marie Slaughter for providing an environment for my project to succeed. I thank Peter Singer for his active support and open door as well as Ian Wallace and Robert Morgus for their team spirit and my former colleagues at New America's Open Technology Institute. John Berger at Cambridge University Press also deserves a special acknowledgment for his belief in this project from the start.

Professor Robert Axelrod and Professor John Ciorciari at the University of Michigan's Gerald R. Ford School of Public Policy provided me with a second home that became a most welcome escape and refuge from the constant buzz and meetings in Washington, DC, especially during the summer of 2016 as I was finishing this book. The regular luncheons with Bob often had me scurrying for a pen or my phone to note down a historical precedent or analogy he mentioned in the midst of a conversation about the latest cyber incident of the day. I am grateful to both for the physical second home and the intellectual community they have provided, which extends to people like Professor Alex Halderman at the University of Michigan's computer science department and its impressive group of PhD students, including Nadiya Kostyuk, Benjamin VanderSloot, and Drew Springall.

I am also indebted intellectually and grateful personally for the mentorship and friendship of a number of people who were sharing their thoughts and advice with me even before this book project started. Professor Joseph Nye, Jr, offered thoughtful feedback on my writings when I first started to focus on this field back in 2010. Professor Martha Finnemore and Professor Duncan Hollis have become particularly important sounding boards growing out of the MIT/Harvard cyber norms community during the past few years. I am particularly indebted to Thorsten Benner, Director of the Global Public Policy Institute, for reasons too numerous to recount here. They all have taken time out of their busy schedules above and beyond what could be expected, and have offered feedback, advice, and criticisms throughout several projects during the past years, including this book.

My thanks also go to Jason Healey at Columbia University's School for International and Public Affairs and the group of scholars that convened for a workshop focusing on proxy actors and cybersecurity in July 2016, who provided me with an opportunity to present my work. Professor Nicholas Tsagourias and Dr. Russell Buchan at the University of Sheffield have my gratitude for inviting me to present at their conference in the autumn of 2015, and for publishing my first article on this subject in Oxford's *Journal for Conflict and Security Law*, alongside a series of articles by international law experts discussing the question of state and individual criminal responsibility and non-state actors in the context of cyberspace. I would also like to thank Kenneth Geers. Not only did he include my short article based on my two research trips to Kiev in his edited volume on cyber operations during the conflict in Ukraine, but he also made the trips so much more enjoyable by sharing his knowledge of the local culture and history.

While I deserve the blame for all errors and inaccuracies in this book, its particularly well written and interesting parts exist thanks to those who reviewed the manuscript and shared their invaluable feedback. These include Martha Finnemore, Duncan Hollis, and Joseph Nye, as well as Matthew Noyes, Max Smeets, Matan Chorev, and George Perkovich. They were all incredibly generous with their time and responses. In addition, I am thankful to Beau Woods, Collin Anderson, Adam Segal, and Nigel Inkster for reviewing specific sections focusing on the capabilities of non-state actors, Iran and China respectively. I owe a particular debt to Isabella Furth and Jonathan Diamond for their assistance with the final manuscript. Finally, I would like to thank the two anonymous reviewers who provided very helpful comments.

Most importantly, I am indebted to the many people who were willing to speak with me as part of the research for this book. During the past three years, I had the privilege of speaking with over four dozen experts from more than a dozen countries on three continents who shared their thoughts, experience, and expertise. Many are referenced in the book by name, others preferred their contributions to be anonymous, and others asked me not to mention them at all. They include white-hat and black-hat hackers as well as former and current officials in the law enforcement and intelligence communities. The list ranges from experts in the private sector, academia, think tanks, and government, as well as computer emergency response teams, security research communities, and journalists. They are what makes this book unique. They helped me separate the wheat from the chaff in the existing literature and often provided additional details and information for this comprehensive account of proxies and cyberspace. Thanks to people like them, publications like this are possible, even on topics that are rather difficult to research.

Last but not least, I would like to thank Eli Sugarman and the William and Flora Hewlett Foundation for having made my research possible. The foundation's Cyber Initiative has become an important source enabling scholars in the United States and abroad to pursue their activities, and the foundation's commitment to general operating support stands out in an increasingly challenging funding environment. Many of the people I have met and interviewed for this book have not remained one-time contacts but have become part of a growing global network of cybersecurity scholars. Additional thanks go to the hosts of the various conferences where I have been invited to speak and participate during the past few years, which often enabled me to add a few more days in the respective country to interview local experts for my book.

Special thanks are reserved for my family and friends who made all of this possible with their support, patience, and understanding. You know who you are and how deeply grateful I am.

Abbreviations

APT	advanced persistent threat
ASEAN	Association of Southeast Asian Nations
CEO	chief executive officer (of a corporation)
CERT	computer emergency response team
CIA	Central Intelligence Agency of the United States
DARPA	Defense Advanced Research Projects Agency (of the United States)
DDoS	distributed denial of service
DoD	Department of Defense (US)
FBI	Federal Bureau of Investigation (of the United States)
FSB	Federal Security Service (of the Russian Federation)
G20	Group of Twenty
G7	Group of Seven
GCHQ	Government Communications Headquarters (of the UK)
GRU	General Staff Main Intelligence Directorate (of the Russian Federation)
ICBM	intercontinental ballistic missile
ICT	information and communications technology
IRA	Irish Republican Army
ISP	Internet service provider
IT	information technology
KGB	Committee for State Security (of the Soviet Union)
MIT	Massachusetts Institute of Technology
NATO	North Atlantic Treaty Organization
NCPH	Network Crack Program Hacker
NGO	non-governmental organization
NSA	National Security Agency (of the United States)
NTRO	National Technical Research Organization (of India)
PLA	People's Liberation Army (of China)
PMC	private military companies
PSC	private security companies
PSMC	private security and military companies

SBU	Security Service of Ukraine
SCADA	supervisory control and data acquisition
SORM	System for Operative Investigative Activities (in Russia)
UN	United Nations
UNGGE	United Nations Group of Governmental Experts
US	United States of America
USD	United States dollars

PART I

Of Brokers and Proxies

1

Cyber Proxies: An Introduction

How societies organize force has intrigued people for centuries. The rise and legitimacy of the modern state itself is tied to the control over coercive capabilities, including those wielded by proxies.[1] As Harvard University professor Joseph Nye reminded an audience in November 2012, "Max Weber did not define the state as having 'the monopoly over the use of force' but 'the monopoly over the *legitimate* use of force.'"[2] This is an important distinction. On paper, the state has become tied to this monopoly, but very few have effectively possessed it. The sociologist Michael Mann even argues that "many have not even claimed it."[3] In other words, the idea of a monopoly over the legitimate use of force is very much linked to the European experience of the emergence of the nation-state and the Westphalian notion of sovereignty that became codified globally after World War II through the Charter of the United Nations (UN). Many countries outside this specific cultural and historical context are better described as brokers than as (aspirational) monopolists.[4] Meanwhile, the nature of the nation-state itself keeps evolving towards what's been called a market-state with increasing and systemic privatization.[5]

Fast forward to the twenty-first century and the new phenomenon of cyberspace. An analysis of how this technology is used to project coercive power and by whom must take Mann's observations into account, especially if the goal is to study this question at a global level. Comparing the proxy relationships in existing cyber powers such as China, Iran, Russia, and the United Sates requires a broader view of the state; it also requires us to revisit distinctions between private and public spheres that are blurred in countries where prebendalism reigns or where communist state structures and the party are still all-pervasive.[6] It also requires contending with Weber's explicit reference to "the legitimate use of *physical* force."[7] While offensive cyber operations can cause physical effects, so far hacking used for political or military purposes has primarily had nonphysical effects. Nonetheless, much of the debate over whether cyber war will take place is focused on the question of force and the likelihood of more than a thousand people dying within a year.[8] At best, this narrow focus ignores the full spectrum of political effects hacking has been used for, as the events in Ukraine and the malicious hacks during the 2016 US elections make clear. At worst, it contributes to a mirror-imaging problem and tunnel vision that prevent a full appreciation of how other countries think about and use these capabilities – with all this implies for crisis prevention, escalatory dynamics, and signaling.

Another important observation to make at the start is that states wanting to project power through cyberspace find themselves in often complex and dynamic relationships with non-state actors. This chapter will therefore explore what non-state actors can be capable of and how they are likely to be used to project cyber power. It will discuss the pool of potential cyber proxies, the case selection for this book, and the attribution problem, and conclude by highlighting the bigger picture.

For the first time, non-state actors can have global reach through hacking, known in the US military bureaucracy's vernacular as "remote offensive cyber operations." Non-state actors can target a third party beyond a state's border with unprecedented ease and at a very low cost compared to conventional weaponry. And the effects can be significant. For example, in February 2016, hackers with alleged ties to North Korea attempted to steal nearly USD 1 billion from the Bangladeshi central bank.[9] If they had fully succeeded, the theft would have amounted to 0.58 percent of Bangladesh's GDP.[10] Attacks on this scale are not unprecedented. In 2015, a single group of cybercriminals stole USD 1 billion from financial institutions worldwide over a period of two years.[11] Moreover, it is clear today that malicious hackers could kill people.[12] Thankfully, not every theoretical possibility becomes reality, but incidents like these demonstrate that it is important to pay attention to these actors, especially when they have relationships with states who might want to use their capabilities and turn theory into practice.

While the Internet was initially a military project to provide a resilient communications network, it is perhaps unique in that the military left its development largely to a few geeks at universities. The military's lack of interest changed when the technology re-emerged out of the obscurity of academic institutions, became commercialized in the mid-1990s, and started to spread around the globe like wildfire. States discovered the Internet's potential not only as a resilient communications network and source for intelligence but also as a platform to project coercive power with an exponentially growing range. Even then, only a handful of states grasped its revolutionary potential and set up structures to take advantage of what would later be declared a new operational domain.[13] Only in 2010, with the front-page public revelations about the Stuxnet malware (reportedly designed by the United States and Israel) damaging centrifuges at the Natanz nuclear enrichment facility in Iran, did most states become aware of the technology's political and military dimension and decide to follow others in its exploitation.

For these reasons, most of the Internet's infrastructure as a global network evolved in private hands, and many of the earliest examples of malicious use are tied to non-state rather than state actors. For example, the first computer emergency response team was established in response to the Morris worm, malware developed by a graduate student, not the malicious activity of a state. The history of cyber conflict itself arguably began with a proxy actor. According to Jason Healey, who edited a book on the topic, the history of cyber conflict "started in earnest in 1986, when German hackers searched through thousands of US computer files and sold their stolen materials to the KGB [the Soviet security agency]."[4] In other words, from the start non-state actors developed offensive cyber capabilities of interest to states and used by states to further the latter's political objectives. And with the dawn of the modern Internet, the pool of non-state actors with such capabilities has been steadily increasing. That is why Alexander Klimburg, director of the Global Commission on the Stability of Cyberspace, has argued that "[t]o create an integrated national capability in cyber power, the non-state sector must be induced to cooperate with government."[5]

Several normative issues cannot be ignored when discussing cyber proxies. Efforts encouraging states to pursue a monopoly over the legitimate use of force, for example, have an obvious normative undercurrent. In a democratic society, the people are sovereign; for effective accountability in a representative system, the state must retain tight control over its agents. Oversight mechanisms and policies defining what are and are not inherently governmental functions ensure such control. Obviously not all states are democracies. But there is a second normative undercurrent that emanates not from a state's political system but from the regime the international community has built to regulate the use of proxies. As far back as the sixteenth century, Niccolò Machiavelli argued that "[m]ercenaries and auxiliaries are at once useless and dangerous, and he who holds his State by means of mercenary troops can never be solidly or securely seated."[6] From his disdain for mercenaries to the nineteenth-century ban on privateering, the international community has clearly expressed a normative view that restricts the use of proxies.

Two of the modern landmark documents providing insight into how the international community thinks about the rules of the road for cyberspace explicitly discourage the use of "proxies." These are the reports by two groups of governmental experts that met under the auspices of the UN. In 2013, a UN Group of Governmental Experts (UNGGE) from fifteen UN member states, including the United States, China, Russia, the UK, France, and India, agreed in a consensus report that "[s]tates must not use proxies to commit internationally wrongful acts."[7] Two years later, a follow-up UNGGE report specified that "[s]tates must not use proxies to commit internationally wrongful acts using ICTs [information and communications technologies], and should seek to ensure that their territory is not used by non-State actors to commit such acts."[8] The new UNGGE group consisted of twenty member states, including the five permanent members of the UN Security Council as well as Brazil, Israel, and Pakistan. Part of the group's rationale was that proxies present new escalatory risks to international peace and security.

The term *proxy* is often limited to non-state actors with comparatively loose ties to governments. However, statements by Chinese and Iranian officials and scholars suggest that they view certain companies and other non-governmental actors as tightly tied to Western governments. This points to the related challenge of distinguishing between private and public. Discussing the meaning of terms such as "mercenaries," "public," "private," "privatization," and "other slippery terms," the international relations scholar Deborah Avant observed that "all of this refers to the world of advanced, industrialized countries where the state, government, and public revolve around some notion of collective good. In parts of the developing world, state institutions and international recognition of them function mainly as mechanisms for rulers to achieve personal (private) gain."[19] This partly explains why distinguishing between political and economic espionage, as in discussions between the United States and China, has been particularly challenging.

Finally, cyber proxies are entangled in the broader normative questions around the definition of information security and cybersecurity; some states like Russia and China consider content an information security threat whereas others, including the United States, consider content and the free flow of information a human right. The latter states exclude content from their definitions and, to highlight this distinction, use the term *cybersecurity*, whereas other states frame their scope of concern as *information security*. Organizational theory and the literature on power are particularly useful analytical lenses that allow us to avoid being drawn into such normative debates.

PROXIES AND CYBER POWER

Some scholars have argued that cyberspace merits being considered its own sphere of power, much as the term "air power" emerged once mankind started exploring the skies. William "Billy" Mitchell, who was a driving force behind the establishment of the US Air Force, considered air power to be "the ability to do something in the air" while two professors at the US Naval Academy defined "sea power" shortly after World War I as "a nation's ability to enforce its will upon the sea."[20] Nye in turn defines *cyber power* as "the ability to obtain preferred outcomes through use of the electronically interconnected information resources of the cyber domain. Cyber power can be used to produce preferred outcomes *within* cyberspace, or it can use cyber instruments to produce preferred outcomes in other domains *outside* cyberspace."[21] Power is broader than just force, as Nye reminded us with his famous distinction between soft and hard power. In fact, in his discussion of cyber power, Nye also mentions circumvention technologies (technologies designed to circumvent government censorship and surveillance) and the Internet Freedom grant-making program by the US Department of State.[22] Cyber power therefore covers a wide range of effects influencing the targeted actor – including but not limited to coercion.

Proxies are used for the projection of power. Cyberspace has become a field for this general exercise of power due to three interconnected but analytically separate trends. First, more and more machines – including cars and control systems in industry – are changing from closed manual and mechanical systems to interoperable digital systems. Second, more and more of these digital devices are connecting to the Internet. And third, ever greater numbers of people are gaining access to the Internet and these devices every day. All three trends expand the network, thereby raising its value, which in turn also increases the incentives for actors to exploit it for their political and military purposes.

The diffusion of reach – the ability to cause effects remotely not only over regional but also global distances – is arguably the most important aspect of cyber power, but it invites the question: what kind of effects can result from it? For example, in the cyber war debate, one of the underlying considerations was whether such a war would result in the deaths of a thousand people in the span of one year, a classic definition in political science.[23] This rather simplistic point quickly gave way to the broader political implications of offensive cyber operations and applications of the political science scholarship[24] discussing the difference between force and violence,[25] political use of force,[26] the power to hurt,[27] and coercive diplomacy.[28] For example, the political scientist K. J. Holsti made the incredibly prescient observation over fifty years ago that "[a]s technological levels rise, other means of inducement become available and can serve as substitutes for force."[29]

The necessary condition for cyber power as used in this book is *unauthorized access*. The notion of consent and authorization is a good baseline for conceptualizing hacking generally.[30] Malicious hacking, or *cracking* as it was once called, can be distinguished from non-malicious hacking in that the former takes place without the consent of the owner or operator of the system whereas the latter takes place with consent. The security researcher, hired to hack the system to identify its vulnerabilities and to subsequently protect it better, receives the authorization to do so.

Given this book's focus on international relations, it is only concerned with offensive cyber actions, which former US military service members Matthew Noyes and Robert Belk[31] term *external cyber operations*: "cyber actions with effects on systems not owned or operated by the actor."[32] Such effects can undermine the confidentiality, integrity, or availability of information.[33] Examples of external cyber action undermining the confidentiality of information include the now frequent data breaches that affect proprietary data of companies from law firms to the natural resources industry, to the hack of the US Office of Personnel Management, which undermined governmental data secrecy; such breaches often also violate individuals' privacy. DDoS attacks, in which targets are flooded with so much data traffic that they become overwhelmed and unavailable, are the most common malicious activity targeting the availability of information or systems. The integrity of information is ultimately the most critical issue. Manipulating the integrity of data is what enables sabotage acts such as Stuxnet and other actions to have potentially severe impacts.

In this book, the definition of cyber proxies is tied to such offensive cyber actions or operations.[34] Offensive cyber operations can be broken down into two components: access and payload. According to Herb Lin, a senior research scholar at Stanford University, "[i]n general, an offensive cyber operation gains access to an adversary's computer system or network and takes advantage of a vulnerability in that system or network to deliver a payload."[35] Malicious hackers can gain physical access or remote access. Remote access can be gained by social engineering, for example by using a fake email (so-called "spear phishing") to trick the user into sharing his or her legitimate credentials with the attacker, or by exploiting a vulnerability in the code. The vulnerability may be unintentional, a bug created due to a programmer's mistake, or it may be intentional – for example a flaw built in deliberately as a backdoor by a government agency. Once a malicious hacker has gained physical or remote access to the target system, the payload determines the hacking's effect and whether the data's confidentiality, integrity, or availability is undermined. The payload's effect can be limited to logical, non-physical observables, or it may have actual physical effects.[36] Proxies can develop, contribute to, and carry out any of the above, although gaining physical access raises the barriers and the cost significantly.

In sum, defining proxy actions as "offensive action" tries to account for the debate about the future of war, whether war necessarily involves physical effects, and the meaning of violence and coercion. Rather than limiting the definition to Weber's "physical force" or "coercion," "offensive action" is meant to include a broader set of activities. It is even possible that a state detecting persistent unauthorized access to part of its critical infrastructure (for example, the electrical grid) could respond by raising its readiness alert condition to the US equivalent of DEFCON 3. This in turn could be misread by other actors and lead to further escalation.

Also, the definition of cyber proxies is deliberately not tied to the effects caused by the offensive actions. While tying the definition to outcomes makes sense in other contexts, such as the discussion about norms or governmental decision-making,[37] it is not particularly helpful for an actor-focused study where the actor's intent and consequently effects of actions might change over time.[38] For example, the Iranian hackers mentioned in the US government's indictments boasted publicly about technically unsophisticated Web defacements made between 2010 and 2012; only three years later, they were trying to gain access to the control system of a dam. In short, the effects of cyber capabilities can evolve quickly compared to most conventional capabilities.

WHAT CYBER PROXIES ARE (THEORETICALLY) CAPABLE OF

An important question is whether non-state actors, and by extension cyber proxies, can wield the same cyber power – and cause similar effects and harm – as states. Some experts, like US Secret Service agent Baranoff, have argued that non-state actors in fact are more powerful. The answer to the question of which is more dangerous is, it depends. First, states aren't equal. The United States has more sophisticated capabilities than Zimbabwe. Even among members of NATO or the G7, there are significant differences in capabilities. Comparing non-state actors to states therefore requires a case-by-case analysis. In addition, the ability to cause harm through hacking is only partially dependent on an actor's level of technical sophistication. Although Stuxnet created an impression that the ability to cause harm is correlated with an attacker's level of technical sophistication, that is only partly true.

The ability to cause harm is accessible to less sophisticated actors beyond a certain minimum threshold. That does not mean that any script kiddie can cause a worrisome degree of harm. As Beau Woods, a cybersecurity expert at the Atlantic Council, wrote in an email to me, "There's a wide gradation between skript kıdd13 [script kiddie] and nation-state adversary. Whether someone acts as a proxy or not, they can cause harm. And they can go from low-skilled carder to taking down hospitals much, much, much faster than the time to react to their capability escalation."[39] In short, there is a threshold at which a small group of people, or even an individual, can acquire the ability to cause harm, including physical harm, across vast distances at a global scale. This threshold is lower for hacking than for most conventional military capabilities.

What Is Technically Possible

So what kind of effects can be caused by hacking today? First, it is important to remember that just because an effect is technically possible does not mean that it will actually happen. Risk is determined not only by the vulnerability, but also by who might have an interest to carry out malicious actions, the threat. Yet, many people still wonder what harm can be caused through hacking. In short, yes, it is possible to cause physical harm with hacking, including killing that occurs indirectly but nevertheless as a consequence of the hacking. Significant vulnerabilities exist, and accidents in the past have shown that people can die as a result of them. For example, in 2015, an Airbus A400 M plane crashed in Spain, killing four people onboard, because data had been accidentally wiped, leading to a software failure.[40] And in 1999, two children were killed when a gas pipeline ruptured because a computer failure prevented the pressure relief function from working properly.[41] Additional examples include the 2015 warning by the US Government Accountability Office that the increasing interconnectedness between aircraft and the Internet "can potentially provide unauthorized remote access to aircraft avionics systems."[42] Also in 2015, two security researchers successfully hacked into cars, a Toyota Prius and a Ford Escape. One assessment suggests that over 2 million Supervisory Control and Data Acquisition (SCADA) systems, the type of systems used in a lot of critical infrastructure, can be accessed remotely through the Internet.[43] Even nuclear power plants are vulnerable to malicious hacking and malware. In 2014, staff at the Monju nuclear power plant in Japan discovered that a computer in the reactor's control center had been infected with malware and was communicating with an outside source.[44] Such vulnerabilities could cause death and destruction if successfully exploited. (However, the safety features that kicked in following accidental software issues at the Browns Ferry nuclear plant in 2006 and the emergency shutdown at the Baxley power plant in 2008 in the United States demonstrate the resilience ideally baked into critical systems.[45])

Such exploitation does not necessarily require highly sophisticated malware. The examples of security researchers being able to hack into and gain control of cars or the effect of unsophisticated disk-wiping malware show that the ability to cause harm does not depend on technical sophistication. In fact, sometimes hackers can succeed simply by trying default passwords or stealing legitimate credentials. For example, a power outage in western Ukraine in December 2015 was caused by hackers using stolen, legitimate credentials. The malware that was used during the operation did not do the actual damage; it served to obfuscate the attack and to delay recovery efforts.[46] Similarly, the hackers targeting the Bangladeshi central bank were able to transfer the money using legitimate credentials. The same technique could be used against chemical plants, dams, or pipelines. For example, hackers reportedly owned the control systems of the Water and Sewer Department of the City of South Houston, Texas.[47] The 2016 Verizon Security Solutions report mentions another example of hackers, reportedly with ties to Syria,[48] having "infiltrated a water utility's control system and changed the levels of chemicals being used to treat tap water. . . The system regulated valves and ducts that controlled the flow of water and chemicals used to treat it. . . It seems the activists lacked either the knowledge or the intent to do any harm."[49] Another example is disk-wiping malware. The cyber attack against Saudi Aramco, one of the world's largest oil companies, is one of the best illustrations. According to news reports, an IT worker at Saudi Aramco clicked on a link in a scam email and, within hours, some 35,000 computers were partially or totally wiped.[50] The effect of the hack included major disruptions of business operations and while oil production continued, the company started giving it away for free in Saudi Arabia. Its purchase of replacement hard drives drove up prices worldwide.[51]

These examples show that the main variable determining whether an actor can cause harm is not technical sophistication, not knowledge of specific vulnerabilities or development of sophisticated codes, but *intent*. If the intent is there, the capability can follow. Zero-day vulnerabilities (vulnerabilities unknown to the public, anti-virus companies, and the software vendor[52]) can be discovered or purchased by state and non-state actors alike.[53] Similarly, government officials and security experts are concerned most about Iran and North Korea as cyber threat actors "not because of their skill, but because they are motivated to cause destruction."[54]

In short, while it is not likely that people may be killed or that significant damage may occur due to accidental or intentional changes to computer code, it is

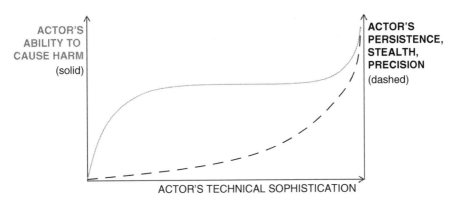

FIGURE 1.1 Relationship between an actor's technical sophistication and (1) the ability to cause harm as well as (2) persistence, stealth, and precision.

nonetheless possible. The likelihood is an open empirical question,[55] which needs to be re-evaluated constantly depending on the threat level from state and non-state actors. At present, there is no known case of somebody having been killed through an offensive cyber operation. The good news is that such acts of sabotage remain rare for most non-state actors, most of whom are criminals and so focused more on profit than on malicious harm. As cybercrime expert Brian Krebs pointed out, "Disabling infected systems is counterproductive for attackers, who generally focus on hoovering as much personal and financial data as they can from the PCs they control."[56]

How Technical Sophistication Matters

Increased technical sophistication can expand an actor's ability to cause harm (after the initial evolution from script kiddie to actual hacker), but in the context of cyber operations, it primarily expands the ability to target precisely and to do so stealthily.[57] Technical sophistication is most important when it comes to three other variables, namely: (1) the degree of persistence, or the ability of an actor to maintain unauthorized access to an infiltrated system; (2) the degree of stealth, or the ability of an actor to hide the malicious activity; and (3) the degree of precision, or the ability of an actor to limit the effect of the malicious activity to the targeted system. The caveat is, of course, that all of this is dependent on the target system's weakness in the first place: technology is constantly changing, a fact which might change the aforementioned dynamics in the future. With regard to the current state of the technology, Figure 1.1 visualizes this argument.

There are some situations where causing harm does require persistence and expertise, especially if the target includes industrial control systems, whose systems often differ significantly from other IT. The scholars Thomas Rid and Peter

McBurney have argued that "developing and deploying potentially destructive cyber-weapons against hardened targets will require significant resources, hard-to-get and highly specific target intelligence, and time to prepare, launch and execute an attack. Attacking secured targets would probably require the resources or the support of a state actor."[58] However, this does not mean that non-state actors cannot cause harm in such situations if they want to. The wording of Rid and McBurney's assessment reveals its limitations. In particular, the references to "hardened targets" and "secured targets" elide the fact that many critical infrastructure systems are not hardened or secured. An astonishing number of incidents in recent years were made possible because basic security measures (such as two-factor authentication) were missing. In such cases, causing harm is certainly within the reach of even relatively unsophisticated non-state actors.

While it is possible for non-state actors and proxies to cause significant harm through the Internet, it does not mean that it is easy. Jon Lindsay, professor at the University of Toronto and former intelligence officer with the US Navy, has observed that "[t]he latency between CNE [computer network exfiltration] and CNA [computer network attack] is more complicated than generally assumed."[59] In other words, just because you are able to access a system to steal data doesn't mean you are also able to carry out a cyber attack. In fact, two experts on industrial control systems, Robert Lee (a former US Air Force cyber warfare operations officer) and Michael Assante, have pointed out that "[industrial control systems]-custom cyber attacks capable of significant process or equipment impact require adversaries to become intimately aware of the process being automated and the engineering decisions and design of the [industrial control systems] and safety system."[60] This requires a higher level of sophistication in terms of persistence of access and expertise because industrial control systems differ significantly from regular IT.[61]

Why Some State Actors Do Stand Apart

Major states do stand apart from other states and non-state actors today in two ways: the level of resources they have available and their access to certain technologies. In terms of resources, for example, the US National Security Agency's (NSA) tailored access operations are carried out by some 600 people working at what is called the Remote Operations Center, which is staffed around the clock seven days a week.[62] The resources required to pay so many highly skilled individuals to work such hours for a prolonged period of time are generally only available to a major state (or corporation). At the same time, states that are able to maintain persistent access thanks to their resources don't necessarily exhibit the same degree of stealth. James Mulvenon, for example, an expert on China and cybersecurity, pointed to an important difference between Russian and Chinese actors in this regard, considering that Russia "abound[s] with highly talented programmers" while Chinese actors use "sloppy tradecraft, leaving behind clear evidence of the intrusion and sometimes even attribution-related information."[63]

Major states again differ from other state and non-state actors with regard to an actor's ability to gain access to certain technologies. Some states have greater ability to manipulate the supply chain to create backdoors enabling future remote access (and companies could act as proxies if they knowingly build backdoors into their products on behalf of a state). Similarly, when it comes to physical access, only major powers with significant human intelligence capacities can use agents to gain physical access and maintain persistence to highly sensitive systems for a cyber operation. Non-state actors could recruit insiders to gain close access – Joaquín "El Chapo" Guzmán illustrated what criminals can achieve – but cyber proxies usually rely on remote access. That is why physical access is neglected in this book.

Apart from these two differences, little distinguishes the hacking capabilities of a non-state actor from those of a state actor. Even zero-days for industrial control systems are available on the market. For example, GLEG Ltd, a Moscow-based company that was established in 2004,[64] openly advertises "Zero-Days for SCADA!"[65] The company website also highlights specifically that "SCADA and related vulnerabilities are very special due to their sensitive nature and possible huge impact involved in successful exploitation. SCADA systems are also 'hard to patch', so even old vulnerabilities are actual," and it offers vulnerabilities affecting industrial PCs, smart chips, and industrial protocols.[66] In addition, a state can provide a non-state actor with access to resources or technologies that the non-state actor might not otherwise have as part of a proxy relationship.

In sum, the ability to cause harm is therefore not a significant differentiator between non-state and state hackers above a certain, fairly low level of technical sophistication. Non-state actors, and by extension potential proxies, can cause significant harm and pose a significant security threat from a national and international security perspective. Compared to conventional means of exercising coercive power, the diffusion of reach and the diffusion of power to the individual level enabled by the Internet have resulted in a qualitative difference in a non-state actor's ability to cause significant harm. Michael Schmitt and Sean Watts similarly argued that cyber operations "appear to present greatly increased opportunities for non-state actors to match, and in some cases even to surpass, state supremacy."[67] At the core of this development is the fact that a hacker's level of sophistication and a given piece of malware's level of sophistication ultimately depend on expertise, not equipment. It is the code that matters, not the keyboard or computer the hacker uses.

The important point here is that a small group of individuals, or even a single individual, can cause considerable levels of harm through malicious hacking and can cause effects remotely. The diffusion of power[68] to the individual level is perhaps the other most salient (if not unique) aspect of cyberspace compared to other security areas. For example, one of the Iranian hackers mentioned in the US government indictment unsealed in March 2016 was charged with having hacked the control system of a small dam near New York City. This malicious hack, which did not use a particularly sophisticated technique, is reminiscent of an incident in 2000 when a disgruntled employee in Australia released millions of liters of raw sewage into local rivers and communities.[69] These are illustrations of the technical reality that even a single individual can cause significant harm through malicious hacking if he or she has the expertise and the intent. According to Juan Zarate, Deputy Assistant to the President and Deputy National Security Adviser for Combating Terrorism from 2005 to 2009, "an individual hacker can emerge as a cyber-power, one whose relative isolation, anonymity, and small footprint is a source of strength."[70] The ability to cause harm is therefore not the primary differentiator that sets an individual apart from a nation-state. In fact, today, some individuals have more sophisticated cyber capabilities than many nation-states.

WHAT CYBER PROXIES ARE LIKELY TO BE USED FOR

Cyber proxies either conduct or directly contribute to an offensive cyber operation. Offensive cyber operations can have a variety of effects. They can be substitutes for conventional weapons – such as a bomb – and they can also enable entirely novel actions – such as manipulating financial data. These effects can be permanent, or they can be temporary and reversible – the latter is a particularly intriguing feature of offensive cyber operations. Eric Rosenbach, former Assistant Secretary of Defense and the Pentagon's principal cyber adviser from 2011 to 2015, underscored these attributes when he said about cyber operations:

> The place where I think it will be most helpful to senior policymakers is what I call in "the space between." What is the space between? . . . You have diplomacy, economic sanctions . . . and then you have military action. In between there's this space, right? In cyber, there are a lot of things that you can do in that space between that can help us accomplish the national interest.[71]

This view is not limited to American thinkers. Scholars at the China Institute for International Studies, the think tank affiliated with China's Ministry of Foreign Affairs, have expressed a similar logic: "[E]ven if there is no act of cyber war in a strict sense, many cyber-attacks that have happened might be regarded as quasi-cyber war."[72] Proxies have been used in the past, particularly in this gray zone of quasi-war. In addition to plausible deniability, using proxies to project coercive power through cyberspace is therefore particularly attractive because the technology enables new coercive effects below the threshold of use of force.

In addition to conducting offensive cyber actions themselves and causing such effects, cyber proxies can also contribute to an offensive cyber operation that a state executes. The modularity of offensive cyber operations is worth highlighting because it presents new challenges for attributing the responsibility of a malicious

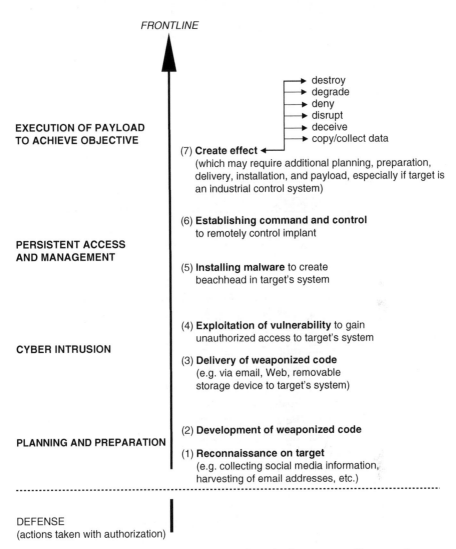

FIGURE 1.2 "Tip-of-the-spear" framework applied to remote offensive cyber operations.[74]

action to a specific actor. Figure 1.2 presents the "tip-of-the-spear" framework as it applies to remote offensive cyber operations and cyber proxies' nongeographic but functional proximity to the battle space. States can and do rely on proxies for any of the seven steps of the "cyber kill chain" outlined in Figure 1.2. For example, a 2009 report prepared by Northrop Grumman for the US-China Security and Economic Review Commission suggested that the different stages of an offensive cyber operation, from gaining access to exfiltrating data, are sometimes split among different

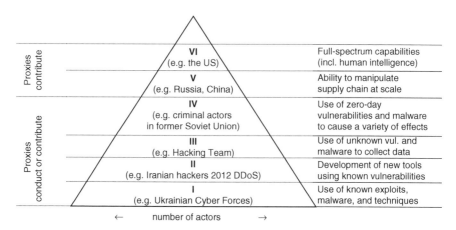

FIGURE 1.3 Situating cyber proxies in threat taxonomy.

groups, including "a mix of uniformed officers, military personnel, civilian intelligence operatives and freelance high-end hackers."[73] Attributing involvement and activity at this modular level of an offensive cyber operation is even more challenging than identifying relationships between actors generally and barely any data is available.

To illustrate cyber proxies' different level of sophistication, Figure 1.3 builds on the US Defense Science Board's cyber threat hierarchy, which differentiates between six tiers (I = lowest tier, VI = highest tier).[75] The graphic summarizes the distinctions made in comparing the capabilities of state and non-state actors.[76] Proxies conducting offensive cyber operations have ranged from tier I to IV. Proxies can also contribute to offensive cyber operations carried out by tiers V and VI actors (the United States, Russia, and China). (Russia and China could arguably also be counted as tier VI but the United States is listed instead to highlight its overall superiority.) The Defense Science Board makes two observations particularly important in the context of cyber proxies. First, "higher-tier actors will use the methods and techniques at the lowest level necessary to accomplish their objectives . . . to avoid exposing their more sophisticated techniques," and, second, "states might employ non-state actors as proxies. In such situations, middle-tier organizations gain access to higher-tier capabilities."[77] This assessment further supports the argument for a certain amount of restraint being automatically built into proxy relationships by the beneficiary.

THE POOL OF POTENTIAL CYBER PROXIES

The pool of non-state actors with offensive cyber capabilities is outlined in Table 1.1. It consists of (1) individual actors, (2) groups of people that are organized informally

TABLE 1.1 *Non-state proxies based on organizational structure*

Organizational unit	Individual	Small, informal networked group of people	More formal, hierarchical group of people
Examples	Individual hacktivist, Individual cyber criminal	Network of hacktivists, Network of cyber criminals	Organized cyber crime groups, militias, private companies

and as a networked structure, and (3) more formal, organized groups of people and hierarchical organizations. Any of these actors can become a cyber proxy, an intermediary that conducts or directly contributes to an offensive action that is enabled knowingly, actively or passively, by a beneficiary.

The individual actors include lone hacktivists and individual malicious hackers-for-hire. "The Jester" (th3j35t3 r) is one of the best illustrations of this kind of lone-wolf hacker.[78] This individual, politically driven hacktivist claims to be a former member of US Army Special Forces deployed to Afghanistan and uses an image resembling the cartoon figure Captain America as his or her avatar.[79] The Jester described his or her motivation in 2015 as follows, "Approximately five years ago I realized that there was a growing threat from Jihadis online using the Internet to recruit, radicalize and even train homegrowners ... I decided to research their favorite haunts, collect intelligence on the users and admins and in many cases remove them by force."[80] The Jester first attracted public attention after targeting terrorist websites like the Taliban's alemarah.info in 2010.[81] Over time, the hacker also targeted WikiLeaks and Anonymous for actions that the Jester considered harmful to the United States and claimed responsibility for targeting Ecuador's stock exchange after Ecuador expressed support for Edward Snowden.[82] In mid-June 2011, he or she also threatened to go after LulzSec and to unmask its members. During the uprising in Libya, the Jester switched techniques and planted false news stories as part of a psychological operation targeting Gaddafi's regime, apparently aimed at undermining morale.[83]

A study of the Jester's activities found that over the span of two years he or she conducted "over 200 attacks on seventy-five unique targets. This means on average that he or she nominates a new target every three weeks and attacks a target just about twice every week."[84] In fact, the report concluded, "The Jester has proved that a single individual is very capable of waging cyber war at a level we previously attributed only to intelligence agencies or crime syndicates."[85] Moreover, having targeted not only terrorists but also fellow hacktivists including Anonymous, LulzSec, and the Syrian Electronic Army, the Jester made him- or herself a target to be unmasked by these actors as well as government agencies.

Nevertheless, the Jester's identity remains publicly unknown to date, despite a very public Twitter persona.[86]

The second category of small networked groups consists of networks of politically driven hacktivists, curiosity-driven hackers, or profit-driven cyber criminals. Importantly, many of these actors operate with mixed intent. Katie Moussouris, who, as the CEO of the cybersecurity company Luta Security, regularly works with hackers, underlined this point when she told me, "It is hard to categorize an actor by intent. He or she might need money at one point in time, and act for political reasons the next day" (or both at the same time).[87] These groups tend to be informal, and generally networked rather than hierarchical.[88] When cyber criminals work in groups, they tend to operate through more informal network structures than do the hierarchical crime organizations dominating the drug trade and other conventional crimes.[89] The former Soviet Union is home to many cyber criminal networks such as the notorious Russian Business Network. A particular feature of such cyber crime networks and the cyber crime underground generally is what cyber crime experts call an increasing commoditization. In effect, there is a marketplace comprising a "loose federation of specialists selling capabilities, services, and resources explicitly tailored to the abuse ecosystem,"[90] including tools providing access to fully developed payloads as well as the service to deploy them inside the target's system.[91]

The third group of formal and hierarchical non-state actors includes private military and security companies, militias, and entities such as the cyber unit of the Estonian Cyber Defense League. Private companies include well-known defense contractors that have expanded their activities to include cybersecurity, such as Lockheed Martin in the United States, BAE Systems in the UK, or Airbus in Europe. But they also include lesser-known companies like ManTech in the United States or NICE in Israel. These companies are included in this discussion of proxy relationships because they are perceived as such in other countries and this perception will inform other governments' behavior. For example, Li Zheng, assistant president of the China Institute for Contemporary International Relations, a think tank affiliated with the Ministry of State Security, has stated, "China is aware that the United States and other Western countries are actively using defence contractors such as Lockheed Martin, Boeing, Northrop Grumman, and Raytheon for cyber-weapon development and deployment... The *Financial Times* recently said that these groups of companies have formed a 'cyber-security military-industrial complex' to 'sell software to the US government that can break into and degrade or destroy an enemy's computer network, as well as programmes aimed at blocking such attacks.'"[92]

Many smaller boutique firms have also sprung up. The most notorious is probably Hacking Team, the Italy-based company that was eventually hacked itself and saw its proprietary data spilled all over the Internet. Media reports revealed that Hacking Team was selling its offensive tools not only to law enforcement and security agencies in Europe and North America but also to countries worldwide – for example, working with NICE and other partners to sell its products to Indian government agencies.[93] In its 2013 annual report, the cyber threat intelligence company CrowdStrike also mentioned that "an India-based security firm known as *Appin Security Group* that may have been contracted by the Indian government" is targeting "numerous entities across the globe that would be of strategic interest to India's government, including heavy targeting of Pakistani military and political entities."[94] According to its informational brochure, Appin Technologies' service offerings include "IT security software for Govt & Defense and Ethical Hacking & Intelligence services," boasting that "Appin has the unique distinction of securing India's President House and all International airports of India."[95]

These reports suggest that private cybersecurity contractors exist all over the world. In fact, after one of the world's leading cybersecurity firms, Kaspersky Lab, exposed an unusually sophisticated hacking operation hitting targets in South Korea and Japan, it cautioned that "In the future, we predict the number of small, focused ... to-hire groups to grow, specializing in hit-and-run operations, a kind of 'cyber mercenaries' of the modern world."[96] A separate but related issue is the continuing discussion in the United States about private sector active cyber defense. This discussion has included proposals such as those by General Michael Hayden, former director of the Central Intelligence Agency (CIA) and the NSA under President George W. Bush. Hayden has stated that "We may come to a point where defense is more actively and aggressively defined even for the private sector and what is permitted there is something that we would never let the private sector do in physical space ... Let me really throw a bumper sticker for you: how about a digital Blackwater?"[97] In short, in addition to the existing market for cybersecurity contractors, this sector might grow in the future if existing laws are changed to give companies greater authority to engage in offensive cyber operations.

Front companies are not considered part of this category or as stand-alone actors, because they are not companies *per se*. Front companies can be defined as "covert public entities with political rather than economic motivations"; they have been around for decades (the CIA created several such companies in the 1960s).[98] A more recent example is the Chosun Neungrado Trading Company based in Shenyang, China, which the South Korean government has claimed is a front company used by North Korea to sell malicious software to customers in South Korea.[99] Iran is also known to use front companies for a variety of purposes.[100] However, they are used by states to cover up the activity of state officials or other proxy actors.

An example of a formalized, hierarchical group that is not a private company is the Estonian Defense League's cyber unit. Set up by the Estonian government after the 2007 DDoS attack targeting the country, the unit describes itself as "a voluntary organization aimed at protecting Estonian cyberspace."[101] It is part of the Estonian Defense League, which counts some 15,000 members today, twice the size of the regular Estonian Defense Forces in peacetime.[102] The Estonian Defense League's function aligns with the classic definition of a militia: "[a] military force that is raised

from the civil population to supplement a regular army in an emergency."[103]
According to Estonia's Minister of Defense, Jaak Aaviksoo, the league's cyber
unit "brings together specialists in cyber defense who work in the private sector
as well as in different government agencies" and would function under a unified
military command in wartime.[104] The cyber unit of the Estonian Defense League
is worth highlighting because it is similar to the militia model the Chinese
government champions. However, while Estonia's cyber unit is clearly structured
to align with the Weberian monopoly on the legitimate use of force, China's
militias and the government's efforts are arguably better described now as an
aspirational monopoly.

PROXY RELATIONSHIPS AND SELECTED CASES

What these actors have in common as cyber proxies is that they act as intermediaries that conduct or directly contribute to an offensive cyber action that is
enabled knowingly, whether actively or passively, by a beneficiary. States organize their relationships with cyber proxies in different ways. In general, states'
relationships with these cyber proxies are extensions of their conventional
approaches to engaging with non-state actors. In the United States and other
countries that witnessed significant privatization over the past few decades, that
privatization did not stop at the door of intelligence agencies; instead, an
industry of spies-for-hire sprang up even as intelligence capabilities began to
build capacity for offensive cyber operations capable of a broader range of
effects. The Chinese government, which has traditionally relied on militias,
expanded them to this new domain, starting to establish information-warfare
militias in the late 1990s. Iran too fell back on old patterns when it suddenly
faced new threats, relying on students to advance its political goals. (Russia, on
the other hand, illustrates how a state can adjust its proxy relationships at a time
of contraction, fragmentation, and increasing corruption, and how it can
become increasingly entangled with criminal networks.) Needless to say, states
have relationships with a variety of proxies. Hacktivists exist in pretty much
every country connected to the Internet, as well as in cybersecurity firms.
However, it is evident that there are primary models for a state's engagement
with proxies.

Three main types of proxy relationships can be identified: delegation, orchestration, and sanctioning, which roughly align with key cases and concepts in international law. Delegation describes proxy relationships where the beneficiary has
significant, at least overall or effective, control over the proxy. Orchestration explains
the phenomenon of proxies on a looser leash, where the state supports the proxy
without necessarily providing specific instructions; generally, the state and the proxy
share a common ideological purpose. Sanctioning or passive support, on the other
hand, captures environments where the state provides an enabling environment for

non-state actors' malicious activity by deliberately turning a blind eye to their activities.

Specifying that the offensive cyber action pursued by proxies "is enabled knowingly, whether actively or passively, by a beneficiary" allows the definition to account for the phenomenon of sanctioning. By contrast, speaking in terms of an action conducted "on behalf of" a state implies a rather narrow relationship, akin to contractual delegation in principal–agent theory or the "effective control" threshold in international law. This would not capture the most challenging real-world aspect of proxies: scenarios where a state either turns a blind eye to an action or deliberately creates so many degrees of separation that it cannot be held responsible in the court of public opinion but is clearly somehow involved. My definition attempts a more precise wording that relies on the analytical and policy-relevant distinction between active and passive support and that qualifies and limits this support by specifying that it takes place "knowingly." For the same reasons, I speak of a "beneficiary" rather than a "principal" to highlight that the relationship is broader than the delegation relationship discussed in principal–agent models.[105] The term "beneficiary" here is meant to subsume the connotations of "principal" and "orchestrator" while also incorporating the notion of sanctioning; this serves to explain why a state might not take action against malicious activity originating from its territory.

Proxy relationships vary across regions and states. In fact, they are dependent on the nature and function of the state itself. Countries where prebendalism[106] reigns differ from those that are evolving into market states, and, following decolonization, militias in newly independent states were shaped by internal and external threats.[107] The threat posed by Iraq, for example, led Iran to tighten control over the Islamic Revolutionary Guard Corps after the 1979 revolution.[108] And as states evolve, so do their proxy relationships. China's transformation during the past four decades, for example, affected its state structures and led it to respond to hacktivist groups emerging in the late 1990s by establishing cyber militias and conducting regular crackdowns on cyber criminals.

Each country selected for the in-depth case studies – the United States, Russia, China, and Iran (plus Syria) – is a prototypical case for one of these main types of proxy relationships. A prototypical case is "chosen not because it is representative but because it is expected to become so."[109] While the number of states expressing their intent to develop offensive cyber capabilities has been skyrocketing during the past five years, only a few have already built mature organizations or used such capabilities. All selected cases are therefore considered established or emerging cyber powers who have not only demonstrated the capability and intent, but have also conducted offensive cyber operations.[110] And while all of these countries use non-state actors to project cyber power, as Admiral Mike Rogers, head of the NSA and of the US Cyber Command, has noted, "[e]ach uses a slightly different structure."[111]

To recap, I classify actors as proxies based on their degree of detachment and control *vis-à-vis* the beneficiary. Other characteristics such as intent or whether a proxy's activities are internal or external to a country's border, are not used for several reasons. Intent is limited as a characteristic because proxies' motives may be multifaceted or may change over time. This is illustrated by hacktivists in China – whose actions shifted from political to profit-driven over time – and the three members of the Syrian Electronic Army, whose indictment explicitly referenced their mixture of personal profit-driven and political ambitions. Due to the diffusion of reach, it is also possible for an actor to engage in a 9 am–5 pm day job and be a proxy from 5 pm to 9 am (or the other way around), and to have differing motivations for the hacking during each period.[112] Ultimately, although some scholars have proposed typologies of proxies based on motivation, these face severe limitations when applied to real-world examples and risk distorting the analysis.[113] The same is true for typologies of proxies based on whether the targets are internal or external to the beneficiary state.[114] A proxy no longer needs to be in physical proximity to its target, making it possible for proxy actors to engage in malicious cyber activity that targets both internal and external perceived threats.[115]

The definition of cyber proxies also does not depend on the relationship between the beneficiary and the proxy or operation being covert or clandestine.[116] Some proxy relationships are overt, as with militias or contractors.[117] Certainly, many proxies operate covertly, enabling plausible deniability by concealing the identity of the beneficiary; some even operate clandestinely without their effect ever being noticed, as in the theft of data. Still, although this discretion is the very reason why proxies are used in many instances, it is not a necessary element for the definition. For example, the Syrian Electronic Army and other hacktivists have publicly claimed credit for specific offensive actions yet offer their sponsors plausible deniability (with the caveat that some of them may also be part of a false-flag operation[118]).

At the same time, characterizing proxies based on the degree of detachment and control has its own limitations. It requires attribution at a level that takes time to establish, and attribution continues to be a challenge, especially when states have asymmetric attribution capabilities. In the absence of detailed and timely information, the three main categories of delegation, orchestration, and passive support can serve as useful approximations for analytical frameworks and national security decision-making.

PROXIES AND THE ATTRIBUTION PROBLEM

Attributing the actions of a conventional or cyber proxy to a state has always been a challenge.[119] Yet following media coverage of cyber incidents on a regular basis, one might think state-sponsored cyber proxies lurk around every corner online. Commentators routinely refer to alleged perpetrators as "state-sponsored actors," especially when an incident first hits the news. However, this wording is often only a work-around for what continues to be a major problem for cybersecurity: the difficulty of attributing malicious activity promptly and doing so in a manner that is independently verifiable and can withstand public scrutiny.[120] Because it is often not known for weeks or months, if at all, whether a malicious online action is the work of a state or is state-sponsored, journalists fall back on the term "state-sponsored" when it seems at least somewhat plausible that a state is involved.

Use of the term "state-sponsored" does not mean that all of these actors are, in fact, non-state actors detached from the state and acting as its proxy. Instead, it reflects journalists' inability to definitively attribute the incident to a state at the time of publication: the term "state-sponsored" is used to describe both state *and* state-sponsored actors as the potential source. A similar logic applies to cybersecurity industry reports: these rarely attribute a specific malware or incident to a state, sometimes more for business reasons than for lack of evidence. Instead, they make general warnings of "state-sponsored attackers" like those Google started issuing in 2012,[121] followed by Facebook,[122] Microsoft,[123] and Yahoo[124] in late 2015.

In 2010, it was still common to hear cybersecurity experts inside the Washington beltway say that attribution was not possible. A few years later, experts argued that attribution capabilities were getting better, and some began to suggest that as many as 80 percent of attacks could be attributed. By 2015, it was clear that this problem was not as insurmountable as initially feared. The question is less *whether* attribution is possible but *by when*. Experts increasingly view attribution not as a binary but as a question of degree, as well as differentiating between its technical and political dimensions.[125] The quality of the attribution depends on the skills and resources available and the complexity of the malware. The many successful law enforcement cases and prosecutions that have occurred over the past two decades stand as an important indicator that attribution is possible.

Improving attribution capabilities does not mean that attribution and designating responsibility is no longer a problem. For example, increasing commoditization makes it more difficult for an individual selling the tool or service to have an insight into what purpose the sale will serve, removing one further potential source for attribution. In Krebs's words, "If there is any truth to the old saying that there is no honor among thieves then it is doubly true for thieves who transact with one another yet never actually meet face-to-face."[126] This increasing commoditization could therefore increase transactions' anonymity and facilitate the use of these capabilities by states, further blurring lines of responsibility. In addition, it is easier to track state actors that are often engaged in long-term operations compared to ephemeral hacking-for-hire jobs.

False-flag operations, in which actors try to cover up their own actions by pretending to be another actor, are an additional challenge. For example, "Guccifer 2.0," a hacker pretending to be Romanian, claimed credit for the hack of the Democratic National Committee in 2016. Later, however, Guccifer 2.0 became widely considered a poor attempt to cover up the direct involvement of the Russian government.[127] The US intelligence community, drawing on signals and human intelligence sources, concluded "with high confidence,"[128] that the

Guccifer 2.0 persona and DCleaks.com had been used by Russian military intelligence (General Staff Main Intelligence Directorate or GRU) to "release US victim data obtained in cyber operations publicly and in exclusives to media outlets and [to relay] material to WikiLeaks."[129] Similarly, when the French television station TV5 was hit with destructive malware, a group calling itself the "Cyber Caliphate" initially claimed credit, pretending to be supporters of the Islamic State. The group turned out to be Russian hackers, whom cybersecurity expert Dmitri Alperovitch considered with "medium level confidence" to be members of the Russian GRU.[130] The Yemen Cyber Army is also worth mentioning in this context. There is ongoing speculation regarding the location and makeup of the Yemen Cyber Army, which, in the words of reporter Lorenzo Franceschi-Bicchierai, "came out of nowhere in the Middle East" and started defacing websites and hacking systems of the Saudi government and posting the data online. While experts disagreed about the identity of the hackers (some researchers argued that the members of the Yemen Cyber Army are Iranian,[131] and others pointed to Russia[132]), they were all united in their skepticism that the members of the Yemen Cyber Army are in or from Yemen.

Perhaps most importantly, while some countries are getting better at attribution, these capabilities will remain asymmetric. The world's great powers such as the United States have been working hard on getting better at attribution.[133] In a 2016 interview, David Sanger, the chief Washington correspondent for *The New York Times*, put it this way: "[t]he NSA's job is to go put implants in computer networks around the world to be able to see what's happening. Think of them as the cyber equivalent of radar stations that we set up around the world to see airplanes."[134] However, such capabilities remain out of reach for all but a handful of the most powerful states. This leaves the rest of the world as much in the dark as before, unless they receive assistance from one of the more advanced powers: assistance that requires significant trust, and that involves significant intelligence trade-offs for the party sharing the information.[135]

In short, robust attribution remains challenging and is often not available within the time frame that decision-makers might need to act, especially in a national security context. Harold Koh, legal adviser at the US State Department, pointed out in a speech at US Cyber Command in September 2012 that "Cyberspace significantly increases an actor's ability to engage in attacks with 'plausible deniability,' by acting through proxies."[136] As John Kerry, former US Secretary of State, remarked in an October 2016 speech, "You can find a location, but you can't necessarily find the person that was working the keyboard or engaged in that . . . what they do is they rent space out, and people come in, and they can come in anonymously and use it and then disappear."[137] Whereas some proxies focus on concealing their activity, others focus on concealing their identity or both. One emerging hypothesis is that the most technically advanced states are likely to achieve plausible deniability through technical means and therefore focus on their activity, whereas less technically advanced states might not have the technical capabilities to be as stealthy and therefore have greater incentives to focus and rely on different organizational models to achieve this objective – for example, the use of proxies that are further detached from the state.

A FEW WORDS ON METHODOLOGY

The qualitative case study approach was a particularly promising method to pursue for several reasons.[138] The study of cyberspace generally is still in its infancy, with limited data available. Data on proxy actors, in particular, is very limited, as it is usually classified or proprietary, and sometimes outright contradictory. In light of this information-poor environment, the case-study approach "gives the researcher an opportunity to fact-check, to consult multiple sources, to go back to primary materials, and to overcome whatever biases may affect the secondary literature."[139] Moreover, the research's protean[140] nature lends itself to a more inductive approach. Closely examining a small number of cases can help shed light on a phenomenon of growing significance. (At the same time, this poses a challenge for reducing selection bias.) As more states build cyber capabilities, these cases are expected to become illustrative ideal-types applying to a growing population of cases.[141] This book attempts to provide a framework that can be populated as more data becomes available.

Sources included primary and secondary literature covering government documents, statements, agreements, peer-reviewed academic articles and books, and media reports as well as nontraditional sources – namely technical reports by cybersecurity companies. The literature-based research was complemented by semi-structured interviews with experts, including hackers such as Hector Monsegur and Vladislav Horohorin; government officials in defense, intelligence, and law enforcement communities; employees at cyber threat intelligence companies; and defense contractors, security researchers and computer emergency response officials.

The year 1995 provides a useful starting point for this inquiry, and for the scholarship of the Internet from an international relations perspective generally. In that year, the National Science Foundation Network (NSFNET) backbone was decommissioned, dividing the early days of the Internet from what I consider the modern Internet.[142] It marks the turning point when a network used by academics for research purposes turned into the global infrastructure that has become the backbone of global communication, trade, and commerce today. The year is significant not only from a US perspective but also from a global one. For example, China only gained access to the Internet a year earlier.[143] It was also the Internet's expansion in the mid-1990s that led the US military to recognize its importance – and ultimately to designate it as a new operational domain in 2010, alongside land, sea, air, and space.[144]

CONCLUSION: CYBER PROXIES AND THE BIGGER PICTURE

Overall, the modern Internet is reshaping relations among states and contributing to the diffusion of power to non-state actors because it creates what I call the diffusion of reach – the ability to cause effects remotely not only over regional but also global distances.[145] For example, the theater of the conflict between North Korea and the United States escalated from a regional to a global scale, from the US perspective, not because of North Korea's development of an intercontinental ballistic missile (ICBM), but because of a malicious hack. In an unprecedented step, on December 19, 2014, President Obama went on television to accuse North Korea publicly of being responsible for the harm caused when the networks of Sony Pictures Entertainment, a company located on US territory, were targeted.[146] Previously, North Korea had been of concern to the United States because of the US security alliance with South Korea, the thousands of US soldiers based in the region, and the potential development of North Korean nuclear weapons. The Sony hack demonstrated that North Korea could cause harm against targets within the United States independent of its development of ICBMs; such harm took place on a much smaller scale but the reach existed nonetheless. Similarly, what ultimately globalized the US conflict with Iran was not Iran's nuclear ambitions, but Iran's growing cyber capabilities, including Iran's ability to target the control systems of a dam in the United States.[147]

   To put it another way, what makes cyber power unique is that in the age of a global network, hacking provides the reach of an ICBM at a cost within the reach of small groups of non-state actors.[148] The natural barriers of geography – distance, oceans, and mountain ranges – that facilitated the effectiveness of the global order after World War II are diminished. For the first time in history, a small group of individuals, or even a single individual, working for a state or not, can exercise power remotely, causing an effect that a state will take note of without any physical proximity. Offensive cyber operations generally have introduced more uncertainty and mistrust into the system and thereby have increased its volatility. They pose new risks of escalation while also enabling new effects short of use of force that can be used to avoid escalation.[149] For example, in 1998, at the height of renewed tension between the United States and Iraq, a hack of the Pentagon was so serious that President Clinton was briefed about it. Some initially believed that the Iraqi government was responsible, but it turned out to be the work of two teenagers in California and one in Israel.[150]

   This diffusion of reach through the Internet complicates traditional analyses of globalization, including the study of global terrorism, which focus on the increasing interdependence of and links among people. The international relations scholar Robert Keohane, for example, wrote that "[s]uch [informal] violence becomes globalized when the networks of non-state actors operate on an intercontinental basis, so that acts of force in one society can be initiated and controlled from very distant points of the globe."[151] In contrast, much as the invention of ICBMs forced nuclear theorists to revisit the notion of "a geographically defined defensive perimeter," a central premise of realist theory, the modern Internet and hacking further undermines this foundational assumption, even the notion of physical proximity still underlying Keohane's words.[152]

The new types of coercive effects explain why cyber operations also affect great power relations. Previously, great powers' behavior was frozen at a certain level due to the strategic nuclear stalemate. There was a clear limit to how far they could go, and they took great care that direct conflicts between them remain below the threshold of an armed attack and use of force – or to carry them out indirectly through proxies in faraway lands. Today, the nuclear stalemate still binds the behavior of great powers. But cyberspace has opened a new realm of possible malicious activity that enables great powers to push the envelope further. They can now engage in activity closer to the threshold of an armed attack, doing so directly or through proxies.

The danger is that this new sphere presents significant escalatory potential – from the cyber dimension of conflicts in the Middle East to President Obama's questions about the Kremlin's possible involvement when JPMorgan Chase was hacked during a time of heightened tensions between the US and Russia in 2014.[153] While the latter's culprits turned out to be cyber criminals, it nevertheless shows that states around the world have not yet learned how to interpret signaling in cyberspace, creating uncertainty, potential for misinterpretation, and novel risk of escalation that destabilizes international security. Yet proxies will be used to project these new coercive effects and the new reach of power, warranting an investigation into how proxy relationships are organized and what they are used for. The diffusion of reach enables proxies to act extraterritorially and to cause effects elsewhere, operating from third countries.

In the years to come, the number of proxies is likely to expand, as are their capabilities and their ability to cause harm. There are several reasons for this. Demand for proxies is likely to increase. There are now over two dozen states with formal military or intelligence units focusing on offensive cyber operations and many more buying off-the-shelf malware from the private market.[154] These numbers illustrate the growing number of countries with an interest in developing capabilities to use the Internet for political and military purposes. Meanwhile, the growth of the Internet of Things, with more and more devices being connected to the Internet, increases the risk of large-scale DDoS attacks and hacking that cause physical effects. The investigative journalist Krebs experienced this effect firsthand in 2016 when his website was subjected to a DDoS attack unprecedented in scale at the time (reaching 620 Gbps). Krebs wrote that this attack convinced him that "one of the fastest-growing censorship threats on the Internet today comes not from nation-states, but from super-empowered individuals who have been quietly building extremely potent cyber weapons with transnational reach."[155]

Proxies' capabilities are also likely to grow in the years to come. Hackers are learning from each other. The *Wired* reporter Kim Zetter revealed in a 2015 article that the US intelligence community suspected that Iran had learned from malware like Stuxnet, Flame, and Duqu, as well as from an attack on its oil industry, and that Iran applied these lessons in its attack on Saudi Aramco.[156] Such learning processes and subsequent transfer of capabilities take place not only among states but also between state and non-state actors. Some non-state actors learn their skills working inside government: for example, one of the security researchers who hacked into the Toyota Prius and Ford Escape had conducted offensive cyber operations for the NSA before moving into the private sector.[157] Others are trained in hacking outside government: courses in India and China offer to teach hacking for a few hundred dollars. According to one of China's first generation hackers and hacktivists, Wang Xianbing, "Hacker school is a bit like driving school – they teach you how to drive but it's up to you if you are going to drive safely or kill someone."[158] That is why a stronger research focus on non-state actors, including proxies, is now more important than ever.

2

Proxies: An Instrument of Power Since Ancient Times

Throughout history, states have been very creative about building and projecting power. From the city-state of ancient Greece to the feudal state of the Middle Ages and the modern nation-state, states have used proxies to help achieve their goals. Thucydides wrote about mercenaries, auxiliaries, and privateers used by the warring parties during the Peloponnesian War.[1] "My enemy's enemy," the title of a book dedicated to proxy warfare, is a phrase taken out of the *Arthashastra*, a treatise on statecraft from India dating back to the fourth century BC.[2] In Chinese military thought, one of the famous "Thirty-Six Stratagems" is to "[k]ill with a borrowed sword."[3] A 2013 article published by the *Shanghai Daily* highlighted the continued relevance of this ancient text, pointing out that "[t]he true meaning of this stratagem is to attack your enemy by using the forces or strength of a third party, or to entice your ally into attacking your enemy instead of doing it yourself."[4] In Europe, "virtually all force was contracted" for five hundred years, although many, including Niccolò Machiavelli, viewed this practice with disdain.[5] In modern history, proxies have been used primarily in the context of the Cold War, with the *Oxford English Dictionary* defining "proxy war" as a US-specific term for "a war limited in scale or area, instigated by a major power which does not itself become involved."[6]

While the term's etymology is Latin and the modern "proxy war" US-centric, it is clear that the phenomenon it describes has varied in its manifestations regionally and over time. This invites the question, what is a proxy actor? What is common to different types of proxy actors?

What is common to proxy actors over time? Why are proxies used, when, and for what purpose? This chapter will present a framework for thinking about proxies comprehensively, explain why proxy relationships exist in the first place, and outline the three main types of state/non-state proxy relationships.

The origins of the English term "proxy" date back to the Latin word *procurare*, "pro" meaning "on behalf of" and "curare" meaning "to attend to; to take care of."

I thank Oxford University Press for granting permission to include material in this chapter from Tim Maurer, "'Proxies' and Cyberspace," *Journal of Conflict & Security Law* 21(3) (2016): 383–403.

The Merriam-Webster Dictionary offers a contemporary definition of proxy as "authority or power to act for another" and "a person authorized to act for another."[7] The international relations literature discusses "proxy warriors,"[8] "proxy forces,"[9] "proxies,"[10] "proxy war,"[11] and "proxy warfare"[12] but without a consensus definition.[13] The term "proxies" is difficult to translate: it does not have a direct equivalent in many other languages, which therefore use another, similar term, circumscribe it, or use it as a loan word. For example, in China, the term "proxy" is usually translated into Mandarin as 代理 (dàilǐ), or "representative," and is combined with either 国 (guó) meaning "country" or 人 (rén) for "people." The first variation, 代理国, is the term used to describe Cold War satellite states. The second variation, 代理人, implies the notion of an "agent" and is used to describe non-state actors.

Most of the existing scholarship on proxies is descriptive; attempts at more theoretical frameworks are rare.[14] Scholars disagree on whether the use of proxies poses greater risks than direct engagement,[15] or fewer,[16] with some even arguing it is "risk-free."[17] During the Cold War, the term "proxy" came to refer to one of the two superpowers using another state (also sometimes called by the related terms "satellite" or "client" state).[18] Since the end of the Cold War, scholars have focused predominantly on non-state actors used by states as proxies.[19] Much like the state, proxies have evolved over time, and they appear quite different and are used differently in different contexts.[20] What proxies have in common is that they are legally not part of the government and are detached from the state to a certain degree. They differ in their motivation, their organizational structure, the environment they operate in, and the historical conditions that have led to their rise and fall. The scholarship on these actors is, at its core, an analysis about their relationship with the state and how they have helped states project power.

Using the proxy framework has two main benefits. First, the concept of proxies can be viewed as an umbrella that includes more historically contingent terms such as "mercenaries"[21] or "privateers" without bearing as many deeply entrenched historical associations. These associations can present an obstacle to analysis. For example, Avant avoided the term "mercenary" altogether in her work, arguing that the changes in the word's implications over time diluted its power as an analytical term.[22] The meaning of "privateering" has varied significantly over time, as well.[23] Whereas in France, privateers were the navy and could not target neutral commerce, in Britain, they were auxiliaries to the navy and were allowed to do so.[24] (One could also use the concept of operational domains and argue that the discussion of mercenaries is essentially about land-based proxies whereas studies on privateering are about proxies on the high seas.) Second, the primary focus of proxy scholarship is on the relationship between two actors rather than on the actors as stand-alone units. Scholars have used many terms to describe this relationship, including sponsor–client,[25] sponsor–proxy,[26] patron–client,[27] patron–proxy,[28] principal–agent, activator–proxy,[29] benefactor–proxy,[30] master–puppet,[31] satellites,[32] auxiliary,[33] surrogates,[34] etc. By approaching the actors as a spectrum rather than from a categorical perspective, this literature therefore builds on scholars' recent call to focus on the relationships between actors rather than on the actor in isolation.[35]

A FRAMEWORK FOR THINKING ABOUT PROXIES

As stated in the previous chapter, a proxy actor can be defined as an intermediary that conducts or directly contributes to an offensive action that is enabled knowingly, actively or passively, by a beneficiary.[36] By extension, the study of cyber proxies must be tied to the domain of cyberspace. A *cyber* proxy is therefore an intermediary that conducts or directly contributes to an offensive *cyber* operation that is enabled knowingly, actively or passively, by a beneficiary who gains advantage from its effect.

This definition builds on the etymological roots of the term[37] that define a proxy as "actor *b* acting for actor *a*." The relationship is asymmetric[38] and distinct from the equal partnership between partners or allies discussed below.[39] Yet, as in all studies on power, measuring the asymmetry of the relationship is a methodological challenge.[40] It is also worth briefly mentioning that this framework excludes technical infrastructure from being considered a "proxy." While this is a fascinating subject, this framework focuses on proxies as actors capable of autonomous decision-making.[41]

Traditional scholarship in this area often couches its analysis in terms of principals and agents. However, decision-makers often face challenging situations in which a state is not technically a principal: the state does not actively support a proxy, but instead turns a blind eye to its activities. This book tries to cover such passive support[42] (or sanctioning) and the complicated policy questions that come with it; therefore, it avoids terminology that implies active sponsorship. Instead, actor *a* is better described as the *beneficiary*, instead of the principal, and actor *b* is the *proxy*.[43] (This does not mean that the proxy does not benefit from this relationship – indeed, a proxy might derive even greater benefit than the beneficiary.[44]) All that the "beneficiary-proxy" pairing implies is a directional element in the relationship as part of the power projection towards others. Figure 2.1 illustrates this framework and places each of the three actors – the beneficiary, the proxy, and the target of the offensive cyber action – into one of two categories: each can be either a state or non-state actor building on related existing frameworks.[45] The bi-directional arrows highlight the fact that no relationship between two actors is a one-way street; each influences the other. This dynamic extends to actor *c* as the targeted party, which in turn can shape the proxy or the beneficiary with its actions. (This will be the focus of Part III of the book.)

Of the four proxy relationships detailed in Figure 2.1, the most relevant in international affairs today is the state/non-state proxy relationship (relationship II). This is the focus of officials working at the White House, the Kremlin, or

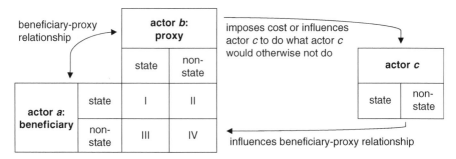

FIGURE 2.1 Beneficiary–proxy relationship directed at a third party.

Zhongnanhai, and it is the focus of this book. In the post-World War II international system, states have enjoyed legal primacy among all other actors because of the global institutionalization of the Westphalian notion of sovereignty. It is therefore easy to argue that states are the beneficiary. Nevertheless, this legally constructed form of statehood should not blind scholars to the empirical realities of a state's domestic control and the implications for proxy relationships.[46]

Expanding the definition of proxy relationships beyond non-state actors used by a state has several advantages. The narrow definition falls short of accurately describing the full phenomenon over time, especially considering the changing nature of the state itself, and risks being subject to a state-centric bias that fails to explain the dynamics in some parts of the world today. The broader framework outlined in the following section is a useful check against such potential biases; it will come into play repeatedly to call into question common assumptions and to demonstrate the real-world relevance of these assumptions. For example, when a state must decide whether to impose sanctions against another state, the decision depends on whether a malicious action was actually a state action or whether the state itself was captured by criminals, for example, and used as a proxy. This is important not only from an academic perspective; it also has direct policy relevance. For example, it is plausible that these factors play into the decision-making process of the US government whether or not to impose sanctions under the April 2015 executive order and against whom.[47]

State/State Proxy Relationships

The first type of relationship (I), state/state, can be widely seen in the literature on satellite and client states of the Cold War as well as that on "state mercenarism."[48] Yet illustrations of this concept date back centuries. The ancient Chinese strategem to "kill with a borrowed sword" refers to Zi Gong, a disciple of Confucius in the fifth century BC, who protected his home state Lu from the more powerful state of Qi. In an elaborate scheme, Zi Gong used neighboring states as "borrowed knives" (i.e., proxies), turning them against each other and the state of Qi, to defend Lu.[49] A participant in a workshop on proxies at Columbia University in July 2016 suggested a cyberspace parallel in reports that the NSA used the UK's Government Communications Headquarters (GCHQ) as a proxy to get data about US citizens, which the NSA was restricted from doing itself.[50]

A recurrent theme in the literature on state proxies is the difference between proxy relationships and alliances.[51] It is clear that asymmetry is necessary to the proxy relationship, although it is difficult to measure. Yet, the discussion about alliances makes this determination more complicated given that the Westphalian system implies that all sovereign states are equal. Nevertheless, alliances that on equal on paper are often asymmetric. This book does not offer a definitive answer on how best to distinguish alliances from proxy relationships. Apart from considering it an open empirical question for each case, a persuasive approach is to exclude formal treaty-based alliances from being considered proxies.[52]

State/Non-state Proxy Relationships

The second type of relationship (II), state/non-state, corresponds with the literature on the private market of force and privatization, including the scholarship on privateers,[53] mercenaries,[54] proxy wars,[55] and proxy warfare,[56] as well as private military and security contractors.[57] This category also includes the body of work on state-sponsored terrorism and scholarship in international law focusing on proxies.[58] The examples are manifold – from the "condottieri,"[59] the quintessential mercenaries used by Italian city-states, to privateers, to the pirates under Jean Laffite's leadership who fought the British in the War of 1812 and the Battle of New Orleans (General Andrew Jackson promised the pirates a pardon from President Madison).[60] More recent examples include the Spanish Civil War, which has been labeled a "world war by proxy,"[61] given its extensive external participants. And Angola's violent past similarly involved three guerilla groups – the MPLA, UNITA, FNLA (and a fourth, the FLEC, to include Cabinda) – and at least half a dozen external sponsors including China, Cuba, South Africa, the Soviet Union, the United States, and Zaire.[62] The most recent illustration is the current conflict in Syria, with its multiple dimensions of internal and external proxies.[63]

A similar array of relationships can be found in the cyber power context despite its relatively short history. For example, in a 2013 interview with Reuters, Costin Raiu, who leads research at Kaspersky Lab, said, "What we have here is the emergence of small groups of cyber-mercenaries available to perform targeted attacks... We actually believe they have contracts, and they are interested in fulfilling whatever the contract requirements are."[64] His firm had just exposed an unusually sophisticated hacking operation primarily hitting targets in South Korea and Japan. Other scholars have compared hackers to privateers.[65] Examples range from the US indictments of Iranian and Syrian hackers to Chinese state-sponsored militia.[66] Among the first extensive analyses of private security companies in the context of cybersecurity are Tim Shorrock's 2008 *Spies for Hire* and journalist Shane Harris's description of what he called the "Military-Internet Complex," which linked the military with a mix of conventional defense contractors and boutique cybersecurity firms.[67] (Examples of this kind of state/non-state relationship are the focus of Part II of this book.)

Non-state/State Proxy Relationships

The third type of relationship (III), non-state/state, diverges from the conventional state-centric approach of most analyses by placing a non-state actor as the beneficiary. The literature on "weak states" and organized crime provides plenty of examples of states being co-opted by organized crime groups that use the state as proxy. This relationship essentially represents the caveat laid out by Avant that a great deal of scholarship does not apply to countries where public institutions have become tools for officials to pursue their private gain and wealth.[68] Kimberley Thachuk, an intelligence analyst focusing on transnational threats, further described this hollowing out of state institutions: "[t]errorists and organized criminals have duped and suborned individuals in governments into virtually selling their sovereignty so as to create 'states of convenience' from which to conduct international operations... In other words, rather than being *agents* of government in their official capacities, individuals *are* the government."[69] Atanas Atanasov, a member of the Bulgarian parliament and a former counterintelligence chief, illustrated this when he said that "other countries have the mafia; in Bulgaria the mafia has the country."[70] In Russia, a similar trend has taken place following the collapse of the Soviet Union. Klimburg pointed to the growing influence of security forces within the Russian government, noting that in 2006 more than three-quarters of top Russian political figures had previous affiliations with the KGB or the FSB, with "strong links between them and criminal elements."[71] This aligns with a remark made by one interviewee knowledgeable about the Ukrainian and Russian hacker scenes: "If you are a small business, FSB will take bribe [*sic*] and an FSB agent will oversee [hacker] like buccaneer [*sic*]."[72]

Non-state/Non-state Proxy Relationships

The fourth relationship (IV), non-state/non-state, reflects the fact that proxy relationships do not necessarily need to include a state at all. Andrew Mumford, for example, pointed out in his book on the topic that "proxy war is not a form of conflict conducted solely by states... The establishment of global al-Qaeda 'franchises' has distinctly affected the mode by which regional conflicts can be influenced by the proxy involvement of such networked cells."[73] It is worth noting that these types of cyber proxies have already been active in the brief history of cyberspace and across the globe. For example, in 2007, the hacker Robert Anderson told *Wired* that the Motion Picture Association of America tried to hire him to hack other websites to crack down on pirated movies.[74] Three years later, similar news about "cyber hitmen" emerged with Bollywood movie companies hiring an Indian company to launch DDoS attacks on sites hosting pirated movies.[75] A third example from yet another corner of the world involves a South Korean company using a DDoS-for-hire service from China against a South Korean competitor. The victim in this instance was ItemBay, South Korea's leading website for game industry trades, with over USD 250 million in trades in 2005.[76] In 2008, ItemBay was the target of an intense DDoS attack that disrupted its business operations for several weeks as part of a blackmail campaign.[77] A few years later, an ItemBay competitor was arrested for the attack.[78]

However, Figure 2.1 does not account for potential changes in the nature of the beneficiary-proxy relationship over time. Such changes do occur as part of the dynamic relationship between the two. For example, a Middle East expert pointed out that "Syria today is more pro-Hizballah than Hizballah is pro-Syria. Hizballah is no longer a card or a proxy; it has become a partner with considerable clout and autonomy."[79] Some proxies, like mercantile companies, become state-like entities. In her seminal study on privateering, Janice Thomson suggested that in the case of mercantile companies, "all analytical distinctions – between the economic and political, non-state and state, property rights and sovereignty, the public and private – broke down."[80] In the digital context, there are similar indications. The relationship between the Iranian hackers named in the US indictment and the Iranian government seems to have evolved. And (as we will see in Chapter 7) Beijing's relationships with cyber proxies has systematically changed over time. It is also worth mentioning that the simplified framework laid out in Figure 2.1 does not reflect scenarios with multiple beneficiaries and a single proxy,[81] or a single beneficiary and multiple proxies. In addition, the affected third party, actor *c*, can itself use a proxy that affects actor *a*, actor *b*, or another actor altogether.

It is also worth mentioning that the beneficiary, proxy, and target are themselves often composed of multiple autonomous actors.[82] Consider, for example, President Xi Jinping's attempt to strengthen his control over various competing factions within the Chinese government. Such complex multi-party environments are common, and they quickly complicate the analysis. In any case, the question arises, why do proxy relationships form in the first place?

WHY PROXY RELATIONSHIPS EXIST

Four conditions must be met for a state/non-state proxy relationship to occur.[83] First, actors detached from the state must be available to act as proxies. Second, the state must have an actual or perceived need for a proxy's activity, or receive an actual or perceived benefit from it. Third, the state must have the ability to mobilize non-state actors to act as proxies or to put an end to a non-state actor's activities. Fourth, the proxy must see a benefit from the relationship. These conditions may seem trivial, but there is more to them than might be apparent at first sight.

Proxy Availability

For a beneficiary to reap benefits through a proxy relationship, non-state actors must be available to act as proxies in the first place.[84] Privateering didn't simply emerge out of thin air: it required vessels and crews to sail them. The degree to which European monarchs were able to use privateers to augment their own navies' power therefore depended on the number of ships that had been built and the number of men available and trained to operate them. The same is true for proxies in cyberspace. Unlike maritime privateering, however, the quantity of manpower matters less than its quality. As the former head of the US Army Cyber Command, Lt. Gen. Rhett Hernandez, has pointed out, "[c]yberspace requires a world-class cyber warrior... [W]e must develop, recruit and retain in a different way to today."[85] A recurrent theme in interviews with technical experts, security researchers, and hackers around the world has been that their estimates of the number of the most sophisticated hackers range in the hundreds or low thousands rather than tens of thousands or more.

Curiously, non-state actors wielding cyber capabilities predate most states' in-house capabilities. With the exception of a few states, such as the United States, who actively funded the development of Internet technologies and adopted them early to further political and military objectives, most states only recently came to consider the Internet as an instrument to project power. While difficult to measure, especially given that many hackers are self-taught, rankings of universities and their respective computer science, engineering, and mathematics departments provide an approximation of how the talent pool is geographically distributed. This distribution is illustrated in Table 2.1 (which is based on rankings by Freedom House and Transparency International to include the type of political system and level of corruption in the analysis, given the role human rights play in the international cybersecurity discussions and their impact on proxy relationships).

States also vary widely in what opportunities are available to their talent pools and how well the supply of skilled labor can be absorbed. For example, in 2013, *NBC News* reported that five teams of students from Russia, Belarus, and Ukraine were among the top ten finalists of the ACM International Collegiate Programming Contest, out of a pool of teams from 2,322 universities in ninety-one countries; students from St. Petersburg National Research University won the prestigious programming contest four times during the previous six years. Meanwhile, a survey from the same year found that only about half of Russia's IT specialists had jobs in the country's IT sector and that "the average [salary] in Moscow for work

TABLE 2.1 *Countries with world's top university departments in computer science, math, and engineering*[86]

Freedom House Index 2016	Order based on Transparency International 2015 Corruption Perceptions Index (100 = very clean; 0 = highly corrupt)		
	100-67	66-34	33-0
Free	Denmark, Finland, Sweden, New Zealand, Netherlands, Norway, Switzerland, Canada, Germany, Luxembourg, UK, Australia, Belgium, Austria, United States, Japan, Chile, France	Portugal, Poland, Israel, Slovenia, Spain, Czech Republic, South Korea, Greece, Romania, Italy, Serbia, Brazil, India	
Partly Free	Singapore	Malaysia, Turkey, Thailand, Mexico	
Not Free		Saudi Arabia, China	Russia, Iran

in information security was 65,000 roubles ($2,000) a month, far less than Western counterparts would earn."[87] Those wanting to earn extra money can advertise their services on the "dark Web," the part of the Internet that requires specific authorization (and sometimes software) to access.

In other countries – for example, the United States – the evolution and trajectory of the private market of cyber capabilities are embedded in a broader shift towards the privatization of government functions. In his 2003 *Corporate Warriors: The Rise of the Privatized Military Industry*, Peter Singer observed that "agents without an information warfare potential could hire it off the open market and then attack unsuspecting or unprepared foes in a completely unexpected realm."[88] This prediction has been backed up by empirical data that has emerged since, ranging from Raiu's encounters with cyber mercenaries to the information about Hacking Team's global business. The broader private cybersecurity industry is now a billion-dollar business.[89] In fact, some governments have decided to actively support and promote this industry. Reuters reported that Israel's cybersecurity industry "attracted a near four-fold increase in venture capital investment since 2010 [amid] a growing overseas market for cybersecurity."[90] Similarly, the British government in 2014 made cybersecurity exports a priority, noting that they account for "30 percent of current UK security exports" and predicting 14 percent growth over the next two years.[91]

In short, many non-state actors already exist and are available as cyber proxies, but states also have the option of creating and cultivating new proxies.[92]

Beneficiary's Benefit

Proxy relationships must yield a benefit to both sides that exceeds their costs, whether in loss of autonomy, cost of mobilization, or reputation. This cost-benefit calculus can change over time and influence or ultimately end the proxy relationship. For the beneficiary state, several potential factors come into play.

One of the most referenced factors is a need for capabilities,[93] either capabilities that the state does not possess at all or that the state does possess but wishes to augment.[94] Expertise is one of the main contributions that proxies bring to the table,[95] with non-state actors providing specific expertise,[96] or direct access to targets.[97] Most states are only starting to build their own cyber capabilities and – like early nation-states struggling to overcome their lack of a navy – are turning to proxies to fill the gap. Today, only a very small number of states have established a cyber command. In fact, it was not until 2010 that the US government formally declared cyberspace to be a new operational domain in addition to land, sea, air, and space, and set up the US Cyber Command. A UN study published in 2013 found only six states with published military cyber strategies in its preliminary assessment. Yet the study also found that the number of states that included cybersecurity in their military planning had risen from thirty-two in 2011 to forty-seven in 2012, demonstrating a worldwide trend to follow the US example.[98] The general need for capabilities and expertise explains why states around the world rely on private actors to build and augment their cyber power. Even established cyber powers like the United States are actively seeking out skilled hackers and support from the private market. A recent contract awarded by the US government enlists six contractors to support the establishment of US Cyber Command. This contract demonstrates many of the advantages afforded by using the private market: access to expertise, the perceived lower cost of relying on the private sector rather than building capabilities in-house, and flexible, time-limited relationships. This illustrates that using private capabilities to create a cyber command or even service not only addresses the initial need but also allows it to be done more cheaply.[99]

States around the world are struggling to attract talent, but it is not only governments that are struggling: there is a general shortage of skilled labor in the field. In 2012, Reuters published an analysis pointing to the cultural challenges faced by military recruiters seeking to hire computer specialists, noting that "whilst money is plentiful for new forces of 'cyber warriors,' attracting often individualistic technical specialists and hackers into military hierarchies is another matter."[100] There have been several impacts of this shortage, including a proliferation of government training initiatives, increased efforts on the part of tech companies to expand work visas to attract more talent from abroad, and a flood of private initiatives to teach ever-younger children how to code. As more and more states develop doctrines for the military use of cyberspace,[101] this competition for expertise is only going to increase. Governments are already competing with the private sector. The governments in the United States, the UK, and Israel all complain about a brain drain from their respective intelligence agencies to the private sector.[102] The cybersecurity expert Irv Lachow pointed out that "The US government has been quite open about its challenge in hiring qualified cyber professionals . . . 2014 was the second consecutive year in which the number of civilian federal cyber employees leaving government eclipsed new cyber hires."[103]

Lachow predicted that "If the military cannot hire enough cyber warriors on its own, and it cannot keep up with the pace of technological innovation set by industry, then it may find itself in a position where it has no choice but to rely on [cyber military and security contractors] to conduct [offensive cyber operations]."[104] In addition, the need for contractors and expertise can change dramatically in the shift from peacetime to war, as the years after the 9/11 terrorist attacks demonstrated.[105] In the context of cybersecurity, it is worth highlighting that it is also relatively easy for actors who usually focus on defense (for example, penetration testers or reverse engineers) to deploy their skills for offensive purposes if, for example, a war breaks out.

States also pursue proxy relationships to gain political benefits. One of the most cited benefits in the literature on conventional proxies is the state's desire to avoid a direct conflict.[106] This preference can be the result of a state's sensitivity to casualties (or, to be exact, its sensitivity to casualties of its own military).[107] This is an important concern not only to politicians in democratic systems such as the United States, where pictures of fallen soldiers can influence voters' behavior,[108] but also in countries such as Russia, where the objections of the Union of the Committees of Soldiers' Mothers of Russia, for example, were considered enough of a threat that the government branded the organization a "foreign agent."[109] Interestingly, it appears that the public is moved primarily on behalf of the state's symbolic representatives: it is not the death of contractors or other proxies that seems to move the people's will, but that of a country's soldiers – thereby creating an incentive for proxy relationships. Beyond this sensitivity to casualties, proxy relationships have also been explained, particularly in the context of the Cold War, by the desire to avoid a direct conflict and limit escalation towards a nuclear conflict.[110] Offensive cyber operations are usually remote in any case, but this desire to avoid direct conflict is nevertheless important in the use of cyber proxies, as it can explain a state's preference for using cyber rather than conventional means for coercion.

States may also use a proxy to enable plausible deniability. Plausible deniability is not a new phenomenon. It has been extensively discussed in historical contexts ranging from privateering to the modern incarnations of terrorism,[111] as well as in the literature on principal–agent analysis.[112] In the digital age, undisclosed principals can exist because the Internet's technical characteristics make attribution difficult.[113] That is why scholars of conventional proxy warfare – Mumford, for example – consider cyber operations "an ideal vehicle for a proxy strategy given the difficulties in tracing the exact origin of cyber attacks."[114] The incentives for an actor to establish plausible deniability vary widely. At times, it may arise out of a wish to avoid the consequences of overt action. Depending on the severity of the effects, openly using proxies, including cyber proxies, may invite condemnation or sanctions, or may spur others to retaliate in kind. Philip Bobbitt's discussion of plausible deniability differs from most other accounts by focusing not on its external but its internal political implications. In his analysis, one of plausible deniability's potential goals is that an action "would avoid the unwelcome scrutiny of Congress because it would not be a government operation," and "a private agency could act more daringly, avoiding the legal prohibitions contained in prior Executive Orders … and in defiance of international norms."[115] Plausible deniability may therefore be pursued as a shield against condemnation not only by external actors but also by internal actors, including oversight bodies.

Interestingly, plausible deniability is practiced almost universally. Russia, China, and the United States, for example, all routinely deny or remain silent about cyber operations they have been accused of. This can be partly explained by the fact that cyber operations grew out of an extension of conventional intelligence and covert operations. Therefore, plausible deniability around cyber operations is also a reflection of the bureaucratic culture of the agencies where those operations originated and continue to be carried out.

A state might also build a relationship to a non-state actor to prevent hacktivists such as the Jester or other non-state actors from interfering with government operations by, for example, shutting down a website forum that the government is monitoring for intelligence purposes.[116] The Jester already revealed that "I don't hit the ones that are being actively monitored and infiltrated on the Human Intelligence side. And I herd more people to them by hitting everything else around them, leaving them no place to go except into the arms of the big boys."[117]

A state does not need to initiate a proxy relationship in order to enjoy its benefits. For example, Eugene Dokukin of the Ukrainian Cyber Forces regularly shared the results of his group's actions with the government. This provided the state with a certain benefit even though it did not directly sponsor or encourage the activities, and the cost of the group's activities was apparently small enough that the government did not use its capabilities to put an end to them. There are many related analyses of states' inaction towards proxy groups. For example, a state may decline to act because it does not perceive a threat from the proxy's activities, as in the case of the US government's inaction towards the activities of the Irish Republican Army (IRA) on American soil,[118] or the Russian government's inaction towards cybercriminals on Russian soil targeting foreign institutions. Alternatively, a state may provide passive support to a proxy not because of a missing threat perception but because of a heightened domestic threat perception. In this case, the cost imposed by external actors targeted by the proxy is perceived to be less than the potential costs that could be unleashed if the proxy were to turn against the state instead. (Consider, for example, a radical Islamist turning against the Saudi government,[119] or Chinese hacktivists targeting the Great Firewall, rather than attacking external targets.) In other words, the perceived benefit of keeping these actors focused on foreign rather than domestic targets makes the host state more willing to absorb the external costs.

Beneficiary's Ability to Mobilize (or Stop) a Proxy

Having a proxy available is necessary but not sufficient; the beneficiary must also be able to mobilize the proxy actor. During my interviews in Ukraine, interviewees from many different backgrounds and sectors all frequently noted the wave of volunteerism that emerged among the population in Ukraine once the conflict escalated across all sectors. Yet, the interviewees also remarked that the government lacked the capacity to effectively absorb these additional resources – it was unable to mobilize them and amplify the state's power. This was a powerful reminder that it is not enough for a country to have resources; the state must also be able to make use of these resources, and this requires effective strategies and institutions. Ukraine certainly had no shortage of actors with cyber capabilities that the government could have mobilized. The country's universities are known for being excellent in the sciences, including computer science, and the country's economy does not generate sufficient demand to absorb this high-skilled labor. The government could also turn to the dark side and strike a deal with local cyber criminals. After all, Ukraine was the cradle of CarderPlanet, which "chang[ed] the nature of cyber crime around the world."[120]

The necessity of tying capabilities to the ability to mobilize them for the projection of power is not a new insight, yet it is worth highlighting.[121] Klimburg focuses on this issue in the context of cyberspace in his excellent article "Mobilising Cyber Power."[122] Failure to meet the conditions for mobilization can explain cases when states failed to reap the benefits of proxies even when they were available, as with the Ukrainian government's apparent inability to effectively leverage the various volunteer groups that spontaneously emerged following the escalation of its crisis in 2014.[123] In addition, the government must not only be able to mobilize capabilities but must also be able to select, monitor, and affect how an agent wields them once they are mobilized, if it hopes to minimize divergence between its own interests and those of its proxies. (In recognition of this necessity, the US Congress established new oversight mechanisms after the Iran-Contra affair, restricting the executive branch's ability to empower proxies.) The ability to mobilize is a function of the weakness or strength of oversight mechanisms.[124] A beneficiary is therefore more likely to mobilize an intermediary actively or passively when institutional control mechanisms are weak.

Proxy's Benefit

Most of the factors influencing a beneficiary's behavior also apply to the proxy.[125] Non-state actors are likely to act as proxies if they derive a benefit; this benefit may consist of either material support (such as augmenting existing capabilities)[126] or ideational support (such as the provision of a sanctuary and legal protections against extradition). Even in the absence of such positive incentives, a proxy relationship may result from shared goals, while negative incentives such as threat of arrest, disruption of funding, or other forms of abandonment can also motivate the non-state actor's behavior.[127] Consistent with the general beneficiary's benefit hypothesis, non-state actors are more likely to enter into proxy relationships (whether actively or passively) when they lack certain capabilities or gain a political advantage. And, just as a state actor can passively enable a non-state proxy by choosing not to stop the proxy's activities, a non-state actor can theoretically be aware of a state's activity and have the ability to stop it – for example, by making details about a specific operation public – but choose not to do so. The feedback loop between beneficiary and proxy also contributes to the dynamic nature of the relationship, whichever form it may take.[128]

THREE MAIN TYPES OF PROXY RELATIONSHIPS: DELEGATION, ORCHESTRATION, AND SANCTIONING

Most states' proxy relationships fall into one of three main types: *delegation, orchestration*, and *sanctioning* (approving or permitting), all illustrated in Table 2.2. It is important to emphasize that these three categories fall along a spectrum of control and detachment between the beneficiary and proxy. An analysis of existing proxy relationships reveals that there is significant variation among them and across countries. Some countries rely more on one set of actors than others. Part II therefore

TABLE 2.2 *Three main types of state/non-state proxy relationships*

Type of proxy relationship		Beneficiary (actor a)	$\longrightarrow$	Proxy (actor b)	$\longrightarrow$	
Active	Delegation	Principal	$\longrightarrow$	Agent	$\longrightarrow$	Target
	Orchestration "*Blitz orchestration*"	Orchestrator	$\longrightarrow$	Intermediary	$\longrightarrow$	(*actor c*)
Passive	Sanctioning	Sanctioner	$\longrightarrow$	Sanctionee	$\longrightarrow$	

focuses on a select number of countries as in-depth case studies to illustrate each of these proxy relationships in greater detail, namely the United States for delegation, Iran and Syria for orchestration, and the former Soviet Union for sanctioning. China is a case study for a state's changing proxy relationships over time.

1 *Delegation*

Delegation captures proxy relationships in their narrowest sense, in which a principal delegates authority to an agent to act on its behalf. In this "principal–agent" relationship – whether the condottieri of the Italian city-states (the archetypical mercenary) or the private security companies that have been extensively studied during the last two decades – principals control the behavior of their agents through contracts.[129] Principal–agent theory[130] has frequently been used to study the governance of organizations, particularly transaction costs and efficiency gains. It is therefore directly applicable in the context of privatization and contractors acting as proxies. The principal–agent dynamic also comes into play in other proxy relationships and, beyond its usual arena of organizational theory in international relations, has recently been applied to study terrorist groups and piracy operations.[131]

In an ideal world, the principal would instruct the agent to act on her behalf and the agent would do so in a manner perfectly aligned with the principal. In reality, the agent's interests are likely to diverge from the principal's, and the agent might act differently from the way the principal intended. The principal usually cannot fully avoid such diverging behavior in the absence of full information about the agent. This divergence of interests is also determined by the number of actors involved, with more principals increasing the agent's autonomy.[132] This is known as the *agency problem* (also known as *shirking, agency slack,* or *slippage*).[133] The agency problem implies that a principal–agent relationship can involve risks and costs for the principal.

First, the agent's divergent behavior can reduce the agent's effectiveness, requiring the principal to provide additional support and pay greater costs.[134] For example, the US military found in 2011 that one of its defense contractors had outsourced part of its work writing "computer software for sensitive US military communications systems" to Russian computer programmers, thus violating "both the company's contract and federal regulations that mandate only US citizens with approved security clearances work on classified systems."[135] At the same time, if a proxy relationship is supposed to be covert to maintain plausible deniability, detecting such violations becomes more difficult or risks revealing the relationship.

Second is what the scholar Idean Salehyan has dubbed the "Frankenstein problem": the risk that "[l]ike Frankenstein's monster, governments might create entities that are beyond their control."[136] An agent that is too eager or takes risks can create an unintended effect, possibly including an escalation and response.[137]

A recent horrific example is the downing of civilian aircraft MH17 over eastern Ukraine, which killed all 298 passengers and crew on board; criminal investigators identified the weapon that brought down the plane as a "Russian-made Buk" missile.[138] It is unlikely that the rebels' sponsor intended this outcome when providing the weaponry to its agent.

The Frankenstein problem is not limited to excessive harm against a third party: it can also involve the agent turning against the principal. As Salehyan observed in the context of delegation to rebels, "Principals walk a fine line between empowering rebels enough to ensure that they can impose costs on the target government but not so much that the rebels do not fear abandonment nor be able to turn against the patron."[139] For these reasons, principals are likely to build restraint into proxy relationships from the start as well as control mechanisms to minimize the risk of such divergent behavior and cost.[140]

To reduce losses and escalatory risks, principals have access to several control mechanisms prior to and during the relationship. The three main instruments principals can use bilaterally to minimize the divergence of interests and behavior are (1) screening and selection, (2) monitoring, and (3) punitive measures.[141] In addition, principals may use multiple agents as an additional instrument, keeping agents weak by introducing competition into the framework.[142]

Principals must screen and select proxies carefully because they don't have full information about the proxies' intentions. According to Salehyan, one screening mechanism is looking for proxies "who share ethnic, religious, and linguistic kinship ties to the state. . . Reduced language and cultural barriers make it easier to gather information on potential agents and avoid misunderstandings; moreover, ethnic kin are more likely to share the patron's preferences, or at least be perceived to do so."[143] Proxies in the context of the former Soviet Union, where sizable groups of Russian-speaking minorities live in now-independent states, illustrate how some of these relationships can cross national boundaries.

Monitoring can rely on a series of tools, ranging from requiring audits and reports of contractors to so-called "fire alarms," third parties that alert the principal to an agent's unintended behavior.[144] Civil society organizations and media often play the latter role – for example, documenting abuse by rebel organizations during a conflict. A "fire alarm" mechanism worth mentioning in the cybersecurity context is the growing number of private cyber threat intelligence firms publishing reports on specific threat actors and their actions. Effective monitoring cannot be achieved in every situation, however: a proxy relationship that is overt or based on a contract offers significantly greater opportunities for monitoring than does a covert proxy relationship striving to maintain plausible deniability.[145]

A principal can also punish a proxy in various ways. These range from reducing material or immaterial support, to abandoning the proxy, to arresting or killing the proxy. In one example of reducing support, the 2014 US Quadrennial Defense Review mentioned that increasing the civilian workforce "reduce[d] excessive reliance on contractor support," arguing that such rebalancing would "ensure organic capabilities and government performance of inherently governmental and critical functions."[146] The increased reliance on civilian workers reflects an attempt to reduce the risks associated with delegation and proxies. In other cases, agents have been punished, as in the jail sentences for the employees of Blackwater Worldwide, the private company working as a contractor for the US government in Iraq, which was held responsible for killing seventeen people in Baghdad in 2007.[147]

Orchestration

Orchestration differs from delegation by emphasizing the ideational dimension of the relationship while still acknowledging the importance of rational interests.[148] Daniel Byman and Sarah Kreps pointed out that the principal–agent model does not describe all real-world situations in the context of their studies of terrorism, a finding that also applies to the study of cyber proxies:

> Rationalist calculations about efficiency gains explain only part of the dynamic between principal and agent in the state–terrorist group relationship. Rarely does a strategic cost-benefit logic, for example, explain the convergence of principal–agent preferences and behavioral outcomes. Rather, a strong ideological bond often reduces divergence and thus reduces the need for other control mechanisms. A shared ideology offers a tremendous source of potential influence for the principal, but may also lead a state not to control the agents' attacks even if they are strategically costly.[149]

Orchestration is the enlistment of intermediary actors on a voluntary basis, by providing them with ideational and material support, and using them to address target actors in pursuit of political goals.[150] In their discussion of orchestration as distinct from delegation, the political scientists Kenneth Abbott and his co-authors argued that the correlated goals between the orchestrator and the intermediary "are constitutive of their relationship."[151] In other words, their orchestration framework is not an attempt to stretch the existing principal–agent model to accommodate various criticisms, but instead proposes a new, complementary framework.[152] Because the orchestrator has fewer direct means of controlling the intermediary, orchestration depends on the existence of correlated goals. Abbot et al. raised the important point that "the model is agnostic as to the source and content of those goals: they may be material or ideational, self-seeking or altruistic; they may reflect a utilitarian logic of consequences or a socially constructed logic of appropriateness; they may be exogenously given or endogenous to actors' social context."[153] The centrality of correlated goals also implies that orchestration consists of identifying correlated goals, selecting and recruiting intermediaries accordingly, monitoring the continued correlation over time, and potentially taking corrective action.[154]

To translate the distinction in terms of international law, the concept of delegation captures the proxy relationships that operate above the threshold of effective and overall control – what is described as "state-sponsored" in the counterterrorism literature. Orchestration, on the other hand, covers the broad spectrum of activities taking place below this threshold – from financing to the provision of arms, intelligence, and logistical support – that nonetheless can be considered "state-supported."

Orchestration implies a beneficiary will carefully evaluate a proxy's past activities during the screening process.[155] For example, do the Web defacements of a specific hacktivist group reflect the political goals of the state? Do the website or videos of a cyber criminal on an underground forum express political views beyond the profit-driven characteristics of his business? Meanwhile, monitoring allows an orchestrator to use indoctrination to minimize divergence of correlated goals. Byman and Kreps mentioned the role of indoctrination in the relationship between Iran and Hizballah: Iranian government officials, they noted, focused on "proselytizing, which served to both screen potential recruits and to reorient the group as a whole toward the principal's interests... The [Islamic Revolutionary Guard Corps] preached the virtues of revolutionary Islam as well as providing military tactics."[156]

An addition to the concept of orchestration is the notion of "blitz orchestration" or "transactional orchestration." Delegation usually describes hierarchical relationships between principals and agents; orchestration reflects network relationships.[157] The term "blitz orchestration" specifically describes orchestration that occurs ephemerally rather than on a prolonged basis. This concept is particularly relevant in the context of cybersecurity: consider, for example, the DDoS attack at the onset of the war between Russia and Georgia, an orchestration relationship that lasted only for a few days. According to Ron Deibert, Rafal Rohozinksi, and Masashi Crete-Nishihata, a group of Canadian experts, "such campaigns have a tendency to take on lives of their own because of the unavoidable participation of actors swarming from edge locations." Describing this phenomenon as "cyclones in cyberspace," Deibert et al. argued that such dynamics "invariably internationalize any cyber conflict."[158] However, while a cyclone suggests a natural occurrence, I prefer the term "blitz orchestration," because it highlights the human role in this phenomenon and the agency of the actors involved.

Sanctioning

Sanctioning builds on the counterterrorism literature's concept of passive support.[159] A state passively supports a non-state actor when it knowingly chooses to tolerate the actor's activities in spite of having the capacity to do otherwise.[160] In this case there is no delegation or orchestration by the beneficiary, yet the state's decision not to act in spite of its ability transforms the non-state actor into a proxy. Sanctioning can also come into play after the fact – for example, in the form of providing a safe haven sheltering the non-state actor from prosecution. A state's toleration of a non-state actor's malicious activity from its territory can be driven by different factors.[161]

First, the activities of the non-state actor might enjoy considerable domestic sympathy, creating costs in case of a crackdown. Byman has cited support for Al Qaeda among the radicals of the Saudi and Pakistani population as well as support for the IRA among Irish-American radicals as examples. In fact, such domestic support can translate into not only toleration but also subsequent endorsement by the government. For example, the Iranian students that took over the US embassy in November 1979 enjoyed support domestically and were initially acting independently, yet their activities were later on endorsed by Ayatollah Khomeini.

Second, a state might tolerate the non-state actor when it does not pose a threat to that state. The radical Iranian students in 1979, for example, belonged to the Muslim Student Followers of the Imam's Line and were supporters of the Islamic revolution and the new government. The IRA was fighting for an independent Ireland that posed no threat to the United States. Al Qaeda had different ambitions than its offspring, the Islamic State, and posed a lower threat to countries like Saudi Arabia and Pakistan,[162] and, in fact, these states recognized that cracking down on Al Qaeda could embolden domestic radicals.

Third, sanctioning occurs when inaction has a low cost or an indirect benefit. As Byman pointed out, "because passive support is far less open than active support, it often is viewed as more acceptable internationally – and thus has fewer diplomatic costs."[163] Inaction might allow a state to score sympathy points at home or have an effect on its adversary that outweighs the cost of the adversary's protest. In the context of cybersecurity, the cost might be low because the effects are non-physical or are not realized until several months after the fact, when tensions might have subsided.

A fourth factor that may drive sanctioning is a discrepancy between the state's projected capacity or aspirational status and its *de facto* capacity and power. In other words, a state might try to project itself as a regional or even global power, implying it has all the correlated domestic capacities, but, in reality, its capacity is significantly more limited. In this case, an ineffective attempt at cracking down on the non-state actor could expose this discrepancy and prove a source of embarrassment.

The phenomenon of sanctioning has influenced some of the underlying assumptions of agency enshrined in existing international law, namely with regard to state responsibility for the actions of private actors. According to Tal Becker, principal deputy legal adviser at the Israeli Ministry of Foreign Affairs and winner of the 2007 Guggenheim Prize for best international law book,

> When President Bush declared, on the evening of September 11th, that the United States would "make no distinction between the terrorists who committed the attacks and those who harbor them" he made no claim that State responsibility was grounded in an agency relationship. The Taliban was held directly responsible for the September 11th attacks because it "allowed" Al-Qaeda to operate, not because it directed or controlled their activities. And yet, the overwhelming number of nations that appeared to endorse this policy, and to support the targeting of both the Taliban regime and Al-Qaeda – seemed remarkably unconcerned by this departure from agency standards.[164]

Becker's remarks underline the growing interest in the concept of sanctioning and state responsibility in the modern age. That is why due diligence has become one of the most contentious issues discussed among the members of the 2016/2017 UNGGE.[165] The debate reflects the risk of stretching the concept of state responsibility too far, especially with regard to the careful balancing of legal and political responsibilities *vis-à-vis* a state's empirical capacities to implement them. Too great an imbalance, in which states are unable to effectively translate expected responsibilities, risks hollowing out the broader normative aspirations. It also makes support from developing countries less likely in the first place given their concerns over being subjected to undue burdens without having or receiving the resources to carry them out. Nevertheless, in an age when ever fewer people can cause ever greater harm across long distances, a state's sanctioning behavior cannot be ignored.

CONCLUSION: IT'S THE RELATIONSHIP THAT MATTERS

Proxies have proven their value to the powerful for centuries. In today's state-centric international system, state/non-state proxy relationships are the most relevant. They exist in countries around the world because there is a sufficient supply of non-state actors with capabilities that can benefit the state. The organization of proxy relationships varies, but all three main types – delegation, orchestration, and sanctioning – can have a substantial impact. Private companies acting as contractors can be an integral part of an offensive cyber operation. Orchestration allows channeling the projection of coercive cyber power at arm's length. And sanctioning can provide the state with a foundation for rapid mobilization for specific operations.

Ultimately, it is important to stress that it is the relationship and not the individual actors that matters most. It is the dynamics between the beneficiary and the proxy that influences the risk associated with any of these proxy relationships (in addition to whatever counteraction the targeted actor might take). For example, if a beneficiary reduces support for a proxy or abandons the proxy altogether, the proxy might no longer feel inhibited in pursuing more advanced capabilities on its own.[166] In addition, reducing support can increase the risk of an agent turning against the principal, which is a particular concern for authoritarian countries worried about internal threats.[167] At the end of the day, proxies are usually but pawns in the broader political game that is being played,[168] but their masters are mindful of any risks they could pose domestically or as potential long-term threats.

3

Cyber Power: Geopolitics and Human Rights

To understand why proxy relationships differ across states and how states use cyber proxies, it is necessary to understand the broader systemic game that is being played and how different governments view information/cybersecurity. This chapter discusses the difference between cybersecurity and information security and the differing perspectives among the world's most powerful states. Whereas most NATO countries prefer the term cybersecurity, Russia, China, and members of the Shanghai Cooperation Organization prefer the term information security, which is tied to the controversy around information operations, control over content, and the free flow of information. To shed light on why and how they use proxies, this chapter will scrutinize how each state that serves as a case study in Part II of this book views the question of information and cybersecurity.

The malicious hack of Sony Pictures Entertainment in the United States provides a powerful example of the geopolitics of cyber power and how hacking gnaws at the foundation of the global security system. That system, formally established after World War II, has roots in long-established traditions of sovereignty and the principle of non-interference in internal affairs that date back to the 1555 treaty of Augsburg and its notion of *cuius regio, eius religio*.

The Sony hack was tied to the impending release of a film comedy, *The Interview*, that satirized the North Korean leader, whose character is killed in the course of the movie. In June 2014, several months before the anticipated release date, the North Korean ambassador to the UN sent a letter to the UN Secretary-General arguing that such a movie "should be regarded as the most undisguised sponsoring of terrorism as well as an act of war."[1] Five months later, personal information of Sony employees and unreleased movies appeared on the Internet. The "Guardians of Peace" (see note 3 below) claimed credit for the hack.

The president of the United States, the most powerful head of state in the world, considered this incident important enough for him to go before a global television audience to address it. Many other companies had suffered data breaches earlier that year without the president becoming involved, however, so what made this case different? First, it became clear that the hack not only leaked embarrassing proprietary data; it had also wiped thousands of hard drives, sending Sony's US operations back to the age of paper and typewriters.[2] Yet even this destructive attack on a private company was not by itself reason enough to bring the US president in front of the cameras. By December, the Guardians of Peace began threatening the physical safety of Americans going to the theaters to watch the movie.[3] Even that was barely a sufficient reason, it being extremely unlikely that there were North Korean sleeper cells in US territory capable of carrying out such action. But the third and arguably most important development came when theaters around the country decided to pull the movie, turning an empty threat into the *de facto* censorship that North Korea had wanted all along.[4] This development transformed costly but reversible damage to a private company into an attack on ideological values the United States considers in its national interest.[5]

The Sony hack is significant for two key reasons: why it occurred in the first place and what the hack was supposed to accomplish. The hackers were trying to force a film studio not to release a movie. That such an aggressive malicious hack had such a motivation surprised many US officials. In hindsight, North Korea's actions, together with several other high-profile incidents during the previous five years, demonstrated that some of the most aggressive cyber actions against the United States were driven not by military concerns but by content. This was a marked departure from the potential scenarios discussed in the Washington beltway, which focused on cyber operations in a military context.

The Sony incident therefore points to an aspect of cybersecurity that has not received sufficient attention: the real-world and operational implications of other states' broader view on information security, the implied connection between cybersecurity and human rights, and a serious mirror-imaging problem among US and Western officials. CIA veteran Richards Heuer defined mirror-imaging as a cognitive phenomenon of "filling gaps in [one's] own knowledge by assuming that the other side is likely to act in a certain way because that is how the United States would act under similar circumstances."[6] In this case mirror-imaging describes Western officials who consider the free flow of content to be a human rights issue and who therefore are limited in their ability to anticipate how other actors that view content as a significant threat might act in response. In other words, some states see the Internet as a threat to the stability of the international system not only because it is possible to cause harm remotely through hacking, which is the concern that has dominated the discussion about cybersecurity in the United States and Europe. These other states, many of which are not considered "free" according to the Freedom House Index, see the Internet's dissemination of information as undermining the principle of non-interference in states' internal affairs and respond accordingly.

This attitude exists not only in smaller states like North Korea but also in major powers, including Russia and China, and it lies at the root of other offensive cyber actions. For example, in March 2015, only three months after President Obama's

televised speech blaming North Korea for the Sony hack, the website GitHub –
a San Francisco start-up that serves as a code-sharing platform[7] – became the target
of the largest DDoS attack it had ever experienced. In its eight years of existence,
GitHub had become a critical tool for software coders. According to the technology
website *Wired*, "Pretty much everyone hosts their open source projects on GitHub,
including Google, Facebook, Twitter, and even Microsoft."[8] So when the DDoS
attack on two specific GitHub pages (http://GreatFire.org, which makes blocked
websites in China available to Chinese users, and a mirror site of the Chinese
edition of *The New York Times*) took the website down for five days,[9] the disruptive
effect reverberated throughout the tech industry.

Reports analyzing the attack traced the source of the malicious traffic back to
China. One in-depth analysis dubbed the attack the "Great Cannon" and concluded
that "[i]t is likely that this attack, with its potential for political backlash, would
require the approval of high-level authorities within the Chinese government."[10]
GitHub itself believed that the attack was intended "to convince us to remove
a specific class of content."[11] The researchers at the Citizen Lab[12] argued that the
malicious behavior aligned with the priorities of the Chinese Communist Party and
its willingness to counter "foreign hostile forces" which, in Beijing's view, included
certain media outlets, NGOs, and other civil society actors.[13]

THE BIGGER PICTURE: SOVEREIGNTY AND INFORMATION

States protesting and taking action against information and propaganda spread by
other countries is obviously not a new issue. The former East German government
tried (unsuccessfully) to block its citizens from accessing West German television,[14]
and the Cuban government has complained for decades about US government-
sponsored radio broadcasts that it considers a violation of its sovereignty. Even the
dissemination of information at a global scale is not new. Decades ago, the advent of
satellites and their global coverage led to a similar controversy at the UN.[15]

At the center of all these disputes lies Article 19 of the Universal Declaration of
Human Rights and whether it allows governments to make information available in
countries where the local government actively suppresses such information.[16] Many
countries argue that it does. For example, the US Congress has appropriated some
USD 770 million over the past thirty years for the purpose of sending radio broadcasts to Cuba.[17] And on the Korean peninsula, loudspeakers on either side of the
border are a regular bargaining chip in negotiations.[18] Such efforts take place in
cyberspace as well. The US State Department's Internet Freedom program has spent
over USD 100 million since its launch in 2010.[19] These can be overt and obvious,
such as the US State Department's Virtual Embassy Iran or its staff openly posting
messages in online forums to counter hate speech and violent extremism.[20] They
may also be covert, as with the US military's use of software that allows military
personnel to maintain up to ten different fake online personas "without fear of being

discovered by sophisticated adversaries."[21] But even some states that try to suppress the free flow of information domestically are engaged in aggressive information operations externally. For example, the Russian government uses information operations including anonymous online commenters who produce and place fake news articles, which one news report described as an "army of well-paid trolls."[22] The activities of these trolls do in some ways parallel those of the US State Department's Digital Outreach team, though with one important difference: as Adam Segal, Director of the Digital and Cyberspace Policy Program at the Council on Foreign Relations, pointed out, "[u]nlike the Internet trolls paid by the Chinese and Russian governments who operate in the shadows, members of the digital team identified themselves as State Department representatives."[23]

Circumvention technologies play an increasingly important role in the struggle over information and sovereignty. According to Monroe Price, Director of the University of Pennsylvania's Center for Global Communication Studies, "Circumvention primarily involves informal efforts to help putatively weak players, including individuals, civil society groups, and other advocates, subvert barriers to access to meaningful information that would help them gain their objectives (including at times, mobilizing to affect the leadership of the country in question)."[24] Circumvention technology is certainly nothing new: when Prussia besieged Paris in 1870, the city's residents used hot-air balloons to continue postal mail traffic with the rest of France and to drop leaflets with political messages onto Prussian troops. In the age of the Internet, the "Twitter revolutions" from Tunisia to Syria, Ukraine, and Hong Kong made circumvention technologies an international political issue. The protests in Iran in 2009 were a pivotal moment in this context, as protestors used their mobile devices to get images and videos to the international news media. Price went so far as to argue that "[t]he Iran event was to the testing of new information technologies what the Spanish Civil War was to experimentation with new military techniques."[25] The US government actively funds and supports the development and deployment of circumvention technologies, as through the 2009 Victims of Iranian Censorship (VOICE) Act, passage of which was perceived by some as part of a broader regime change effort.

Yet, the spread of information itself can trigger an escalatory response. According to a contemporary account, one of the leaflet-dropping Parisians in 1870 was fired upon by the Prussians when his balloon passed over them.[26] Similarly, today, not only do Russia, China, and other governments have very different perspectives on content and circumvention than do the United States and other countries conceptually, but these issues drive their actions, including offensive cyber actions. That is why it is important to discuss circumvention technologies, as Nye has done in his scholarship on cyber power. It is therefore not surprising that when US Secretary of State Hillary Clinton delivered a speech in 2010 making "Internet Freedom" a new rallying cry for US foreign policy, feathers were ruffled in Moscow and Beijing. Price explains,

Secretary Clinton's argument depended on a tree of logic in which US interests are served by the increase in democratic values in states throughout the world. A long-standing theory holds that a world that is more dependably democratic is more stable, possibly more prosperous, and less likely to lead to conflict with other democracies. Related to this is the belief that openness to information, and press freedom more specifically, is linked to democracy, as a system of information diffusion that empowers individuals, leads to greater accountability and improves or enhances the demand side for democratic governance. "Internet freedom" is, at least in part, shorthand for a series of policies concerning the Internet that would advance these democratic values and expedite more democratic political outcomes.[27]

Secretary Clinton's speech would resurface in the January 2017 assessment of the US intelligence community that President Putin had ordered an influence campaign targeting the 2016 US elections. The US intelligence community concluded that the campaign was intended to "denigrate Secretary Clinton," "harm her electability and potential presidency," and "undermine public faith in the US democratic process."[28] They named several reasons for Putin's decision to launch this campaign, including his conviction that Secretary Clinton had encouraged protests against him and his government in 2011;[29] the leak of the "Panama Papers," which revealed that individuals around the world (including officials close to Putin) had secretly channeled their wealth through offshore firms and a law firm in Panama; and the exposure of Russia's state-sponsored doping system.[30] The Obama administration assessment was that these activities had put Putin in "offensive mode beyond what he sees as his sphere of influence" and had led him to try to undermine institutions in the United States, the European Union, and the NATO alliance.[31] In Putin's eyes, they concluded, the release of the Democratic National Committee emails was likely a tit-for-tat for what he saw as information operations directed against him.

One of the best illustrations of the tension between sovereignty and the free flow of information, as well as their relationship to cybersecurity, is the different terms different states use in international forums. Russia and China have championed the term "information security," and they have expanded their definition of the concept beyond its original technical definition.[32] As Ilya Rogachev, Director of the Department of New Challenges and Threats at the Russian Ministry of Foreign Affairs, made clear at the EastWest Institute in September 2015: "For the Russian government, information security is also about content."[33] The draft International Code of Conduct for Information Security that the Russian and Chinese governments have been promoting since 2011 through the Shanghai Cooperation Organization therefore expects states to pledge cooperation in "curbing the dissemination of information that incites terrorism, secessionism or extremism or that undermines other countries' political, economic and social stability, as well as their spiritual and cultural environment."[34] Under this code, states would cooperate to restrict content deemed to pose a threat to a country's "social stability." In contrast, the US government and many other governments prefer the term "cybersecurity" over "information security," in part out of concern over the human rights implications of the latter term's extended definition.[35]

These different views are reflected in governments' national strategies and policies, which in turn shed light on how different states are likely to act in and through cyberspace, including through proxies, and therefore merit closer examination.

THE US GOVERNMENT'S PERSPECTIVE

Offensive cyber operations grew out of conventional activities by intelligence agencies, including intelligence collection and information operations, and were initially viewed through this prism. Yet over time, the US national security community developed the mainstream view that offensive cyber operations are distinct from classic information and psychological operations and electronic warfare. Martin Libicki, a long-time scholar on cybersecurity, wrote in 2012,

> A dozen years ago, a … misguided notion plagued the defense community. The concept of information warfare created a false unity binding diverse activities such as cyberspace operations on the one hand and psychological operations on the other. Fruitless hours were spent developing a comprehensive theory covering this agglomeration. When questioned about whether such a unity was not illusory, high defense officials retorted: be that as it may, the concept was established and that was that. But things did change. The term information warfare, in the process of morphing into "information operations," created "influence operations," which covers psychological operations and concomitants, such as strategic communications. The cyber part of this formulation, computer network operations, married the "cyber" prefix and separated itself completely from matters psychological. Electronic warfare returned to its own aerie. So, at least the term, information warfare, has been rectified.[36]

Today, the Pentagon calls computer network operations "offensive cyber effects operations," a term that replaces the previous terms "computer network attack," "computer network exfiltration," and "computer network defense."[37] Marco Roscini, who has written an extensive review of how the various terms evolved over the past two decades, pointed out that "computer network" was starting to be replaced with "cyberspace" or just "cyber" with the 2011 International Strategy for Cyberspace and the 2011 US DoD Strategy for Operating in Cyberspace. Part of the reason behind this evolution is that the new terminology recognizes the fact that cyber operations do not take place only in cyberspace: they can be conducted "not only remotely through networks, but also through local installation of malware by agents that have physical access to the system."[38]

The current terminology defines *cyber effect* as "the manipulation, disruption, denial, degradation, or destruction of computers, information or communication systems, networks, physical or virtual infrastructure controlled by computers or information systems, or information resident thereon."[39] According to this broad definition, offensive cyber effects operations can range from Web defacements to operations causing physical effects and death.[40] How these definitions are applied and outlined in DoD memos is an open question, especially given the overlap of cyber operations with other types of operations, processes, and chains of command. Susan Hennessey, a former attorney at the NSA, has stated that "[t]he chain of command is clear on paper. It's much more difficult in practice," holding up the distinction between a cyber operation and electronic warfare as an example.[41]

The US government's desire to clearly distinguish cyber espionage from cyber attack remains complicated, as reflected by the terminology differentiating cyber collection operations, operational preparation of the environment, and cyber effects operations.[42] As Gary D. Brown and Andrew O. Metcalf, both legal advisers to the armed forces, have pointed out, "One of the first practical issues confronting a cyber operations lawyer is the artificial distinction between espionage and operations... Often the only difference between military cyber operations intended to collect intelligence and those designed to deliver cyber effects is the intent."[43] This legal challenge is because often an intrusion could serve both purposes: intelligence gathering and creating a disruptive or destructive effect.

Nevertheless, the US government has explained at great length that it considers political espionage legitimate (while considering espionage for commercial competitive advantages illegitimate). Even so, when China aimed its political espionage at the Office of Personnel Management, some decision-makers in Washington declared "enough is enough." As Christopher Painter, Coordinator for Cyber Issues at the US Department of State, said in Congressional testimony on May 25, 2016, this "kind of intrusion is just too big to ignore and too disruptive and it is a real concern."[44] President Obama considered using the new Executive Order 13694 he had signed in April 2015, which allowed the US government to impose sanctions against individuals or groups engaging in malicious cyber-enabled activities.[45] At the same time, senior intelligence officials, such as James Clapper, expressed admiration and envy of the operation, suggesting that they considered it an act of political espionage that is not prohibited under international law.[46] In short, even the US government continues to debate whether there might be a level of political espionage where the difference in quantity starts to constitute a difference in kind.

The most recent attempt by the US government to formulate a coherent and practical view of offensive cyber operations was Presidential Policy Directive 41, released in July 2016. The directive drew a distinction between *cyber incidents* and *significant cyber incidents*. A *cyber incident* was defined as "[a]n event occurring on or conducted through a computer network that actually or imminently jeopardizes

TABLE 3.1 *US Presidential Policy Directive 41.*

	Description
Level 5 Emergency (Black)	*Poses an imminent* threat to the provision of wide-scale critical infrastructure services, national gov't stability, or to the lives of U.S persons.
Level 4 Severe (Red)	*Likely to result in a significant* impact to public health or safety, national security, economic security, foreign relations, or civil liberties.
Level 3 High (Orange)	*Likely to result in a demonstrable* impact to public health or safety, national security, economic security, foreign relations, civil liberties, or public confidence.
Level 2 Medium (Yellow)	*May impact* public health or safety, national security, economic security, foreign relations, civil liberties, or public confidence.
Level 1 Low (Green)	*Unlikely to impact* public health or safety, national security, economic security, foreign relations, civil liberties, or public confidence.
Level 0 Baseline (White)	Unsubstantiated or inconsequential event.

the integrity, confidentiality, or availability of computers, information or communications systems or networks, physical or virtual infrastructure controlled by computers or information systems, or information resident thereon." A *significant cyber incident* was "[a] cyber incident that is (or group of related cyber incidents that together are) likely to result in demonstrable harm to the national security interests, foreign relations, or economy of the United States or to the public confidence, civil liberties, or public health and safety of the American people."[47] The level of severity was assessed with the chart shown in Table 3.1. The reference to a "group of related cyber incidents" occurring together reflected the "accumulation of events" doctrine in international law, which has also been used to justify counterterrorism activities.[48] A more popular wording would be to call it the 'death by a thousand cuts' logic.

What remains subject to intense debate among policymakers is to what extent these various tools, including influence and offensive cyber effects operations, require stand-alone policies and strategies, and to what extent they should be viewed in an integrated manner as components of "hybrid warfare."[49] In addition, while Directive 41 tried to separate data exfiltration from other effects, questions remain about how best to implement the framework in scenarios where data is both exfiltrated and released to create a specific political effect, as it was in the case of the hacks into Sony and the Democratic National Committee. Such leaks have not only led to high-level resignations in both organizations, they can also lead to the bankruptcy of a company, as in the case of HB Gary, whose reputation was irrevocably damaged after its internal communication was exposed by Anonymous.[50]

THE RUSSIAN GOVERNMENT'S PERSPECTIVE

In 2009, Timothy Thomas, a senior analyst at the US Army's Foreign Military Studies Office at Fort Leavenworth, Kansas, warned that, "[p]erhaps more than any other country, Russia is alarmed over the cognitive aspects of cyber issues as much as their technical aspects."[51] This warning, delivered seven years before the hack of the Democratic National Committee in the United States, quoted a speech given by V. I. Tsymbal at a US-Russian conference in Moscow in September 1995, in which the Russian military theorist suggested that Russia would respond to an "information attack" from the United States with a nuclear weapon.[52] Making the analogy between a nuclear strike and an information operation might seem bizarre to Western observers, yet it continues to feature in presentations by Russian officials, as I witnessed at a conference in 2016.[53] What explains this hyperbolic parallel between content and a weapon of mass destruction?

Analysts of Russian policy emphasize that the Russian government has been primarily concerned about internal stability and external efforts to undermine it.[54] Thomas, a long-time observer of Russian (and Chinese) information security policy, pointed out that "[Russian b]ooks and articles claim that the death blow to the Soviet Union came, not from NATO conventional forces, but from an imperialist 'information war' that Russia lost. By 2000, therefore, Russian state specialists had written the country's first information security doctrine (perhaps the first of any nation in the world), which focused on laws and regulations and the information security of individuals as much as on the information security of industry."[55] This historic narrative of what led to the fall of the Soviet Union is driving Russia's current efforts to control information and the Internet in Russia. It is therefore no surprise that Russia's Information Security Doctrine of 2000 focused not only on the external but also on the internal threat dimension, defining information security as "protection of [Russia's] national interests in the information sphere defined by the totality of balanced interests of the individual, society, and the state."[56] The Kremlin's focus on internal threats also explains why one of the first known instances when the Kremlin used an offensive cyber operation in combination with conventional kinetic force occurred not during the 2008 war with Georgia but during the 2002 standoff with Chechen rebels holding hostages in the Moscow Theater; in that instance, the websites of Chechen rebels were taken down in an attack timed to coincide with the Russian special forces' attack on the theater.[57]

Internationally, Russia's diplomatic initiatives reflect both domestic concerns over the free flow of information and the military's approach to information operations and cybersecurity. In the mid-1990s, the Kremlin approached the White House with a proposal for an international information security treaty. Although the US government rejected the proposal, this has not kept the Russian government from pursuing and promoting the idea globally. Moscow put the implications of information and communications technologies for international peace and security on the agenda of the UN General Assembly's First Committee in the late 1990s and worked with the member states of the Shanghai Cooperation Organization to further advance its proposal for such a treaty. Together with China, Russia developed the aforementioned 2011 draft International Code of Conduct for Information Security, along with a draft Convention that circulated at a conference in Yekaterinburg in autumn 2011. Remarks made by Sergei Smirnov, the first deputy director of the FSB, at a meeting of the Shanghai Cooperation Organization revealed the motivation behind these efforts: "New technologies [are being] used by Western special services to create and maintain a level of continual tension in society, with serious intentions extending even to regime change... Our elections, especially the [2012] presidential election and the situation in the preceding period, revealed the potential of the blogosphere."[58]

The Russian perception that information constitutes a threat dates back to the Bolsheviks. As Andrei Soldatov and Irina Borogan, two Russian investigative journalists, have pointed out, "The Bolsheviks wanted newspapers to organize and mobilize the masses, not to inform them."[59] The Communist Party therefore focused on establishing an effective censorship regime partly based on using intimidation to encourage self-censorship. There is evidence that President Putin has similarly been concerned about Russia's political stability since his days as Yeltsin's protégé and director of the FSB in the late 1990s.[60] Putin's ascent to power coincided with the Russian government's push to strengthen its control over the media following the demise of the Soviet Union. Soldatov and Borogan have traced how, over the years, the government worked with friendly oligarchs to buy media companies and Internet platforms and control them through ownership.[61] These renewed efforts to increase the state's control over information coincided with the establishment of pro-Kremlin youth organizations, partly as a counterbalance to potential popular uprisings.[62] This concern over domestic stability also affected the bureaucratic structure of the state itself. For example, in the wake of the global financial crisis of 2007–2008, Dmitry Medvedev, President of the Russian Federation at the time, created a new Interior Ministry department that focused, together with the FSB, on monitoring early signs of popular unrest.[63]

The color revolutions in Georgia and Ukraine and the Arab Spring of 2011 fueled the Kremlin's perception of threat. As Soldatov and Borogan pointed out, "It was not lost on Putin and his people that the events in Tunisia and Egypt were widely characterized as Facebook and Twitter revolutions. Putin and his entourage became worried that this time the United States had found a truly magic tool that could bring people to the streets without any organizing structure: the Internet."[64] In response, the Russian government started to further tighten its control on the Internet. In addition to DDoS attacks against blogging platforms,[65] an increasing number of technical controls were put in place. In July 2012, a new law was signed allowing the government to filter content on the Internet.[66] The law also used a narrative of sovereign democracy and digital sovereignty to pressure companies like Google and Facebook to store data on Russian territory. Placing servers within Russia's borders would enable the government to gain access to the data via the SORM (literally 'System for Operative Investigative Activities') black boxes that were already running on Russia's telecommunications infrastructure and allowing the government to surveil communications.[67]

The 2014 ouster of Ukrainian president Yanukovych struck even closer to home than the Arab Spring.[68] In response, an April 2014 decree led to the combination of the existing SORM-based surveillance system with deep packet inspection, and added a legal requirement that servers be located on Russian territory. A new Russian information security doctrine adopted in 2015, the first since 2000, articulated the heightened sense of threat, stating that "[t]he special services of certain states provide information and psychological influence, aimed at destabilizing the political and social situation in various regions of the world, resulting in the undermining of the sovereignty and the territorial integrity of other states."[69] Even so, Soldatov and Borogan pointed out, the Russian government's efforts to control information are much subtler than in other countries. Actual arrests of journalists or raids by the police are rare; according to Soldatov and Borogan, "The Putin approach is all about intimidation, more often than actual coercion, as an instrument of control."[70]

When it comes to the Russian military, the same focus on the control of information shines through. The 2010 Military Doctrine of the Russian Federation, for example, described information warfare as an instrument "to achieve political objectives without the utilization of military force," and in combination with conventional means as a tool to create "a favorable response from the world community."[71] In 2011, the Russian Ministry of Defense also published "Conceptual Views on the Activities of the Armed Forces of the Russian Federation in Information Space." This document defines information war as "[c]onflict between two or more States in information space with the goal of inflicting damage to information systems, processes, and resources, as well as to critically important structures and other structures; undermining political, economic, and social systems; carrying out mass psychological campaigns against the population of a State in order to destabilize society and the government; as well as forcing a State to make decisions in the interests of their opponents."[72] The following year, Deputy Prime Minister Dmitry Rogozin announced the establishment of a new branch in the Russian military and creation of a cyber command.[73]

A shift in Russian thinking apparently occurred in 2013 that moved them even further away from a focus on cyber attacks on infrastructure and toward information operations. That year, Valery Gerasimov, Chief of the General Staff of the Russian Armed Forces, published his influential essay that outlined what has been coined "hybrid warfare." In the words of Pavel Zolotarev, a retired Russian general, "we had come to the conclusion, having analyzed the actions of Western countries in the post-Soviet space – first of all the United States – that manipulation in the information sphere is a very effective tool." The Internet had provided a new set of tools that could replace what Zolotarev called "grandfather-style methods: scatter leaflets, throw around some printed materials, manipulate the radio or television."[74] The Ukrainians have experienced the full force of this new strategy. Ever more details are being documented about the Kremlin's army of trolls that is paid to confuse, disinform, and subvert its target audiences. Reports suggest that this approach was expanded in autumn 2013 and driven by Vyacheslav Volodin, the deputy chief of the presidential administration in Moscow.[75] The trolls number in the hundreds, work in 12-hour shifts and are required to post 135 comments a day on online message boards and media websites.[76] They are part of a broader network of proxies the Russian government has been using to project soft power in its pursuit to retain regime hegemony.[77]

In other words, this solidification in the Russian government's views on information security and the use of information operations is reflected in its actual behavior. While it stands accused of causing a power outage in western Ukraine with a cyber attack, such disruptive events have been rare. Instead, as the Ukrainians observed in my interviews in 2015, Russia is more focused on using information operations to achieve its political goals. Ukrainians were much more concerned over the long-term strategic effects of such operations than they were about the potential effects of a cyber attack against critical infrastructure.

THE CHINESE GOVERNMENT'S PERSPECTIVE

When the Chairman of the US Joint Chiefs of Staff, Martin E. Dempsey, visited China in April 2013, the head of China's General Staff Department, Fang Fengshui, reportedly told him "that a major cyber attack 'may be as serious as a nuclear bomb' and that 'anyone can launch the attacks – from the place where he lives, from his own country, or from another country.'"[78] The similarity to Russian statements is striking, and, indeed, the Chinese government exhibits a similarly pronounced tendency to view information as a threat. In China, the Communist Party still reigns supreme, and its survival and regime stability are paramount. The use of two different terms in the context of cybersecurity underlines this perspective: *xinxi anquan* for information security emphasizes content, and *wangluo anquan* focuses on the more technical network security.[79]

However, Russia and China differ noticeably when it comes to the projection of cyber power internationally. Russian documents focus overwhelmingly on information warfare; Chinese writings, while prominently featuring information warfare, also include extensive discussions of offensive cyber operations. This is illustrated by a publication of the China Institute of International Studies, which is affiliated with the Ministry of Foreign Affairs. The report's authors, Teng Jianqun and Xu Longdi, distinguish between "strategic cyber-warfare," which takes place on the Internet and aims to "paralyz[e] state apparatus and [bring] about social unrest and the downfall of enemy countries' governments," and military operations focused on "cyber-warfare on the battlefield."[80] The differences are also rooted in the country's culture and history. As China expert and former director of operations and intelligence of the British Secret Intelligence Service Nigel Inkster points out, "Chinese dynasties have always been predominately inward-looking, and foreign intelligence collection as it has become understood in the West was not a major feature of China's intelligence culture until fairly recently."[81] This also explains why China's Ministry of State Security, for example, has an internal surveillance mission as well as a foreign collection mission.[82]

Although the Chinese security apparatus had traditionally focused on domestic security, in the mid-2000s, reports about Chinese cyber espionage started to emerge, coinciding with the creation of cyber militias.[83] Inkster noted, "[m]uch has been written within China on the subject of cyber warfare. By contrast, virtually nothing has appeared in print on the subject of cyber exploitation, or cyber espionage."[84] Meanwhile, Chinese economic espionage quickly grew to such a scale that it attracted head-of-state level attention and criticism. In fact, it became such a priority that the United States and China reached an agreement on the issue at the head of state summit in September 2015.

Like Russian officials, Chinese representatives see the US government-sponsored Internet freedom projects as a threat.[85] But Internet freedom activists receiving funding from the US State Department are not the only targets of suspicion. For example, an article published by *China Economy Weekly* (itself part of the *People's Daily*, the China Communist Party's official newspaper) branded Apple, Cisco, Google, IBM, Intel, Microsoft, Oracle, and Qualcomm as the "eight guardian warriors"[86] (*bada jingang* 八大金刚) supporting the NSA's intelligence collection efforts.[87] And a report by the Chinese Academy of Social Sciences stated that Facebook and Twitter foment instability.[88] The government's preoccupation with the free flow of information and "anti-social activities" among its citizens is openly acknowledged by China scholars.[89] As in Russia, the government's efforts result in significant self-censorship, to the extent that in Beijing even stand-up comedians exclude politics from their humor.

It is noteworthy that whereas much of the literature discussing Russian information security thinking in the late 1990s focuses on the Kremlin's domestic concerns, the scholarship on China focuses on China's perception of external threat from US military operations during the 1991 Gulf War and later in the Balkans. This difference may have several possible sources: different interests and focus among the different scholarly communities, the scarcity of public data in either Russia or China, or an actual difference in governmental focus. What seems clear is that the Chinese military witnessed a debate about information versus cyber operations much like that which plagued the US military in the 1990s.[90] However, whereas in the US silos emerged between electronic warfare, psychological operations, and cyber operations for collection and effects, China pursued an integrated framework – its Integrated Network Electronic Warfare (*wangdian yiti zhan*) – in which the concept of information operations was subsumed into the category of "information confrontation."[91] General Dai Qingmin, former head of the People's Liberation Army (PLA) General Staff's Fourth Department, is credited with developing this approach.

One of the most disruptive cyber actions China has allegedly taken to date echoes the North Korean Sony hack in the reasons for its launch. The "Great Cannon" DDoS attack on GitHub specifically targeted two pages offering "services designed to circumvent Chinese censorship": GreatFire and the Chinese version of *The New York Times*. GreatFire, which monitors and provides access to blocked websites in China,[92] has been labeled a foreign anti-Chinese organization (境外反华组) by the Cyberspace Administration of China.[93] And the Chinese-language *New York Times* began being blocked by the Chinese government after it ran stories exposing the enormous wealth of former Chinese Premier Wen Jiabao and his family.[94] The Great Cannon's use against GitHub can be considered an act of "extraterritorial censorship."[95] One of the most detailed investigations into the DDoS attack, published by the Citizen Lab, concluded that there is "compelling evidence" that the Chinese government was responsible:[96] "In recent public statements, China has deflected questions regarding whether they are behind the attack, instead emphasizing that China is often itself a victim of cyber attacks... We tested two international Internet links into China belonging to two different Chinese ISPs, and found that in both cases the GC [Great Cannon] was co-located with the GFW [Great Firewall]. This co-location across different ISPs strongly suggests a governmental actor."[97] The DDoS attack was so massive that the website was unavailable intermittently for five days, prompting the news outlet Ars Technica to state, "[g]iven GitHub's status as the world's biggest host of open-source projects, it might not be hard for some people in Washington DC to argue the DDOS assaults meet the threshold of an attack that disrupts key American interests."[98]

Some experts have speculated that from the Chinese government's perspective, the Great Cannon action was not a first strike but a retaliation against the perceived deliberate attempt to undermine the regime, a position resembling Russia's view on the cyber attack in Ukraine.[99] Such a stance would align with the Chinese Communist Party's focus on ensuring domestic stability. And, as the Citizen Lab scholars pointed out, Beijing's efforts are not limited to potential threats to regime stability at home but also target "foreign hostile forces."[100] Even if one argues that there cannot be a moral equivalency between content and disruptive or potentially destructive, malicious cyber actions, this argument itself will not prevent governments that do consider them to be equivalent from taking aggressive actions in the future. This has important implications for conflict dynamics and escalatory risks. Imagine, for example, a scenario where content leads a civilian branch of the Chinese government to launch a similarly disruptive action, but that this time it leads to a US military response, which in turn triggers aggressive action by the Chinese military. Scenarios like these are why it is important to be particularly sensitive to potential mirror-imaging problems.

The cooperation between the Russian and Chinese governments in the field of information security is therefore not surprising. The two nations' mutual interest even extends to the development of joint definitions. A synthesis by the Russian government of its bilateral agreement with China, for example, includes a definition of information attack as "[t]he deliberate use of software (software and hardware) tools to target information systems, information and telecommunications networks, electrical communications networks, and industrial process automated control systems, carried out for the purposes of disrupting (halting) their operation and (or) breaching the security of the information being processed by them."[101] In spite of the two countries' heavy focus on regime stability and content, this joint definition resembles the relatively technical and narrow terminology of cyber operations found in US military doctrine. Indeed, the terminology reflects a point of common concern among the great powers regarding potential harm and damage resulting from malware that stands apart from the contentious issue of content and human rights.

THE IRANIAN GOVERNMENT'S PERSPECTIVE

Compared to its counterparts in Russia and China, the Iranian government has been a late bloomer. It was not until the 2009 Green Movement and the discovery of the Stuxnet malware in 2010 that it seemed to fully grasp the technological change that was underway. Tehran's efforts since then demonstrate how quickly a state can make significant advances when the government throws its full weight behind them.

The Iranian government has been motivated by the same concerns over US government-funded projects that drive the Russian and Chinese governments. For example, in June 2011, *The New York Times* ran a front-page story about the

"Internet in a suitcase," a project aimed at developing mesh networks that would enable people to communicate even if the government had shut down the regular network. The story described the development of the technology, an effort of the Open Technology Institute based in Washington, DC, funded by the US Department of State.[102] The Iranian minister for communications Reza Taghipour labeled these efforts "cyber terrorism,"[103] and one month later, the Iranian government updated its domestic censorship system.[104] Tehran had already announced its plans to establish a nationalized "halal" Internet. In fact, Heidar Moslehi, Iran's intelligence minister, suggested that "[w]e had predicted these actions, such as the Internet in suitcase, and we have planned proper ways to combat them."[105]

These strong reactions are not too surprising when viewed from the Iranian government's perspective. After all, when Ramin Mehamanparat, spokesman for Iran's foreign ministry, addressed the issue, the news ticker running along the bottom of the television screen was simultaneously announcing that the trial of ousted Tunisian president Ben Ali would start on June 20.[106] The memories of the protests in Tunisia six months earlier were still fresh in everybody's mind – especially the fact that those protests, unlike those in Iran in 2009, had succeeded in toppling the government and had ignited protests throughout the Arab world.

Due to the uprisings across the Arab world toppling one regime after another, the Iranian government, like its Russian and Chinese counterparts, has been particularly focused on information operations and what it called "Soft War." In 2010, the Islamic Development Organization of Iran defined Soft War as "any kind of psychological warfare action and media propaganda which targets the society and induces the opposite side to accept the failure without making any military conflict. The subversion, Internet war, creation of radio-television networks and spreading the rumors are the important forms of Soft War. This war intends to weaken the ... thought processes of the given society and also causes the socio-political order to be annihilated via the media propaganda."[107] Like the Russian government, the Iranian government has viewed civil society organizations as potential proxies of the West, and (similar to the Russian government's crackdown on NGOs and foreign funding) in 2010 declared sixty of these organizations to be "Soft War agents" and prohibited Iranians from collaborating with them. Indeed, Tehran views circumvention technologies and the US government's Internet freedom agenda not as an expression of human rights but as a regime-change policy. This view has since also informed efforts by the government, including the paramilitary volunteer militia Basij, to build its capabilities.[108] By 2014, the cyber threat intelligence company FireEye reported that it was already tracking six threat actors in Iran (compared to twenty-two in China).[109]

In addition to its pursuit of the "soft war," the Iranian government has allegedly had its hands in several malicious cyber activities, including the attack on Saudi

Aramco.[110] The US government indictment of Iranian hackers also accused the Iranian government of having targeted financial institutions in the United States with massive DDoS attacks and of attempting to infiltrate the control systems of a dam. Like Stuxnet, these incidents illustrate the cyber dimension of the conflict between Iran, Saudi Arabia, and the United States unfolding in the shadow of the negotiations over Iran's nuclear program.[111] The speed and effect of Tehran's action stunned analysts in the United States and Israel, especially in its projection of coercive cyber power internationally.[112] It is a cautionary tale in how quickly a state can cause significant harm through cyberspace when it intends to do so.

CONCLUSION: CYBERSECURITY IS IN THE EYE OF THE BEHOLDER

States seem to agree that the new ability to cause physical harm remotely via cyber operations constitutes "malicious" activity of concern to the international community. Yet they are split on the status of digital communications, with democracies considering them a new tool to promote and protect human rights, and other governments considering them to be "malicious" and a threat to regime stability. This dispute echoes past debates about the media and the free flow of information *vis-à-vis* sovereignty. The US government is still haunted by its own actions, like those described in a 1950 White House document that demonstrated its willingness to conduct "operations by covert means in the fields of economic warfare and political and psychological warfare with a view to fomenting and supporting unrest and revolt in selected strategic satellite countries."[113] While the US government's approach has evolved significantly since then, this history continues to shape other countries' perceptions of US behavior and to haunt US government policy today.[114] Which activity is considered "malicious" and what constitutes a source of instability for the international system is therefore in the eye of the beholder, and UN documents are similarly vague in defining what constitutes "malicious use of ICTs."[115] From an international law perspective, information operations, including those targeting civilian populations, are not prohibited as long as the activities do not incite crimes.[116] Yet, information operations surfaced as the biggest concern among the Ukrainians I interviewed in Kiev and have subsequently been a focus of European governments planning elections.

Ultimately, for some governments, international cybersecurity negotiations are a two-level game, important on the international level but with an equally if not more important domestic dimension. Reviewing Russian, Chinese, and Iranian perspectives on cyber power reveals that their foreign policies on cybersecurity are largely driven by domestic concerns. There is no black box separating the domestic from the foreign. These four nations' different perspectives also explain their different reasons for forming proxy relationships and how those relationships play out. Depending on the perspective and priorities of the state, cyber proxies may be useful in the internal or external projection of cyber power, for domestic surveillance or law enforcement purposes, or as part of externally focused military or intelligence activities. It is important to highlight that the definition of cyber proxies used in this book considers unauthorized access a necessary element of an offensive action (apart from a DDoS attack). It therefore excludes actors carrying out information operations that do not include unauthorized access, such as the trolls in St. Petersburg or companies such as the one hired by US Central Command to post on websites. Part II of this book examines specific case studies of these relationships in greater detail.

Cyber Proxies Up Close

4

Cyber Proxies on a Tight Leash: The United States

In April 2015, the US Cyber Command solicited proposals to award contracts to private companies for up to USD 475 million "to stand up Command."[1] According to the solicitation, the US military was looking for outside expertise, tools, and administrative services, including the provision of "technical expertise to assist in the deliberate planning, coordination, and synchronization of Offensive Cyber Operations (OCO), Defensive Cyber Operations (DCO), and operation of the DODIN [Department of Defense Information Networks]... Additionally, the Contractor shall assist in providing maneuver, fires and effects through the application of capabilities in and through the cyber domain."[2] These contracts, much like the creation of the US Cyber Command itself, are closely watched around the world. Private security contractors are the classic example of delegation and principal–agent relationships. This model of the state relying on the private market is particularly pronounced in the United States, the UK, and other European and NATO countries, as well as Israel. This chapter will briefly review the growth of conventional private military and security contractors and discuss the rise of private cybersecurity contractors, including those working with the US Cyber Command. It will conclude with an examination of the predictable proliferation of capabilities that results from these relationships.

Cybersecurity differs from most other security fields in that a private market for cybersecurity services and tools already existed by the time governments really started to consider cyberspace a domain for military operations. For example, in the United States, the predecessor of the US Cyber Command, the Joint Task Force–Computer Network Operations, became operational in 2000 and consisted of 150 members, a time when the Dot-com bubble was already at its height and cybersecurity companies such as McAfee and Symantec listed on the stock market.[3] Meanwhile, the rise of private cybersecurity contractors built on a twenty-year trend of privatization, including military and intelligence functions, which provided fertile soil for the private cybersecurity industry to emerge.

The broader trend of privatization dates back to the administration of Prime Minister Thatcher in the UK and President Reagan in the United States and has continued in the United States under Republican and Democratic administrations alike.[4] Over time, the trend to privatize government functions and the emergence of the "new public management" movement extended into the security realm.[5] As a result, what began as an internal, domestically driven evolution in the role of government spilled over into arenas with external implications, affecting foreign policy and international security. As the conflict researcher Zeljko Branovic put it, "In the last three decades the privatization paradigm has spread around the world like wildfire. Emphasizing better efficiency and effectiveness, privatisation is often styled as a panacea for the clumsy and cost-intensive performance of public administrations."[6]

Private military companies (PMCs) increasingly appeared in conflict zones around the world in the 1990s.[7] At first many of these companies provided aggressive tip-of-the-spear services, but after a series of scandals the industry as a whole tilted towards defense; this shift reduced the number of companies providing armed military operational support and increased the number of military consultant and support firms.[8] In the process, the concept of PMC broadened to include private security companies (PSC), and eventually the two became known collectively as private military and security companies (PMSC).[9] Sarah Percy, who wrote a book on the history of mercenaries, noted that the market for PMCs dried up even as the market for PSCs grew dramatically, and she argued that the norm against mercenarism "explains why PMCs disappeared from the international stage almost as abruptly as they had arrived upon it."[10] In addition to firms changing their service offerings, Percy argued, this shift was driven by an international trend towards states exercising increasing control over contractors, as seen in the 1998 South Africa Regulation of Foreign Military Assistance Act, which prohibited mercenary activity. As governments realized that principal–agent problems resulted in unanticipated negative consequences, they tightened the leash, and the market restructured so that firms worked much more closely with their home country or within the country's alliance network.[11] Nonetheless, some issues remain unresolved. For example, the staff of private military and security companies working in Iraq enjoyed immunity from local prosecution and at the same time were exempt from the US Military Code. This illustrates an important gap in one of the key mechanisms for minimizing principal–agent problems: punishment or the threat of it.

Even as firms shifted from military to security services, the private market for security services grew dramatically, driven by the push for privatization, a general reconceptualization of the role and size of the state, increased economic incentives for outsourcing, and the specific political incentives to use contractors as overt or covert proxies. Demand from the intelligence community grew as well,[12] and the 9/11 terrorist attacks provided an additional catalyst. A 2010 fact sheet published by the US Office of the Director of National Intelligence noted the particular impact of 9/11:

The growth in contractors was a direct response to an urgent need for unique expertise post-9/11. The surge in contractors allowed the IC [Intelligence Community] to fill the need for seasoned analysts and collectors while rebuilding the permanent, civilian workforce. It also allowed agencies to meet required skills, such as foreign languages, computer science, and electrical engineering... The stark reality is that more than 50% of the Intelligence Community workforce was hired after 9/11.[13]

A few years later, this explosion in contracting started to attract greater scrutiny in government circles. The international relations scholar Allison Stanger wrote in 2009 that "[e]ven the Pentagon itself was until recently unaware of the explosion in non-uniformed personnel deployed on its behalf; its prior estimate of 25,000 was off by a factor of at least seven."[14] The intelligence community conducted its first-ever annual inventory of core contract personnel in 2006. As a result of this inventory, government policy reinforced its rules against using contractors to carry out "inherently governmental activities," but continued to allow their use for "activities such as collection and analysis."[15] In 2010, these core contract personnel represented 28 percent of the intelligence staff's total workforce.[16] Under the Obama administration, the US government conducted another review. This led to the creation of a new category of "critical functions" and new policy guidance regarding what types of functions can be outsourced to private actors and under what circumstances.

Today, the dynamic relationship between the state and private actors remains characteristic of the market for cyber capabilities, in spite of the broader trend to walk back some of the privatization that has occurred. The market for cyber threat intelligence alone is expected to reach USD 1 billion by 2017 from USD 255 million in 2013.[17] Private cybersecurity companies can be put into two broad categories based on their size and customer base. The first category consists of the biggest companies, sometimes called "pure plays." Shorrock, an expert on intelligence agencies and contractors, defines a pure play company as one "focused on a single market and earning most of their revenue from that market [with] up to 90 percent of their revenue from contracts with the Pentagon, the CIA, and the national collection agencies."[18] The staff of these contractors are often embedded with their government clients, working on-site at government facilities alongside their government colleagues. The second category of companies are those with a broader, more diverse customer base beyond governmental agencies as well as smaller boutique firms.[19]

PRIVATE CYBERSECURITY CONTRACTORS

As the broader private security industry expanded, private cybersecurity contractors[20] began to emerge – some as subsidiaries of existing contractors and others as new stand-alone companies. As early as 2003, the US Army's professional journal was arguing that the US military should "hire specialized PMCs for specific offensive

information campaigns, providing a surge capability instead of attempting to maintain limited-use, cutting-edge skills in the regular force, far removed from its core
activity."[21] A decade later, the US Army awarded a one-year, USD 125 million
contract for cyber operations.[22] Two factors have been driving this trend. First, the
traditional pure-play defense contractors have been expanding their activities to
include cybersecurity. These include ManTech, CACI, BAE Systems,[23] and
Northrop Grumman. ManTech, for example, was awarded a USD 250 million
contract in 2015 to "prepare the next generation of cyber warfighters for the
Department of Defense."[24] Second, smaller boutique firms and start-ups emerged
and either became established contractors or were bought by larger companies such
as HBGary, QuesTech Inc., Immunity, and Hacking Team.[25] In one such case,
ManTech acquired Oceans Edge Inc., which it called "a leading provider of cyber
network operations (CNO) solutions... This acquisition will increase ManTech's
significant presence in this highly sought after segment of the US government cyber
solutions market to include service components of US Cyber Command."[26] Another
example is Raytheon, which in 2014 paid USD 420 million for Blackbird
Technologies Inc., a company established in 1997, which provides "services across
the full range of cyber operations."[27] The United States is not alone in this pattern:
Israel, France, and the UK also rely extensively on private contractors. In all these
countries, political systems, legal traditions, and history distinguish strongly between
the public and private spheres, and the states have been under pressure to privatize
and outsource state functions to save costs.

These companies offer a broad range of services. While the contracts and services
provided by the contractors for national security agencies are usually classified and
secret, company and employee websites offer some clues. ManTech's work, for
example, covers "intelligence and operations, counterintelligence, information
operations, and cyber-warfare."[28] The company openly advertised "Computer
Network Operations" among its capabilities, saying "We carry out incident response,
analysis and investigations, and provide information assurance and full spectrum
CNO information operations. These operations include cyber forensics and exploitation, SIGINT and cyber operations support."[29] Similarly, Northrop Grumman
states on its website that its staff is "developing systems and solutions to meet the ever-
evolving threat and providing full-spectrum cyber operations for our customers,
worldwide."[30] When I asked an employee of a major defense contractor about the
type of services his company and others in the market offer, he replied,

> A journalist asked me at a defense trade conference whether my company also offers
> offensive cyber tools and services. Having gotten media training, I replied that we
> tell all of our clients that they need to focus on defense – so a classic "neither
> confirm nor deny" answer. As a company, we generally don't comment on such
> questions but obviously we are building this stuff. We are a defense contractor. It's
> a natural extension of our business. How else could the government procure this?[31]

More interesting than traditional private military and security companies expanding and diversifying their service offerings to include cybersecurity is the explosion of small start-up companies in this field. Unlike the development of conventional weaponry, which usually requires substantial investment and manufacturing capabilities, the development of malware for offensive cyber operations has much lower barriers to entry. Governments around the world are therefore not only working with large companies when it comes to cybersecurity but often also with small boutique firms. These firms, like cleared defense contractors, can have prolonged relationships with government clients, but the relationships can also be much more ephemeral and transactional. These smaller firms deserve special attention because they have a much lighter footprint in terms of information available about them, creating less transparency and scrutiny than the well-known conventional private security companies.

Take, for example, ReVuln, a small company run by two Italian security researchers on the Mediterranean island of Malta. According to *The New York Times*, ReVuln sells zero-day vulnerabilities for industrial control systems, like those used in water treatment facilities, oil and gas pipelines, and power plants, "to countries that want to break into the computer systems of foreign adversaries." [32] The article mentions the NSA and government agencies in Brazil, India, Israel, Malaysia, North Korea, Russia, Singapore, and the UK as being active in this market. (Companies providing zero-days that have exclusive or prolonged relationships with governments can be considered proxies, given their continued involvement and integration in offensive cyber operations; however, companies conducting business on a transactional, one-off basis without being integrated into an offensive cyber operation are more accurately compared to conventional arms dealers than proxies.)

Vupen, a similar company focusing on zero-day vulnerabilities, was established in 2004, with locations in France and Maryland, USA. The company openly advertised that it "provides government-grade zero-day exploits specifically designed for law enforcement agencies and the intelligence community to help them achieve their offensive cyber missions and network operations."[33] (Vupen stopped business in 2015 after appearing in a series of media articles that raised critical questions about its business affairs, but its founder created a new company called Zerodium shortly thereafter, in a move reminiscent of Blackwater's rebranding itself as Xe Services.)

Another company, Immunity Service, headquartered in Miami, Florida, lists penetration testing as its "premier consulting option."[34] Founded in 2002, the "one hundred percent American-owned business" offers its services to Fortune and Global 500 companies and "serves government departments from all over the world." It prides itself as concentrating "on purely offensive techniques," such as "develop[ing] new penetration technologies including exploits, implants, and evasion techniques. Immunity's product line remains focused on attack and penetration. Immunity delivers consulting services including penetration testing, vulnerability management, and Immunity's experts provide regular training classes."[35] (It is also the Russian company GLEG's "exclusive reseller outside Russia"[36] and GLEG resells Immunity's products in Russia.)[37]

The company Endgame, on the other hand, focused on another element of the spear-tip taxonomy by identifying which computer systems could be potential targets in a range of countries from China to Russia, the Middle East, and Latin America. Harris noted that "Endgame doesn't conduct the attack, but the intelligence it provides can give clients the information they need to carry out their own strikes."[38] Endgame's business, in a move reminiscent of companies' shifting from PMCs to PSCs in the late 1990s, also evolved. When Nate Fick, a former member of the US Marine Corps, was appointed as its CEO in 2012, he decided to shift the company's focus away from the controversial zero-day trade.[39]

DELEGATION UNDER THE SPOTLIGHT: US CYBER COMMAND AND
CYBERSECURITY CONTRACTORS

The solicitation by the US Cyber Command provides the most detailed insight publicly available to date about the contractual relationship between a government and private cybersecurity contractors regarding offensive cyber operations in a military context. It serves as a useful case study to apply principal–agent theory in the context of private cybersecurity contractors. Contractual agreements of this type are ideal-type versions of the delegation relationship and examples of how governments can keep a tight leash and control over proxies.

To start, it is worth highlighting that the US Cyber Command itself is still a very young structure. It became operational in 2010, the same year that the Pentagon publicly declared cyberspace to be a new operational domain and ten years after the creation of the Joint Task Force. From the Joint Task Force's initial staff of 150, the 2016 budget for the US Cyber Command lists 963 civilian and military government employees and 409 contract employees.[40] That is a ratio of 70 percent government employees to 30 percent contractors, similar to the ratio found among core contract personnel in the intelligence community in 2010. A comparison between the intelligence community and offensive cyber operations for military purposes is appropriate here, because the US Cyber Command is a hybrid organization: its commander is also director of the NSA. Like the military, the NSA makes use of contractors: a NSA spokesman stated that "we engage heavily with the industrial and academic research communities to develop new and innovative technologies to help us in securing critical networks, in exploiting the communications of foreign adversaries and in providing vital foreign intelligence to our warfighters."[41] The US Cyber Command's still-nascent structure is also reflected in the contract itself, which stated that part of its objective was "to streamline USCYBERCOM's acquisition of cyber mission support capabilities and services, information technology services, and cyber professional services … under a centralized structure."[42]

Of the seventeen companies competing for the five-year contract with US Cyber Command, six won part of the USD 460 million awarded: Booz Allen Hamilton, CACI, KeyW, SAIC, Secure Mission Solutions, and Vencore.[43] Booz Allen Hamilton, headquartered in Tysons Corner, Virginia, has some 22,000 staff world-wide and USD 5.41 billion in annual revenue in 2016. It is one of the largest defense companies in the United States and a contractor for both intelligence and military agencies. Its cybersecurity business was developed by John M. McConnell, who retired from the Navy as a Vice Admiral and as Director of the NSA in 1996. McConnell later rejoined government as the second Director of National Intelligence from 2007 to 2009. CACI was founded in the 1960s by a former RAND employee and counts some 20,000 employees among its staff today, with USD 3.7 billion in revenue. Headquartered in Arlington, also in Virginia, CACI advertises on its website that it supports all aspects of cyber operations. Shorrock has described CACI as "a private supplier of signals intelligence, human intelligence, imagery, and black ops, all rolled into one enterprise."[44] KeyW is headquartered in Hanover, Maryland, with both government and private sector customers; it is smaller than Booz Allen Hamilton or CACI, with 1,100 employees. SAIC, mean-while, boasts 15,000 employees and annual revenues of USD 4.3 billion. Secure Mission Solutions is headquartered in Reston, Virginia; it is the smallest of the six, with only 500 employees, but it was acquired by Parsons, a large engineering company, in 2014. Vencore, on the other hand, is a spin-off from Lockheed Martin Corp[45] with some 4,000 employees and USD 1.3 billion revenue.[46]

The services offered by these companies range from defensive to offensive to administrative. Lachow found that "contractors play critical roles in two key func-tions: intelligence/reconnaissance and planning/mission support."[47] While he high-lighted the primarily defensive nature of the contractors' activities, it is clear that they are involved in offensive cyber operations as well; in fact, they openly advertise it. CACI's website, for example, states that its "personnel analyze systems, networks, and platforms to facilitate cyber targeting for the purpose of identification and penetration of target environments, from data centers to platforms."[48] Meanwhile, SAIC job advertisements include those for cyberspace operational planners, who are expected to develop "Offensive Cyberspace Operations and Defense Cyberspace Operations policy, plans, processes, procedures, and government directives," as well as "lead the creation of strike packages, and the vetting and validation of targets" at Fort Meade.[49] In short, Singer's description of conventional private military and security companies offering services along the full length of the spear, with the exception of the deadly tip, appears to apply to private cybersecurity contractors as well.[50] However, it remains unresolved what exactly constitutes "inherently govern-mental functions" in the context of cyber operations and which types of activities can and cannot be outsourced. (This question is discussed in Part III.)

Applying principal–agent theory to the government's use of cyber operations contractors is straightforward. The US Cyber Command's contractual requirements outline the selection and screening process in detail. For example, firms must be US-owned or, if foreign-owned, "possess a favorable National Interest Determination"; however, all individuals performing the work must be US citizens and must have "Top Secret personnel security clearances with SCI access eligibility."[51] Just as conventional private military and security companies often structure themselves to be particularly appealing as government contractors (for example, guaranteeing that they will not do business with other governments that are rivals or adversaries), so do cybersecurity contractors.[52] Netragard, for instance, a Massachusetts company that focuses on exploits, has said that it works only with US customers. Yet, how much companies limit themselves varies greatly. Vupen, for example, reportedly imposed fewer restrictions upon itself and conducted business in any country that was not "subject to European Union, United States or United Nations restrictions."[53]

Monitoring of contractors is implemented through a variety of means. Contractors often work physically alongside their government counterparts. In fact, the US Cyber Command solicitation specifies that "[c]ontractors designated as critical to successful completion of mission essential functions, or as emergency personal may be required to travel with government counterparts to work for extended periods of time from a remote contingency location during a continuity of operations event." In addition, remote work is forbidden, making monitoring easier. The contract provides that "[u]nder NO CIRCUMSTANCE will a home office be considered an alternate work location [emphasis in original]."[54] Because of provisions like these, these types of relationships are among the closest beneficiary–proxy relationships, with the strongest degree of control by the state. Mechanisms are also in place to monitor whether contractors and private security companies share any specific expertise or tools with any other actors as part of their business. These include export controls requiring registration, licensing, and other checks (for example, the US Munitions List or the Commerce Control List for dual-use technology).

Punishments can also take various forms. For example, the defense contractor and subcontractor that outsourced part of their work to Russian software developers paid USD 12.75 million in civil penalties.[55] The government can decide not to review a contract and to exclude a contractor from future bidding. The US government can also arrest individuals, as occurred with the August 2016 arrest of a Booz Allen Hamilton contractor who allegedly stole and disclosed code used for offensive cyber operations by the NSA.[56]

PRIVATE CYBERSECURITY CONTRACTORS AND INTERNAL SECURITY

Governments use contractors not only to project power abroad, but also for internal security. Hacking Team, for instance, develops products that allow remote access to a person's devices to monitor emails, calls, keystrokes, and location. The company's chief communications executive, Eric Rabe, has repeatedly stated that the company sells exclusively to government law enforcement or security services and that the company has internal guidelines to ensure its products are not misused.[57] In addition to selling its products to the US military,[58] the company has sold them to the Federal Bureau of Investigation (FBI) and marketed them to hundreds of local police departments.[59] Other clients include the Royal Police in Thailand and the Turkish National Police as well as government agencies in Mexico, Singapore, South Korea, and several European countries.[60]

Controversially, Hacking Team also counted among its customers security agencies in countries such as Azerbaijan, Bahrain, and Sudan, in spite of these states' well-known poor human rights records and limited rule of law – and Hacking Team products have been used to target dissidents out of concern they might influence a country's domestic politics.[61] The case of Ahmed Mansoor, a pro-democracy activist in the United Arab Emirates, illustrates the implications of this trade. Mansoor was targeted with the remote control system sold by Hacking Team, and he was arrested in the United Arab Emirates and subjected to torture.[62] His case demonstrates that the use of hacking tools does not necessarily stop with data theft and violation of privacy but can have physical consequences. Data leaked when Hacking Team was itself hacked in 2015 suggests that the United Arab Emirates paid Hacking Team USD 634,500 for the use of its products, with which they surveiled over 1,000 people.[63] It is worth pointing out that Hacking Team relied on a number of zero-day exploits for its products, demonstrating its level of sophistication.[64] (One side effect of Hacking Team's data being leaked was that its library of zero-days was also disclosed and subsequently used by malicious threat actors around the world.)

Rabe stated in an email to me that Hacking Team attempts to learn about any possible abuse by vetting clients, monitoring reports of abuses, and "requir[ing] certain behaviors which we outline in our contract"; if they detect abuse, they "may decided [*sic*] to suspend support for that client's system rendering it quickly ineffective."[65] His comments highlight that, while some companies claim that they have no control over how their products are used once they are sold and shared with the client, many companies offer customer service and product updates that require a continuing relationship and provide insight into the products' use. Depending on the company and product, it may therefore be possible for a company to terminate its relationship and product's functionality; in some cases, it may even be easier to do this than to take back the sale of conventional tangible goods.

CONCLUSION: PREDICTABLE PROLIFERATION OF CAPABILITIES

Private cybersecurity contractors are in many ways a mere extension of the existing practice of outsourcing functions to the private sector and defense contractors. As the military expert Sean McFate pointed out, in the United States, "barring mandatory conscription, the superpower cannot wage war without the private military industry."[66] However, cybersecurity contractors raise new issues. For one, existing mechanisms for monitoring a firm's business with other clients (especially clients overseas), such as export controls, face big hurdles when it comes to tools and services related to code. Many of the companies involved are small, boutique firms with staff numbers in the dozens rather than in the hundreds or thousands, making it harder to identify and monitor all the players in the marketplace. Lachow highlighted this important point: "[i]t is conceivable that an offensive cyber operation could be completely researched, constructed and conducted by a company outside of any government's purview," echoing an earlier finding that "[t]he simple fact is that there are no guarantees over where or for whom the firms will work."[67] Moreover, it is unclear how effective oversight can be established and sustained when the government is facing a general shortage of staff who possess the expertise needed to effectively carry out their monitoring function.[68] It is therefore questionable that an effective oversight regime – ranging from individual program officers to the oversight responsibilities of the US Congress or other legislature – currently exists.[69]

Beyond the immediate challenges of the principal–agent problem, a larger question looms on the horizon: how will the increasing number of governments building cyber capabilities affect the broader market, and how will this reshape the landscape when people leave government and contractors? The experience and efforts of the Israeli government, which date back to the 1970s, could be a fascinating case study given its prolonged experience of tackling this challenge.[70] In nearly all other countries, the revolving door in and out of cyber-related jobs in government is still a fairly recent phenomenon. But an increasing number of US military and intelligence employees, for example, are now moving on to start their own companies. For example, Vahna, a computer security service, was founded by Brendan Conlon, who had spent ten years focusing on offensive cyber operations at the NSA.[71] Jeff Tang, Vahna's chief scientist, lists on his official company biography that he worked at the NSA in global network exploitation and vulnerability, "including computer network operations related military targeting support and US Government computer network attack efforts"; subsequently, he worked at ManTech as a computer network operations developer.[72] Media reports have documented a big private sector demand for people with backgrounds like Tang's or Conlon's.[73] This development matters because, as Lachow pointed out, these private companies "have more advanced cyber capabilities than the vast majority of countries around the world."[74] Managing this inevitable proliferation of capabilities around the world will be a challenge in the years to come.

5

Cyber Proxies on a Loose Leash: Iran and Syria

Iran is an excellent case study of a country whose government started focusing on cyberspace only recently and subsequently established proxy relationships typical of orchestration. The massive protests in 2009 and the discovery of the Stuxnet malware in 2010 suddenly presented officials in Tehran with both internal and external threats enabled by a technology they had not made a top priority before. As a result, Iran shifted its policy and attention, as can be seen in Ayatollah Khamenei's decision in March 2012 to establish the High Council on Cyberspace, consisting of senior government officials "with the mission of instituting high-level policies on the cyberspace."[1] Two years later, *Russia Today* reported that Khamenei in a speech "urged his country's students – whom he called "cyber war agents" – to prepare for battle... 'You are the cyber-war agents and such a war requires Amman-like insight and Malik Ashtar-like resistance. Get yourself ready for such war wholeheartedly.'"[2]

This rapid evolution of Iran's ability to project power through cyberspace came as a surprise to officials in other countries, including the United States and Israel. Less surprising is the way the Iranian government has used proxies to achieve its goals. This chapter traces how Iranian officials have described the perceived internal and external threats over the years and analyzes various Iranian threat actors, including the group of Iranian hackers orchestrated by Tehran named in the recently unsealed US indictment. Another section of the chapter is dedicated to the Syrian Electronic Army as an example of a proxy and orchestration in wartime, and the chapter concludes by identifying key lessons learned from the unexpected escalation of both Iran's and Syria's malicious behavior.

Overall, Tehran's actions are driven by its focus on domestic regime stability. Internal developments like the large-scale demonstrations during the 2009 Green Movement fueled major concerns among Iranian officials. Witnessing the catalytic role that Internet-based information and communications technologies played during the protest, the government soon responded with a systemic effort to monitor, censor, and hamper those communication channels online. This included requiring Internet cafes to collect their users' personally identifiable information, and requiring Internet service providers and Internet cafes to share data on their customers.[3] Hackers were used to target opponents of the regime, a fact acknowledged by the commander-in-chief of the Islamic Revolutionary Guard Corps, Mohammad Ali Jaafari.[4] The Iranian police, like the Islamic Revolutionary Guard Corps and the Basij, established units focusing on access to and use of the Internet. Government controls on information also included more creative instruments such as throttling people's bandwidth so videos could no longer be uploaded.[5]

Projecting coercive cyber power abroad also became more frequent. As Hossein Mousavian, a former Iranian diplomat, put it: "The US, or Israel, or the Europeans, or all of them together, started war against Iran... Iran decided ... to establish a cyberarmy, and today, after four or five years, Iran has one of the most powerful cyberarmies in the world."[6] In 2011, Mojtaba Zolnoor, the former deputy representative of the Supreme Leader, mentioned that Iran's cyber army had successfully hacked "enemy sites." A year later, Tehran reportedly held its first countrywide cyber defense exercise while also substantially increasing its investment in building cyber capabilities.[7] This is remarkable considering that a comprehensive review of Iran as a cyber threat actor in 2005 found no evidence that Iran was able to conduct offensive cyber operations against its enemies,[8] adding that "outside of the security courses being taught to university students, there was no direct evidence of state-sponsored training."[9]

It did not take long for new actors to appear on the scene. In 2009, the Iranian Cyber Army targeted the Chinese search engine Baidu, causing great tension between Chinese and Iranian hacktivists.[10] (To date, the Iranian government has not claimed responsibility for the Iranian Cyber Army.) By 2014, CrowdStrike was reporting in its Global Threat Intel Report that the Iranian government was hosting hacking contests to identify skilled hackers, much as the People's Liberation Army (PLA) had done a decade earlier. In particular, the report noted that Sharif University of Technology had "conducted a contest for 'innovative methods' of computer network intrusions and defense against such intrusions," and that "Iranian government cybersecurity authorities had access to the students' submissions in the contest, [which] were not released to the public but rather kept private to only those with access to the contest submissions."[11]

In addition, *Forbes* reported in 2011 that "[t]he government of Iran has recently decided that the Basij ... must recruit more hackers to fight what it calls the 'soft war' in cyberspace."[12] Originally paramilitary volunteers, the Basij volunteers became institutionalized; the militia's armed units were absorbed by the Islamic Revolutionary Guard Corps in 2007, while its civilian units focused on the "soft war" discussed in Chapter 3. The activities of the Basij cyber units include writing content in praise of the regime on designated blogs or publishing commentary in support of the government on other websites, much as the Russian trolls have done.[13] According to one analyst, the Basij and the Islamic Revolutionary Guard Corps have been expanding their efforts, with the former, composed of "mostly inexperienced individuals" engaging in "less complex hacking or infiltration operations on sites and emails" and the Islamic Revolutionary Guard Corps focusing on "the more sophisticated operations."[14] And the 2013 FireEye report adds, "There is increasing evidence to suggest that the hacker community in Iran is engaged in a transition from politically motivated defacements and denial of service attacks to cyber espionage activities."[15]

Tehran's focus on domestic regime stability also explains one of the most aggressive external offensive cyber operations associated with Iran, the hack of the Dutch company DigiNotar in 2011, which revolved around an attempt to gain access to the personal online communications of tens of thousands of Iranian citizens. DigiNotar issued SSL (secure sockets layer) certificates used by institutions worldwide to create secure communication channels. Once the attacker had successfully infiltrated DigiNotar, the access was used to issue fraudulent certificates allowing the attacker to launch a man-in-the-middle attack against whoever relied on the certificates. This included Google, and the attacker attempted to gain access to the communications of Iranians using Google services. On August 29, 2011, Google published a post on its Security Blog: "Today we received reports of attempted SSL man-in-the-middle (MITM) attacks against Google users. . . The people affected were primarily located in Iran. The attacker used a fraudulent SSL certificate issued by DigiNotar."[16] There is perhaps no better sign of the systemic nature of these efforts aimed at suppressing regime opponents both inside Iran and extraterritorially than the fact that Google started to warn its users of state-sponsored attackers in October 2012.[17] In 2013, Google issued a new announcement that they had discovered "a vast Iranian spy campaign that had been targeting tens of thousands of Iranian citizens over the last three weeks" and said that they were "confident" that these attackers had also perpetrated the 2011 DigiNotar attack.[18]

Iranian hacking has a notably extraterritorial dimension. Apart from the extraterritorial effects of the offensive cyber operations themselves, the members of some groups are apparently spread across different countries, and some groups focus on third-party conflicts. Research by Cylance, a cyber threat intelligence company based in California, suggested that members of Cutting Kitten, also known as Operation Cleaver, are located not only in Iran but also in Canada, the Netherlands, and the UK.[19] This group consists of an estimated twenty people,[20] most likely "a mix of existing team members and new recruits pulled from the universities in Iran."[21] The Cleaver team focuses specifically on critical infrastructure, including aviation-related systems in South Korea, Saudi Arabia, and Pakistan,[22] and it is also thought responsible for creating a series of fake LinkedIn profiles to use as a beachhead for more targeted spear phishing.[23] Iranian actors are also active in third-party conflicts. A report published by Citizen Lab in August 2016 described the activity of a new threat actor its authors called "Group 5," which is targeting the Syrian opposition. After a careful analysis, the authors concluded that "an Iranian group newly active in Syria . . . provides the best explanation for what we have observed," considering it likely that either the Iranian or the Syrian government sponsors the group.[24]

In short, the Iranian government relied on its existing approach and structures dating back decades, much as the United States built on its private security contractor model and Beijing expanded its conventional militia system. Close analysis of the US indictment of seven Iranian hackers provides unprecedented detail about this evolution in Iran and the relationship between the state and private actors.

ORCHESTRATION UNDER THE SPOTLIGHT: THE US
INDICTMENT OF IRANIAN HACKERS

The indictment by the US government unsealed in March 2016 marks the first time the US government has unsealed an indictment against state-sponsored proxy hackers.[25] According to the US Department of Justice, the seven Iranians named "were employed by two Iran-based computer companies ... which were sponsored by Iran's Islamic Revolutionary Guard Corps."[26] The details described in the indictment, plus additional research, suggest strong path dependence in Iran's approach to cyber proxies; in establishing these new relationships, the state is building on its decades-old conventional approach. In particular, there are similarities between the contemporary use of proxies and the students' role during the November 1979 hostage crisis.

On November 4, 1979, a group of Iranian students stormed the US embassy in Tehran, taking 66 Americans hostage for what would become a 444-day ordeal.[27] Three students – Ibrahim Asgharzadeh from Sanati Sharif University, Mohsen Mirdamadi from Amir Kabir University, and Habibullah Bitaraf from Technical University – came up with the plan to take over the embassy.[28] Like the Chinese hacktivists we will see in Chapter 7 and Eugene Dokukin in Ukraine, the Iranian students expressed a desire to be affiliated with their respective governments and to become their agents. In this case, however, there was an additional wrinkle of the competing factions within Iran at the time. Asgharzadeh and his cohort called their group Muslim Students Following the Imam's Line to "be recognized as a strictly Islamic organization, one loyal to Khomeini."[29] And while local police supported the students' actions by not interfering,[30] Khomeini himself did not know about the students' plan.[31]

The question of the Iranian state's responsibility for the students' actions was at the center of the case brought before the International Court of Justice in 1981.[32] The US government argued that the Iranian government was "permitting, tolerating, encouraging, adopting, and endeavouring to exploit, as well as in failing to prevent and punish, the conduct described."[33] On November 4, 1979, the Iranian government did not step in to disperse the crowd around the embassy as it had on previous occasions; instead, several hundred people took over the compound which would remain under their control for more than a year.[34] Khomeini reportedly initially condemned the students' actions in a private conversation with Foreign Minister Yazdi, but within the span of a few hours he reversed to take a hard-line position.[35] On the day following the takeover, Yazdi announced that "the action of the students 'enjoys the endorsement and support of the government, because America herself is responsible for this incident.'"[36] According to the International Court of Justice, that policy fundamentally transformed the legal situation created by the embassy occupation.[37]

In a conclusion also relevant to the US indictment of the Iranian hackers, the International Court of Justice ultimately distinguished between two phases of events. Before the embassy occupation and during its first hours, the court found, the students were acting independently.[38] The period *ex post* the immediate take-over of the embassy, however, the court saw as a separate phase, arguing that "[t]he approval given to these facts by the Ayatollah Khomeini and other organs of the Iranian State, and the decision to perpetuate them, translated continuing occupation of the Embassy and detention of the hostages into acts of that State. The militants, authors of the invasion and jailers of the hostages, had now become agents of the Iranian State for whose acts the State itself was internationally responsible."[39] This finding is now supported by the students' own recollections. After Khomeini endorsed the students' actions and turned them into his proxies, the students' leader Asgharzadeh "sensed that control of the event had already slipped out of his and the other students' hands, that powerful men had moved into position behind them."[40] Asgharzadeh also experienced the potential escalatory risk involved in trying to orchestrate a network of actors. In an interview with *TIME* magazine in 1999, he recalled, "Things got complicated... We couldn't make decisions on our own anymore," and it was difficult to maintain "discipline in the ranks."[41]

Reading the 2016 indictment of the seven Iranian hackers carefully in combination with additional publicly available information reveals striking similarities between that case and the events of November 1979. It appears that a group of students acting independently as hackers since at least 2010 became proxies of the Iranian government in autumn 2012 (as shown in Figure 5.1).

The indictment lists seven Iranian citizens – Ahmad Fathi (age 37), Hamid Firoozi (34), Amin Shokohi (25), Sadegh Ahmadzadegan (23), Omid Ghaffarinia (25), Sina Keissar (25), and Nader Seidi (26)[42] – who were part of two companies, ITSecTeam and Mersad Company. According to the grand jury indictment from the Southern District of New York, ITSec Team and Mersad Company "performed work on behalf of the Iranian Government, including the Islamic Revolutionary Guard Corps, on computer hacking charges related to their involvement in an extensive campaign of over 176 days of distributed denial of service (DDoS) attacks," targeting primarily financial institutions including SunTrust, JPMorgan Chase, CitiGroup, Wells Fargo, US Bancorp, Capital One, PNC, and HSBC.[43] The massive DDoS attacks cost victim institutions millions of US dollars in remediation costs. In addition, Firoozi was accused of gaining unauthorized access to the

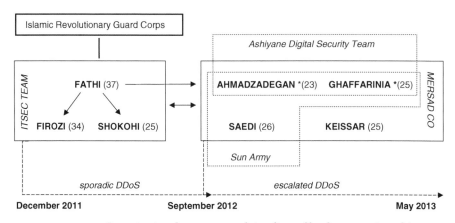

FIGURE 5.1 Organizational structure and timeline of hackers mentioned in US indictment in 2016 of seven Iranian hackers.

Bowman Dam, located 20 miles north of New York City.[44] A year prior to the unsealing of the indictment, *The New York Times* had already reported that "American intelligence officials say Iran's most sophisticated hackers are limited in number, but work for both front companies and the government."[45] While the DDoS attack and intrusion of the dam were not particularly sophisticated from a technical perspective, it seems reasonable to assume that ITSecTeam and Mersad Company acted as front companies or companies whose employees became proxies of the Iranian government.

One of the most fascinating elements of the parallel to the events of 1979 is buried in the indictment: Ahmadzadegan (also known by his online pseudonym "Nitrojen26"), Ghaffarinia (a.k.a. "PLuS"), and Saedi (a.k.a. "Turk Server") were members of two hacker groups, the Ashiyane Digital Security Team and Sun Army. The Ashiyane Digital Security Team is one of several Iranian hacker groups established before the Iranian Cyber Army's rise in 2009; it has been involved in political hacktivism and cyber crime for many years.[46] In fact, some of the earliest Web defacements committed by a member of the Ashiyane Digital Security Team were indexed by Google's search engine as early as 2001.[47] According to the security researcher Iftach Ian Amit, members of the Ashiyane Digital Security Team have been involved in a variety of malicious activities, from Web defacements to hacking to copying data, as well as criminal intrusions into industrial control systems.[48] A 2005 study found that members of the Ashiyane Digital Security Team were young (mostly between 16 and 28) and that "[s]everal of these members conducted classroom training for a fee on topics such as basic, advanced, and professional levels of hacking; hacking tools; and a list of other programming languages, operating systems, and professional certifications."[49] The training took place at a vocational school in Tehran and cost USD 200–355 for 40 hours of training.

The relationship between this group of hacktivists and the Iranian government seems to have evolved over time.[50] Members of the Ashiyane Digital Security Team and the Sun Army have publicly boasted about their Web defacements on Zone-H, a global repository for Web defacements created in March 2002 by Roberto Preatoni, an Italian living part-time in Estonia.[51] I was surprised to find several dozen entries posted on Zone-H, which included screenshots of websites defaced by Sun Army between February 17, 2010 and March 17, 2012 and which listed the three hacker pseudonyms mentioned in the indictment – Nitrojen26, PLuS, and Turk Server.[52] An entry dated March 10, 2012 displays a website owned by Mehdy007, MagicCoder, Nitrojen26, PLuS, BodyGuard, tHe.Mo3tafA, KinG, and Turk-Server with "special thank" to Farzad_Ho, rAbiN_hoOd, and R3D.Mind.[53] Similar entries date back to 2010, including defacement of the website for NASA's Langley Research Center in April of that year.[54] While ITSecTeam and Mersad Company appear to be front companies, it seems strange that the Iranian government would allow a group it actively sponsors to publicly boast about such activities. The postings end in the spring of 2012, the same year that the US government's indictment accuses the hackers of beginning their involvement in the malicious activity targeting US financial institutions. This finding also coincides with the speculation in the CrowdStrike 2014 Global Threat Intel Report that the closing of various Iranian hacker forums could be the result of "a desire to decrease the public profile of individuals in the Iranian underground."[55]

The data suggests that it was only after the addition of the four Iranian hackers that were part of the Mersad Company that the DDoS attack escalated, "transforming the equivalent of a few yapping Chihuahuas into a pack of fire-breathing Godzillas."[56] The indictment stated that while the DDoS attacks against the financial institutions in the United States began in December 2011, they escalated in both frequency and scale from September 2012 through May 2013, causing thousands of customers to temporarily lose online access to bank accounts.[57] This escalation is noteworthy because the indictment also stated that the four members of Mersad Company, three of whom were also members of Sun Army, did not join the DDoS attack against the US financial institutions until September 2012 through May 2013.[58] Also aligning with this timeline is the fact that, starting in September 2012, the group Izz ad-Din al-Qassam Cyber Fighters took credit for the DDoS attacks while as early as 2013, media reports referenced American intelligence officials saying that the Izz ad-Din al-Qassam Fighters are "a cover for Iran."[59]

There are several noteworthy differences between ITSecTeam and Mersad Company. First, the ITSecTeam members were older: aged 25–37 while the members of Mersad Company were aged 23–26. Second, the indictment listed hacker pseudonyms only for members of Mersad Company, implying that the pseudonyms for ITSecTeam members were unknown or did not exist (or that the US government did not want to disclose them). Third, ITSecTeam appeared to be organized more hierarchically. According to the indictment, Fathi was the leader of ITSecTeam and "responsible for supervising and coordinating ITSecTeam's participation in the DDoS attacks against the US financial sector and AT&T" as well as "responsible for managing computer intrusion and cyberattack projects being conducted on behalf of the Government of Iran."[60] Shokohi, on the other hand, developed the malware that the others installed on compromised devices; Shokohi allegedly received "credit for his computer intrusion work from the Iranian government towards completion of his mandatory military service in Iran."[61] Firoozi built and managed ITSecTeam's botnet, much as Ghaffarinia and Keissar had done for Mersad Company.[62]

Firoozi stands out from the other six named in the indictment for having also obtained unauthorized remote access to the SCADA system of the Bowman Dam between August 28, 2013 and September 18, 2013. This access "allowed him to repeatedly obtain information regarding the status and operation of the dam, including information about the water levels and temperature, and the status of the sluice gate, which is responsible for controlling water levels and flow rates."[63] Contrary to some media reporting, the techniques used to identify and gain access to this critical infrastructure were not very sophisticated. However, the intrusion is worth highlighting because it shows the desire and intent to target such systems in the first place, which is also the reason it caused concerns among White House officials.[64] In addition, the scope of Firoozi's intent remains unclear: some have speculated that Firoozi actually intended to target the much larger Arthur R. Bowman Dam in Oregon rather than the Bowman Dam in New York, and that the intrusion of the latter was a mistake. Another hypothesis is that he meant to target the smaller dam but that this was "a dry run for a more disruptive invasion of, say, a major hydroelectric generator."[65]

The proxy relationship between Mersad Company and the Iranian government reflected in the US government's indictment aligns with more general descriptions of the Iranian government's efforts to build and project coercive cyber power. The structure and evolution of the malicious activity between December 2011 and May 2013 would fit this description, especially since another hacker mentioned in the indictment "provided training to Iranian intelligence personnel."[66] There are also other groups whose activity seems to align with this broader strategy of orchestration. For example, the Ajax Security Team followed a similar trajectory to that of Mersad Company, shifting from an early focus on Web defacements to more sophisticated and aggressive malware-based intrusions in 2013.[67] Its suspected size of between five and ten members is similar in size to the IT Sec Team and Mersad Company, and some of its members have also been part of the Ashiyane Digital Security Team.[68] In terms of level of sophistication, the group develops its own malware but does not use zero-day exploits.[69] And in another sign of the relationship with the government, CrowdStrike's 2014 Global Threat Intel Report points out that the Ajax Security Team targets the defense sectors of foreign countries and "Iranian dissidents in foreign countries, as well as in Iran itself" in line with the Iranian government's threat perceptions.[70]

ORCHESTRATION IN WARTIME: THE SYRIAN ELECTRONIC ARMY

Two days before the indictment against the Iranian hackers became public, the US Department of Justice also unsealed another indictment against three Syrian citizens, members of the Syrian Electronic Army, one of whom resided in Germany. The three Syrian nationals are Ahmad Umar Agha, aged 22, also known as "Th3 Pro"; Firas Dardar, 27, also known as "The Shadow"; and Peter Romar, 36, also known as Pierre Romar (his online pseudonym is unknown, if he has one at all). In this case, the US government did not explicitly state that the accused were "sponsored" by the Syrian government but instead alleged that two of the three defendants acted "in support of the Syrian Government and President Bashar al-Assad."[71] This indicates that within the spectrum of orchestration, the Syrian government's relationship to these hackers was closer to passive support than to active orchestration. In essence, the relationship between the Syrian government and these hackers began as orchestration and devolved towards passive support as the country descended further into chaos and all-out war.

The Syrian Electronic Army first established a Facebook presence in April and May 2011,[72] describing itself as "a group of enthusiastic Syrian youths who could not stay passive towards the massive distortion of facts about the recent uprising in Syria."[73] Establishing this social media presence was only possible because the Syrian government had lifted the ban against Facebook and Twitter two months earlier, after blocking access for three years.[74] Facebook quickly disabled the Syrian Electronic Army profile for violating its terms of use, but the group has continued to create new profiles whenever its existing one is taken down.[75] Much like the Russian trolls and some of the Chinese actors, members of this group started placing pro-Assad content on other Facebook and social media accounts as well as in the comments sections of websites. The group also launched DDoS attacks against media organizations seen as critical of the Assad regime and targeted Assad opponents with spyware that, "coupled with geo-location services . . . puts those targets at risk of kinetic [i.e., active physical] attack."[76]

Many researchers believe that the members of the Syrian Electronic Army today are not the same ones who conducted those earlier attacks.[77] Based on internal data dumped online by the hacktivist group Anonymous, which hacked the Syrian Electronic Army in April 2013, these researchers concluded that the Syrian Electronic Army's activities from 2011 to 2013 were carried out by a hierarchically organized group, which has since disappeared.[78] The subsequent group of hackers involved, the researchers said, "consists of roughly a dozen new actors led by hackers who call themselves 'Th3 Pro' and 'The Shadow' [who appear in the US indictment] and function more like Anonymous, the loose hacking collective, than a state-sponsored brigade."[79] CrowdStrike also mentioned this change in its 2013 Global Threat Report, which referenced a shift away from opportunistic malicious activity to targeted spear phishing. Furthermore, in June 2013, the server hosting the Syrian

Electronic Army's website switched to a Russian server.[80] The Shadow, now also known as Firas Dardar, wrote in an email to ABC News in August 2013 that "[w]hen we hacked media we [did] not destroy the site but only published a message on it if possible or published an article that contains the truth of what is happening in Syria"; referring to potential US military responses to Syria's use of chemical weapons, he added that "if the USA launches attack on Syria, we may use methods of causing harm, both for the US economy or [in] other [ways]."[81]

The US indictment accused the two hackers based in Syria of acting in support of the Syrian government and President Bashar al-Assad; however, it did not say that they were state-sponsored. Assad has referred to the Syrian Electronic Army as "a real army in a virtual reality,"[82] and he has made supportive statements publicly, but these comments are vaguer than those made by Ayatollah Khomeini in 1979, which the International Court of Justice considered too general to constitute legal responsibility. As a result, based on the information that is publicly available today, the Syrian government's relationship with the Syrian Electronic Army can be characterized as orchestration. The relation extends beyond mere tolerance or passive support because members of the Syrian Electronic Army also belong to the Syrian Computer Society, which Assad has led since 1994.[83] Despite this connection, however, it is not clear whether any specific instruction or oversight existed during either the first phase from 2011 to 2013 or after the apparent change in 2013.[84] As John Carlin, US Assistant Attorney General for National Security, has pointed out in the context of the indictment, "While some of the activity sought to harm the economic and national security of the United States in the name of Syria, these detailed allegations reveal that the members also used extortion to try to line their own pockets at the expense of law-abiding people all over the world."[85]

Of the three Syrian nationals named in the indictment, Romar stands out because, unlike Agha and Dardar, who are believed to reside in Syria, he was living in Waltershausen, a small town of 13,000 in the center of Germany, until his extradition to the United States by German authorities in May 2016.[86] Romar is not accused of directly acting in support of the Syrian government but of acting as an intermediary helping Agha and Dardar evade sanctions and engage in extortion schemes for personal profit.[87] That the affiliation with the Syrian Electronic Army was not mentioned in every case of malicious activity suggests these actors had mixed motives that included political as well as profit-driven rationales. According to an affidavit filed in support of the arrest warrant, Romar contacted Agha via Facebook in April 2013 and expressed a desire to affiliate himself with the Syrian Electronic Army, and asked for advice on how to target systems in Saudi Arabia, Turkey, and Qatar.[88] Romar subsequently collaborated with Dardar, who "conducted computer intrusions from his location in Syria and sent threats and demands for payment to each victim," while Romar "received and attempted to retransmit the extortion proceeds to [Syrian Electronic Army] members in Syria, in violation of US sanctions against Syria."[89]

Agha and Dardar targeted their victims with spear-phishing emails to gain unauthorized access to systems of the US government, media organizations, and other private companies.[90] The effects of their activity consisted of Web defacements and taking over social media accounts. Their techniques were not very sophisticated but nevertheless made headlines when they managed to hijack the Twitter account of the Associated Press (which apparently was not protected by simple two-factor authentication). Once in control of the account, they used it to place a tweet with the fake announcement that a bomb had exploded at the White House, injuring President Obama. This caused the Dow Jones Industrial to plunge by 100 points and wiped USD 136 billion from the S&P 50 index before it bounced back several minutes later.[91] While Agha and Dardar were not necessarily particularly skilled compared to other hackers, the effects they caused were nevertheless grave enough for them to be added to the list of the FBI's Cyber Most Wanted, and the US government offered USD 100,000 for information leading to their arrest.[92]

The indictment did debunk prior speculation that the Syrian Electronic Army, as far as these three individuals were concerned, was "actually Iranian,"[93] "based in Lebanon,"[94] or that 'The Pro' was from Morocco.[95] It is true that other members of the Syrian Electronic Army (if any) might fit this description and that any of the three indicted subjects might have been in Lebanon at one point. A tie to actors in Lebanon is a particularly plausible hypothesis. A team of researchers at the cyber threat intelligence firm FireEye described a three-day training course offered in Lebanon in 2012 that included

> [e]stablishing an "Electronic Army" to infiltrate Syrian activists' computers, websites and Internet accounts, and attempting to use stolen personal information against them. Setting up opposition social media accounts to spread false information and make accusations and counter-accusations to create conflict between opposition members in and out of Syria. The use of women to entrap opposition members and activists using social media sites such as Skype and Facebook.[96]

With regard to the broader Syrian conflict, the Syrian Electronic Army is not the only threat actor involved. In addition to Group 5, which targets Syrian opposition, there are also the Security Lions Hackers[97] and malicious activity focused on stealing information that "can provide actionable military intelligence for an immediate battlefield advantage … revealing the Syrian opposition's strategy, tactical battle plans, supply needs, and troves of personal information and chat sessions."[98] As Dokukin argued in Kiev in the summer of 2015, this information can help the military plan kinetic operations and influence the war on the ground.

CONCLUSION: UNEXPECTED ESCALATION AND LIMITED
OPTIONS FOR RESPONSE

Remarkably, the malicious actions carried out by the Iranian and Syrian hackers have all occurred only in the past five years. It is clear that the Iranian and Syrian governments are not merely tolerating and providing passive support to hackers operating out of their territories. They are aware of the hackers' activities and, to echo the words of the International Court of Justice finding from 1980, they are "fail[ing] altogether to take any 'appropriate steps' to protect [the hackers' targets] . . . or to persuade or to compel [the hackers] to withdraw."[99] Whether this is sufficient to hold Tehran responsible for the hackers' actions under international law remains unclear. While the International Court of Justice did not consider the Iranian government legally responsible for the students' behavior until their actions had been subsequently endorsed, it did note that the hostage takers explicitly referenced an announcement made by Khomeini on November 1, 1979, in which he urged students "to expand with all their might their attacks against the United States and Israel, so they may force the United States to return the deposed and criminal shah, and to condemn this great plot."[100] Even though the court found this statement insufficient to consider it an authorization of the students' specific actions under international law, it certainly mattered politically, and it showed the ability of the beneficiary to orchestrate intermediaries' actions.

The relationship between Tehran and the hackers involved fits the orchestration model, whereas the available information regarding the Syrian Electronic Army suggests the relationship with the Assad regime is looser, qualifying either as orchestration or sanctioning (approving or permitting). Both states' proxy relationships reveal shifts over time, and both demonstrate that proxies on a relatively loose leash can have a major impact.

Perhaps the most interesting aspect of the Iranian and Syrian stories is that actors in both countries were able to project coercive cyber power so quickly. The two indictments showed that non-state actors have played a significant role in carrying out malicious activity against internal opponents and external adversaries alike, and also in training government officials. Collin Anderson, an expert on Iran and the Internet, substantiated this point: "Following in the model of Ashiyane, smaller defacement groups formed private companies that offered cybersecurity and IT services. Several of these companies can be attributed to espionage and disruption campaigns that are connected to the Iranian government, primarily the Islamic Revolutionary Guard Corps and the Ministry of Intelligence. These companies only constitute a few individuals, who are not members of the security services."[101] These non-state actors provided a latent capability ready to be mobilized by the government. And Assistant Attorney General Carlin highlighted the nexus between criminal and political activity when he said, "The allegations in the complaint demonstrate that the line between ordinary criminal hackers and potential national security threats is increasingly blurry."[102] These non-state actors rely on tools available in underground forums or commercial off-the-shelf tools. Some analysts have also claimed that Iran has been receiving help from Russia;[103] this claim is unsubstantiated, although there is at least evidence that Iran and North Korea are cooperating in this area.[104]

At the end of the day, the indictments have provided unprecedented insight into the identities and activities of Iranian and Syrian hackers. At the same time, they are unlikely to have any immediate impact. One defendant has been extradited to the United States, but the remaining nine individuals remain at large and are believed to be in Iran and Syria; they can be arrested only if they travel to a country that has an extradition agreement with the United States. At this point the indictments therefore serve primarily as a naming and shaming exercise, demonstrating that attribution is possible and enabling the government to take punitive action if the opportunity presents itself in the future.

6

Cyber Proxies on the Loose: The Former Soviet Union

Countries in the former Soviet Union serve as the best illustrations of proxy relationships based on sanctioning. Sanctioning occurs when a state consciously but indirectly benefits from a malicious activity targeting a third party, an activity which the state could stop but chooses not to. Sanctioning describes environments where the state indirectly creates a fertile ground for such malicious activity to occur in the first place. This chapter first outlines the various reasons that sanctioning has become a prevalent phenomenon in the former Soviet Union. The events in Estonia in 2007, in Georgia in 2008, and in Ukraine since 2014 will further illustrate the impact sanctioning can have in peacetime as well as during an armed conflict. The details revealed in the March 2017 US indictment of Russian hackers will shed light on how sanctioning provides the foundation for a state's more active engagement.

Former Soviet states stand out for their many individuals with highly developed technical skills and their university departments in math, engineering, and computer science, which have ranked among the world's best for decades. It is the result of systematic literacy campaigns after the 1917 revolution, with the campaigns boosting the literacy rate from 22 percent at the beginning of the twentieth century to full literacy by the time the Soviet Union collapsed. While states that used to be part of the Soviet Union still rank among the world's most literate and educated societies, unemployment has risen, and the economy has not been able to absorb this technically skilled workforce.[1] The economic crash in 1998 exacerbated the problem, with only an estimated 50 percent of Russian software companies surviving the downturn and concomitant rise in cyber crime.[2]

The same challenges persist today. For example, someone in his twenties holding a cybersecurity job in the Ukrainian government today would earn roughly $3,000 – a year, not a month. And while Samsung has one of its largest R&D centers in Kiev, the private IT industry is neither large nor attractive enough to absorb the available skilled labor.[3] As Alexei Borodin, a 21-year-old hacker, put it, "People think: 'I've got no money, a strong education and law enforcement's weak. Why not earn a bit on the side?'"[4] In sum, there is no labor shortage in the region when it comes to information technology and hacking, but the legitimate industry is not big enough to absorb all of the labor, and government salaries of a few thousand dollars a year pale in comparison to reports of thousands or millions made in the latest cyber heist.

At the turn of the century, several hundred Russians had already participated in hacking competitions such as the one organized by http://www.hackzone.ru, and hacker magazines had a monthly circulation in the tens of thousands.[5] A decade later the Moscow-based cybersecurity company Group-IB estimated the size of the cyber crime market in Russia alone to be USD 2.3 billion.[6] Since hackers take great care not to target people within the area of the former Soviet Union but focus on victims in the United States and Europe, it is not surprising that few arrests are made by Russian law enforcement agencies.[7] The latter often do not respond to requests for assistance from foreign law enforcement agencies and frequently protest when Russian nationals are arrested abroad.[8] For example, when Vladimir Drinkman was arrested while vacationing in Amsterdam in 2012, the Russian government tried to block the US government's extradition request by filing its own extradition request, thereby at least delaying prosecution.[9]

The cyber crime expert Misha Glenny has expressed doubt that Russian law enforcement is weak and the government unable to take action. He argued that "Russian law enforcement and the FSB (Federal Security Service) in particular have a very good idea of what is going on and they are monitoring it, but as long as the fraud is restricted to other parts of the world they don't care."[10] The FSB's role is particularly important given its management of the SORM monitoring system, and as Thomas has documented, the FSB law has been amended to allow it "to conduct police investigations to counter threats to Russia's information security."[11] Another indication that the Russian government can effectively enforce the law if it so chooses is the fact that malware used by Russian and east European cybercriminals is often designed so that it "purposefully avoids infecting computers if the program detects the potential victim is a native resident."[12] For example, "http://installscash .com" pays people money for installing their adware and spyware on machines in dozens of countries but points out on its website that "[w]e do not purchase Russian and CIS [Russian Commonwealth] traffic."[13] (When Russian hackers do target victims in Russia, Moscow's response is swift and harsh. In 2012, eight men were arrested by Russian police after stealing some USD 4 million from several dozen banks, including some in Russia. According to Krebs, "Russian police released a video showing one of the suspects loudly weeping in the moments following a morning raid on his home."[14])

The toleration of criminal activities by the state, or rather people abusing state authority for private gain, can become even more convoluted. Take the example of Dmitry Ivanovich Golubov (Dmytro Holubov), a 32-year-old Ukrainian national from Odessa. Wanted by US law enforcement as a top cyber criminal accused of credit card fraud, Golubov was briefly imprisoned in 2005 "until two influential Ukrainian politicians convinced a judge to toss out the case," according to a former FBI agent who investigated the case.[15] After founding the

Internet Party of Ukraine in 2007, Golubov has been a member of the Ukrainian parliament since 2014.[16] The reason he pursued a seat in the Ukrainian parliament? According to Krebs, "Gaining a seat in the Ukrainian government would grant [him] automatic immunity from prosecution for criminal activities under Ukrainian law."[17]

A similar example is Roman Valerevich Seleznev, a 32-year-old Russian national and the son of Valery Seleznev, a member of the Russian parliament and the ultra-nationalist Liberal Democratic Party.[18] He was convicted by a US federal jury of financial cyber crime that reaped millions in profit.[19] The US Secret Service arrested him while he was on vacation in the Maldives rather than trying to work with the Russian government to arrest him – perhaps because of his family connections and certainly because of Russian law enforcement agencies' general reluctance to cooperate. Seleznev's arrest caused significant tension between Moscow and Washington. The Russian Ministry of Foreign Affairs accused the US government of having "kidnapped" Seleznev when it arrested him as he was boarding a plane in the Maldives, and transferred him to Guam and then to Seattle. (In court in the United States, Seleznev's defense tried to challenge the circumstances of the arrest but was unsuccessful.)[20]

The Russian Ministry of Foreign Affairs maintains that "the practice of detaining Russian citizens following US requests to third countries all over the world is a legal abuse and violation of internationally recognised proceedings."[21] When the US government used a fake job interview to trick a suspect, Vasily Gorshkov, into traveling to the United States, and US law enforcement agents accessed Gorshkov's computer in Russia, the Russian government therefore also protested. Such action, they said, "violated a 1997 agreement that mandates 'investigation and prosecution of international high-tech crimes must be coordinated among all concerned states, regardless of where harm has occurred.'"[22] In the weeks leading up to a December 2015 visit by US Secretary of State John Kerry, the ministry demanded that "US law enforcement authorities stop the hunt for Russian citizens in other countries."[23]

Such sanctioning can turn into more proactive interest from the government. In some cases, entering a proxy relationship allows a non-state actor to avoid arrest, as described by Oleg Gordievsky, the former head of the KGB office in London, who said in 1998 that "[t]here are organised groups of hackers tied to the FSB and pro-Chechen sites have been hacked into by such groups. . . One man I know, who was caught committing a cyber crime, was given the choice of either prison or cooperation with the FSB and he went along."[24] In such cases, in return for their cooperation, the hackers not only avoid prison, but are actively defended by the Russian government. Alexander Klimburg and Heli Tirmaa-Klaar described one such case in which the Tomsk FSB office described malicious activity against pro-Chechen websites in 2002–2004 as being legal."[25] This system of the FSB turning hackers into proxies for internal and external offensive cyber operations was also reaffirmed by Sergei Pokrovsky, the editor of the hacking magazine *Khaker*, and Vasilyev, a convicted hacker and the head of the Moscow Civil Hacking School.[26]

How this systemic sanctioning can affect international relations became evident in 2007, when Estonia was hit by a significant DDoS attack.

SANCTIONING IN PEACETIME: THE 2007 DDOS ATTACK ON ESTONIA

The DDoS attack targeting Estonia in 2007 was a wake-up call, especially since its disruptive effect occurred in peacetime. The incident began after the Estonian government decided to move the Bronze Soldier, a Soviet-era World War II memorial, sparking vocal protest by the Russian government and among many Estonians of Russian origin. The anger quickly spilled onto the streets and riots broke out in Estonia's capital, Tallinn, on August 26 and 27. These physical protests were accompanied by a virtual riot in form of a DDoS attack that brought down websites of the Estonian government and businesses.[27] According to the excellent analysis by Eneken Tikk, Kadri Kaska, and Liis Vihul,

> The first phase took place from April 27 to 29 and was assessed to have been emotionally motivated, as the attacks were relatively simple and any coordination mainly occurred on an *ad hoc* basis. The first phase was followed by the main, co-ordinated attack phase lasting from April 30 to May 18, which was much more sophisticated, and where the use of large botnets and professional coordination was noticed... In various Russian-language Internet forums, calls and instructions were presented to launch *ping* commands (simple commands to check the availability of the targeted computers) with certain parameters on the MS Windows command line.[28]

There is no conclusive proof of the Kremlin's direct involvement in this attack, but there is considerable evidence to argue that it was a case of sanctioning.[29] In March 2009, Sergei Markov, a deputy of the State Duma, acknowledged that his assistant had been involved in the DDoS attack, together with other members of the pro-Kremlin youth movement Nashi. Created during the 2000s by the Kremlin as a pro-Kremlin political force, Nashi featured a "school of bloggers" consisting of "eighty people from all over Russia, each working with two or three activists, and their graduates were supposed to organize information campaigns online."[30] Two years later, one of Nashi's leaders, Konstantin Goloskokov, himself confirmed Nashi's involvement.[31] Importantly, the Russian government did very little to stop the malicious activity – unlike, for example, the Chinese government, which regularly reined in its hacktivists with public statements calling on them to stop their campaigns. Moreover, Russia did not cooperate with Estonia and rejected Estonia's request for a bilateral investigation. To date, only a single person has been prosecuted for participating in the DDoS attack: Dimitri Galuskevich, an Estonian IT student at Tallinn University of Technology, who was 19 years old at the time and was sentenced under the Estonian Penal Code.[32] In spite of the absence of concrete proof linking the Kremlin to the attack, the 2007 incident started the discussion among NATO members as to whether Article 5, which commits alliance members to collective defense against attacks, could be invoked in case of a cyber attack. (Seven years later, the alliance's heads of state would declare that Article 5 does apply to cyber attacks, though without defining "cyber attack" or what threshold would have to be met.)

While Estonia suffered the consequences of this malicious cyber activity in peacetime, Ukrainians experienced it as an element of the broader conflict with Russia.

SANCTIONING IN WARTIME: THE CONFLICT IN UKRAINE (2014–TODAY)[33]

The conflict between Ukraine and Russia illustrates the actions of cyber proxies during wartime. Simmering political tension escalated in November 2013, when the former Ukrainian president Viktor Yanukovych abandoned plans to sign a trade agreement with the European Union. Yanukovych's decision incited mass protests that were met with a violent government crackdown. In November, several months before Yanukovych's flight in February 2014 and the build-up of Russian troops on the Crimean border, reports emerged that Russian hacker groups were executing DDoS attacks and defacing websites critical of the Yanukovych government's relationship with Russia. This period was characterized by low-level hacking targeting highly visible websites, either rendering them unavailable or changing their content.

On February 28, shortly after Yanukovych fled the country, unmarked soldiers (which Russia's President Vladimir Putin later acknowledged to be Russian troops)[34] seized a military airfield in Sevastopol and Simferopol International Airport. Concurrently, armed soldiers tampered with fiber-optic cables and raided the facilities of the Ukrainian telecom firm Ukrtelecom, which stated afterward that it had "lost the technical capacity to provide connection between the peninsula and the rest of Ukraine and probably across the peninsula, too."[35] In addition, Ukrainian parliamentarians' cell phones were hacked, and the main Ukrainian government website was shut down for 72 hours after Russian troops entered Crimea on March 2. Patriotic Ukrainian hacker groups such as "Cyber Hundred" and "Null Sector" retaliated with DDoS attacks of their own against websites of the Kremlin and the Central Bank of Russia.[36] The day before the presidential election, Ukraine's Security Service (SBU) discovered malware in the systems of the Central Election Commission designed to compromise data collected on the results of the election, revealing how close hackers had come to sabotaging the results.[37] The pro-Russian hacker group "Cyber Berkut" claimed responsibility.[38]

Dokukin's Ukrainian Cyber Forces is among the most prominent Ukrainian hacktivist groups. It consists primarily of ordinary citizens without a technical background using ICT to track pro-Russian forces in the east, brute-force cameras and publish CCTV footage of troop movements online, and leak data from the Russian Ministry of the Interior.[39] At one point, the Ukrainian Cyber Forces threatened to shut down the Internet in the Crimea and other cities in eastern Ukraine.[40] Given Dokukin's public statements, the Ukrainian government could have interfered but instead turned a blind eye and thereby sanctioned his activities. One explanation is that the government quietly appreciated the benefit. Based on my research interviews, however, it seems more likely that the government did not take Dokukin seriously enough to warrant devoting attention or scarce resources to him.

In at least one instance, a government official offered more specific assistance, though it is not clear if this was in an official or personal capacity. Kostiantyn Korsun, Chairman of the Ukrainian Information Security Group and former Head of Ukrainian CERT and former Deputy Head of Computer Crime Division at the Security Service of Ukraine, posted the following request on his LinkedIn profile: "Because of the military intervention of Russia against Ukraine I ask everybody who has the technical ability to counter the enemy in the information war, to contact me and be prepared for a fight... Will talk to the security forces to work together against the external enemy." Maxim Litinov, Head of the Ukrainian Interior Ministry's cyber crime department, replied "You can count on me" and offered facilities and staffing assistance.[41] Others, however, have received no such support. On the contrary, a member of a hacktivist group called RUH8 has said that after hackers shared hacked data with Ukraine's Security Service, "criminal proceedings were instituted on a couple of episodes, including under Art. 111 ('treason' in the Criminal Code of Ukraine), and some arrests were made."[42] In short, in addition to lacking an overall strategy to mobilize these additional capabilities and provide active support, the Ukrainian government has also been inconsistent in its stance towards passive support.

On the pro-Russian side of the conflict, the most prominent actor is Cyber Berkut,[43] which emerged after President Yanukovych fled the country and Berkut, the Ukrainian special police force, was disbanded. Assessments about Cyber Berkut's location, origin, and state sponsorship vary. Some consider the group to consist of Ukrainians,[44] possibly former SBU employees; others suspect it to be Russian hackers.[45] Cyber Berkut's activities, along with those of other pro-Russian hacktivist groups like Cyber Riot Novorossiya and Green Dragon,[46] resemble those of the pro-Ukrainian hacktivist groups – launching DDoS attacks[47] and hacking Ukrainian government networks.

It remains unclear whether the most significant cyber attack that has occurred as part of the conflict to date was the result of proxy activity or was carried out by the Russian government. In December 2015, a cyber attack against the Ukrainian electrical grid cut power in the western part of the country for about six hours.[48] It is possible that this attack was carried out by a proxy actor to increase plausible deniability; however, given its significant potential to lead to escalation, there are also strong incentives for any government not to outsource this type of operation to a proxy. And while the power outage itself was enabled by the simple theft of credentials, the fact that the attack also used malware to delay recovery efforts and a coordinated effort to interrupt communications points to a tighter level of communication and a link with the state. At the same time, the cyber attack against the electrical grid must be put into perspective. Despite its significance in the history of cyber incidents, it had little effect in the broader scheme of the conflict. In fact, it occurred only a month after conventional bombs physically destroyed pylons supporting the power supplies to Crimea. This kinetic attack did not cause a brief power shortage that lasted for hours; it continued for months, affecting not only the Russian naval base located there but also the people in Crimea.[49] Therefore, while the cyber attack targeting the power supply in western Ukraine was an escalation viewed through the prism of cyber conflict, it was only a blip in the broader "cybered conflict." ("cybered conflict" is a term coined by Chris Demchak to describe a conventional conflict that includes but is not confined to offensive cyber operations.)[50]

Ultimately, the Ukrainian example illustrates the presence of significant cyber capabilities in private hands, the activity of proxies during a hot conflict, and incentives for the states involved to use these private capabilities. However, the amount of cyber proxy activity has remained relatively low. The most prominent proxy actors on the pro-Ukrainian side have been hacktivist groups including pro-Kiev OpRussia, Ukrainian Cyber Forces, Cyber Hundred, and Null Sector.[51] Their activities have been limited to DDoS attacks, Web defacements, and the occasional leaking of government files. It is notable that the conflict does not appear to have politicized and mobilized the most sophisticated non-state actors with cyber capabilities – the cybercriminals – to change their profit-driven behavior to more politically driven action to any significant degree. According to one hacktivist, "We do not cross ways with hackers operating on the black market. There have been some polemics on the closed commercial underground forums, but the admins purged them mercilessly."[52] For its part, the Ukrainian government has not had the capacity and strategy in place to mobilize the capabilities provided by volunteers. One explanation for the Ukrainian government's limited ability to mobilize non-state actors is the general poor state of the military. Once considered one of the most powerful conventional military forces in the world, the Ukrainian military has been falling apart since the end of the Soviet Union, and Kiev was ill-prepared for a conflict with Russia.[53]

Indeed, Ukraine was not the only state ill-prepared for conflict with Russia; Georgia found itself woefully unready to counter malicious activity online when war broke out with Russia in 2008.

BLITZ ORCHESTRATION: THE WAR AGAINST GEORGIA IN 2008

The short war on the ground between Georgia and Russia lasted only five days, August 7–12. It coincided with an episode of blitz orchestration, the rapid mobilization of non-state actors to project coercive (cyber) power, in the form of a DDoS attack. The importance of the event was summed up by Heather Harrison Dinniss at the Swedish Defense University: Georgia 2008 was "the first time that there had been a coordinated cyber component to an international armed conflict; however, despite the obvious links to the ongoing conflict, there is only circumstantial evidence that the Russian Federation was in any way involved in the attacks."[54] Because of the close relationship between criminals and agencies of governments that have emerged in the former Soviet Union, several experts argued that the offensive cyber operations against targets in Georgia between Russia and Georgia were carried out by Russian criminals but orchestrated by the Russian government.

Tensions between Russia and Georgia had escalated following the Rose Revolution of 2003, one of the first color revolutions that would create such concern in the halls of the Kremlin and Zhongnanhai in the years to come. Georgia's president Mikheil Saakashvili, elected in 2004, was trying to unify the country's territories, but with the breakup of Yugoslavia in the 1990s and NATO's recognition of Kosovo in 2008, Moscow started pushing back, and tensions escalated on both sides. On August 7, Georgian troops were sent to South Ossetia, and Russian troops crossed the border the next day. At the same time, the DDoS attack crippled the government's ability to communicate with its population and its military.[55] This lack of communication sowed panic among the population of Tbilisi, especially after rumors circulated that Russian forces were about to enter the Georgian capital.[56] Four days after Russian troops crossed the border, the Russian president Medvedev declared the objectives of the Russian military operation had been met and the two countries signed a peace agreement on August 15.[57] Overall, the DDoS's effects "played a significant, if not decisive, role in the conflict – as an object of contestation and as a vector for generating strategic effects and outcomes."[58]

Analysts disagree as to whether the proxy relationship during the 2008 Russo-Georgian war is better characterized as a case of sanctioning by the Russian government or as covert orchestration of non-state cyber proxies.[59] A study by the US Cyber Consequences Unit, a non-profit research organization with ties to the US government, argued that "there had to be close cooperation between people in the Russian military and the civilian cyber attackers" as well as advance knowledge, because the timing of the cyber operation coincided with military advances on the ground; this report also explicitly mentioned the involvement of Russian criminals.[60] The analysis by Deibert et al., while it agreed that the Russian government benefited from the DDoS attacks, was more skeptical and questioned the Kremlin's involvement in carrying them out.[61]

Analysts agree that the command-and-control servers for the DDoS attack were located in Russia, that at least part of the DDoS infrastructure relied on DDoS-for-hire services used and operated by cybercriminals, and that the DDoS attack was coordinated via Russian hacker forums.[62] Instructions and scripts were posted on several Russian-language websites, making it so easy to participate that Evgeny Morozov, a writer on technology in the United States, managed to become part of the operation within an hour.[63] According to Deibert et al., "this would not have precluded Russian authorities from contracting these botnets; however, no open-source evidence exists to support such a claim. Moreover, it can be conclusively ruled out that the DDoS network was purpose-built for the August 2008 conflict."[64] They considered orchestration a possible scenario, despite their skepticism in the absence of direct evidence in open sources;[65] however, they considered it more probable that the DDoS attack was carried out by an independent third party in the form of a network of patriotic hacktivists.[66]

Based on the aforementioned historical evidence of the FSB's relationship with hackers, a review of the analysis of the events in 2008, and additional research interviews, I have concluded that both scenarios are possible, but the scenario of orchestration is more likely. Orchestration, however, does not necessarily imply a prolonged campaign or a lot of planning having gone into preparing the operation: rather, the nature of DDoS attacks enables blitz orchestration – a quick mobilization of non-state actors already engaged in such work for their own purposes. Such actors are undoubtedly on the scene. For example, it is is entirely possible that a cyber criminal such as "BadB," also known as Vladislav Horohorin, a 33-year-old with citizenship in Ukraine, Russia, and Israel, could have been involved in such an operation. Known as one of the founding members of CarderPlanet and making millions through credit card fraud, BadB, like many cybercriminals in the region, was not motivated solely by the desire to make a profit. In one of the cartoon videos posted on his website titled "A BadB Welcome Cartoon," he depicts himself as a Russian patriot whose criminal actions deliberately cause harm against the United States as part of a fight against "US imperialism." The video also shows Putin giving medals to hackers and the video calling on viewers to "join army now" and to "invest US funds in Russian economy and make it grow bigger." (CarderPlanet also followed the simple rule "[y]ou don't mess with the Commonwealth of Independent States."[67]) This further illustrates the close nexus between the criminal underground and the Russian government, a point substantiated in the indictment of the Russian hackers by the US government announced in spring 2017.

In sum, the events in Estonia in 2007, in Georgia in 2008, and in Ukraine starting in 2014 represent examples of governments, namely Russia and Ukraine, providing at least passive support to non-state actors whose actions the governments benefit from. The governments are fully aware of the malicious activities taking place yet do not act to stop malicious activity or to prosecute hackers except in a few isolated cases. This raises the question of an established pattern of behavior, which in turn would make judicial concepts such as the denial of justice more relevant for those who are being targeted by such actors.

Yet again, such proxy relationships between a state and criminals are not unprecedented.[68] During World War II, the US government grew increasingly concerned about potential sabotage by Nazis who had infiltrated the United States or by Nazi sympathizers. After the ship *Normandie* burned, capsized, and sank at the pier in New York in February 1942, the government turned to the mafia and its network of informants,[69] forming a secret alliance with criminals that echoed the pact between General Jackson and the pirate Lafitte 130 years earlier. Meyer Lansky, the mafioso who was credited with setting up the proxy relationship, like Horohorin, was not motivated solely by profit. Lansky explained that "[t]he reason why I cooperated [with the US government] was because of strong personal convictions. I wanted the Nazis beaten. I made this my number one priority even before the United States got into the war. I was a Jew and I felt for those Jews in Europe who were suffering. They were my brothers."[70]

It is also not unprecedented for senior officials to be in the dark about the details of such relationships. For example, Captain MacFall, the Chief of US Naval Intelligence in New York in 1942, decided to keep information about the relationship with the mafia to himself and his immediate unit, not reporting it to his superiors.[71] MacFall argued that "[t]he use of underworld informants and characters, like the use of other extremely confidential investigate procedures, was not specifically disclosed to the Commandant or other superior officers as such use was a calculated risk."[72] At the same time, "[t]o ensure that the relationship between the US government and the underworld was working correctly, wire taps were authorized to monitor telephone calls."[73] In 1942, as today, monitoring was used to minimize the agency problem.

These historical analogies have their limits, however. The US indictment of the Russian hackers provides rare insight into the systematic nature of these relationships over a prolonged period of time. Reports about mutual monetary benefits from cybercrime for beneficiaries and proxies alike suggest a relationship more akin to privateering than the collaboration with the mafia that occurred in New York during World War II. Furthermore, the US indictment illustrates how such relationships of sanctioning can evolve and affect other people and countries.

SANCTIONING AND MOBILIZING: THE MARCH 2017 US INDICTMENT OF RUSSIAN HACKERS

In March 2017, the US government unsealed an indictment that offered unprecedented insight into the relationship between FSB officials and cybercriminals. It reinforced previous anecdotal evidence and offered new details why and how this proxy relationship was beneficial to all parties involved. The indictment listed three Russian citizens living in Russia, including two FSB officers, as well

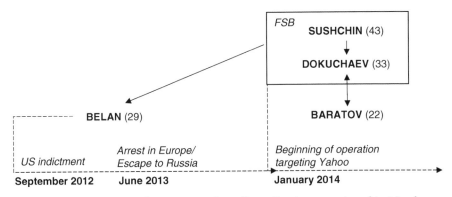

FIGURE 6.1 Organizational structure and timeline of hackers mentioned in March 2017 US indictment of Russian hackers.

as a Canadian national residing in Canada, accusing them of cyber crime and espionage primarily targeting Yahoo, starting in January 2014.[74] The two FSB officers were Igor Anatolyevich Sushchin, 43, and Dmitry Aleksandrovich Dokuchaev, 33 – both belonged to the FSB's Center for Information Security. (Sushchin was Dokuchaev's superior.) They were accused of targeting the online accounts of specific individuals, including journalists and government officials in the United States and Russia, as well as private sector officials in the financial, transportation, and other sectors.[75] To achieve their objectives, they worked with two cyber criminals: the Russian citizen Alexsey Alexseyevich Belan, also known as "Magg," 29; and the Canadian, Karim Baratov, also known as "Kay," "Karim Taloverov," and "Karim Akehmet Tokbergenov," 22.[76] According to the indictment, the two FSB officers "protected, directed, facilitated and paid [the] criminal hackers to collect information through computer intrusions in the United States and elsewhere."[77] The organizational structure of the hacking is illustrated in Figure 6.1.

What was the benefit for Belan and Baratov to work with the FSB? For Belan, it was avoiding a US prison. He had been indicted in the United States in 2012 and 2013 for various cyber crimes[78] and was arrested in Europe in June 2013. However, he managed to escape to Russia before being extradited. In spite of Interpol issuing a Red Notice for his arrest in July 2013 and the FBI adding him to its Cyber Most Wanted criminals list in November 2013, the Russian government refused to arrest him. The indictment reveals that the Russian government instead "used him to gain unauthorized access to Yahoo's network."[79] In addition to avoiding having to face charges in a US court, Belan benefited from information shared by the FSB officers that helped him "avoid detection by US and other law enforcement agencies outside Russia, including information regarding FSB investigations of computer hacking and FSB techniques for identifying criminal hackers."[80] Finally, Sushchin and

Dokuchaev turned a blind eye to Belan's enriching himself on the side: in addition to providing them with access to Yahoo accounts, "Belan used his access to steal financial information such as gift card and credit card numbers from webmail accounts; to gain access to more than 30 million accounts whose contacts were then stolen to facilitate a spam campaign; and to earn commissions from fraudulently redirecting a subset of Yahoo's search engine traffic."[81]

For Baratov, residing in Canada, the incentive was money. Whereas Belan was used by Sushchin and Dokuchaev to gain access to targets' Yahoo accounts, Baratov was asked to gain access to a target's accounts with other providers and paid a bounty in return.[82] According to the indictment, "When Baratov successfully obtained unauthorized access to a victim's account, he notified Dokuchaev and provided evidence of that access. He then demanded payment – generally approximately US $100 – via online payment services. Once Dokuchaev sent Baratov a payment, Baratov provided Dokuchaev with valid, illicitly obtained account credentials."[83] Baratov was arrested in Canada on March 14, 2017.[84]

Technically, the operation relied on spear phishing and using programs to clean log files to hide traces of the illegal activity.[85] And while the relatively modest payments to Baratov show that the cost of the operation itself was low, it caused significant economic damage to Yahoo. Yahoo, which was in the process of being acquired by Verizon, had to cut its deal by USD 350 million when the data breach became known.[86] In addition, it is unclear whether the access to individuals' accounts led to any further damage or injury. It is noteworthy that the accounts included targets of interest to the FSB, both from an external standpoint, such as US government officials, as well as an internal standpoint, such as Russian journalists and politicians critical of the Kremlin.[87] Finally, Acting Assistant Attorney General McCord pointed to a particularly egregious element of this story: Sushchin and Dokuchaev's FSB unit is the FBI's point of contact in Moscow on cyber-crime matters. This, McCord remarked, "is beyond the pale."[88]

CONCLUSION: SANCTIONING AND STATEHOOD

The use of cyber proxies in the former Soviet Union today tells us a lot more about the political realities in those countries than just the role that hackers play. Even twenty-five years after the Soviet Union's collapse, it is clear that the economic situation remains dire enough to provide fertile ground for criminal activity – activity that in the digital age can be far removed from the victim and allow the perpetrator to avoid arrest, and often even detection. The amount of money at stake has also made it attractive for corrupt local officials to work with those technically savvy enough to pull off cyber heist after cyber heist. The new possibilities enabled by offensive cyber operations and those able to conduct them have also drawn the attention of intelligence agencies. The combination of economic hardship, relative impunity, and high reward has created an environment in which malicious activity is permitted, as long as certain rules are followed, primarily finding victims abroad rather than at home.

The availability of highly skilled and technically well-versed individuals also presents a pool of potential proxies that can be mobilized at a moment's notice. Often, people will mobilize themselves and take political action in support of the government, as happened in Estonia in 2007 and in Ukraine since 2014. Governments differ in their ability to catalyze such activity and the extent to which they are in a position to merely endorse, orchestrate, or actively direct their outcomes. In countries where public institutions and the state's ability to exercise control have deteriorated, it is an uphill battle to break the increasingly entrenched incentive structures reinforcing existing proxy relationships. Meanwhile, the controversy over law enforcement cooperation, including mutual legal assistance and extradition, shows the limits of international cooperation and external influence. The phenomenon described in this chapter is therefore a cautionary tale of the potential pitfalls when a state significantly weakens or collapses and the consequences that will reverberate for decades to come.

7

Change Over Time: China's Evolving Relationships with Cyber Proxies

Usually, it takes a state a long time to systematically shift its approach to the organization of coercive power capabilities. In China, this shift took place within the span of only two decades, in tandem with the expansion of the modern Internet and the rise of cyber proxies. No other country has seen such a quick transformation and ascendance to global power status. China is therefore an excellent case study to trace how a state moved from permitting the malicious behavior of hackers, to creating institutions and structures to orchestrate private actors, and eventually to tightening the leash even further and moving from orchestration to delegation. Beijing's changing attitude towards proxies occurred alongside China's general rise. This chapter identifies three periods during which these shifts occurred, coinciding with the tenures of three Chinese leaders. The period from 1994 to 2003, during Jiang Zemin's presidency, is characterized by the government permitting the activities of the growing number of hacktivists while laying the foundation for what would become a fully institutionalized militia system. During Hu Jintao's tenure (2003–13), Beijing started to tighten its control over non-state actors wielding cyber capabilities; since Xi Xinping took office in 2013, Beijing has further consolidated its power through sustained crackdowns and institutionalized incentive mechanisms.

The external and internal dimensions of cybersecurity are somewhat blurred by China's policies and bureaucracy. The activities of the Ministry of State Security, for example, have both an internal and external dimension. According to Li Fengzhi, a member of the ministry who defected to the United States in 2009, in addition to dealing with external threats, the ministry's mission includes "bolster[ing] Beijing's Communist Party rule by repressing religious and political dissent internally."[1] The real-world impact of these blurred lines is illustrated by reports about a graduate student hacker at Sichuan University, Gu Kaiyuan, who targeted companies in India and Japan of interest from an external security perspective as well as Tibetan activists tied to Beijing's internal security concerns.[2] It is worth bearing in mind the observation by Scott Henderson,[3] an expert on Chinese hackers, that "[f]rom a Western perspective, the idea of active espionage against another nation requires government initiative, involvement, and direction. It is hard for us to conceive of links being formed between state authorities and quasi-freelance intelligence operations, simply because it does not fit our preconceived notion of the proper relationship."[4] In China these links between state and private are also blurred. Inkster pointed out that telecommunications companies like Huawei and ZTE "aspire to be 'normal' companies but like all Chinese private sector companies have what is in effect a 'shadow board' in the form of a Communist Party cell which can override management decisions and enforce adherence to national strategic priorities."[5]

For its part, the Chinese military serves the party and not the nation first. The Third and Fourth Department of the PLA's General Staff are responsible for what the US military calls cyber collection and cyber effects operations, respectively. The Science of Military Strategy, a crucial document published about once a decade by China's Academy of Military Sciences, points to the blurred lines between military and civilian actors in Chinese thinking. The most recent of these documents, as paraphrased by Elsa Kania, a cybersecurity scholar focusing on China, stated that "since 'military and civilian attacks are hard to distinguish,' the PLA should 'persist in the integration of peace and war [and] the integration of the military and civilians,' such that 'in peacetime, civilians hide the military, [while] in wartime, the military and the people, hands joined, attack together.'"[6] This approach is reflected in a number of high-level documents such as "Locating Military Potential in Civilian Capabilities" in the Tenth Five-Year Plan, or "Civil-Military Fusion" as part of the Eleventh Five-Year Plan, although these documents focus primarily on the defense industrial base.[7] As in many other countries, the PLA relies on university research and has built a network of over forty universities;[8] in addition China has also systematically built militias that interact with the PLA and universities since at least 2002.[9] These militias were explicitly mentioned by the Academy of Military Science in 2006.[10]

To better understand how these policies and bureaucratic structures affect proxy relationships in China, it is helpful to review how the status quo has evolved.

THE RISE OF HACKTIVISTS IN CHINA AND THE GOVERNMENT'S
PASSIVE SUPPORT (1994–2003)

The year 1994 is seen as the true starting point of the Internet in China; China's initial connection to the Internet and the emergence of its first hacker groups took place during Jiang Zemin's presidency from 1993 to 2003. China's first known hacker group, the Green Army, was founded in 1997 and counted some 3,000 members until its founders had a falling out in 2000.[11] While, at the outset, the government's attitude to such groups was largely one of sanctioning, in 2001 the government was issuing statements to stop hacktivists, outraged by the death of a Chinese fighter pilot whose jet collided with a US surveillance plane, from targeting the United States – illustrating the government's evolving relationship with non-state actors wielding offensive cyber capabilities. The Golden Shield, which was built to control information internally, also dates back to the late 1990s.[12]

In 1998, anti-China protests in Indonesia became the catalyst for the creation of other prominent hacktivist groups in China like the Red Hacker alliance, which brought together individual hackers and existing hacker groups (including the Green Army).[13] As Indonesia's local Chinese population was made a scapegoat for the country's economic problems, Indonesia witnessed a wave of violence, including rapes and killings, against them. This in turn incited anger in China, but the Chinese government was so afraid of any form of public protest that it turned down requests to stage demonstrations. Some people took to the streets anyway, for what became the largest demonstrations since the 1989 Tiananmen Square protests, although orders of magnitude smaller and with a very different political objective.[14] The Internet provided a new outlet for Chinese citizens to express their anger at the Indonesian leadership through spam emails, Web defacements, and DDoS attacks.[15]

The 1998 events reveal the strong, even foundational role of patriotism in China's hacktivist groups, an attitude that stands in stark contrast to many Western hackers' shared ideology of opposition to governments. The rise of the Red Hacker Alliance and the Honker Union of China[16] in the early 2000s reflected a growing number of hackers defacing foreign websites and launching DDoS attacks against them while also targeting domestic critics of the state.[17] At that point, the Honker Union of China counted some 60,000 users on its forums and 20,000 people on its mailing list.[18] The China Eagle Union formed in 2000, its members pledging, "I solemnly swear to put the interests of the Chinese nation above everything else. I am willing to do everything in my power to make the Chinese nation rise up."[19] Members of these groups were often students at universities, such as Jiaotong University in Shanghai, which has close links to the Third Department of the PLA and counts former PLA officers on its staff.[20] However, Henderson's research has debunked the myth that these hacktivists formed a unified, monolithic group, instead demonstrating they were a rather loosely organized network held together by shared ideology. By 1999, Chinese hackers were no longer dependent on malware developed abroad but had started developing their own tools.[21]

The expansion of the Internet in China and the rise of patriotic hackers created a fertile ground for more formal proxy relationships. Up to that point, government support for hackers had been limited to turning a blind eye and occasional after-the-fact endorsements. For example, after patriotic hacktivists from the Chinese mainland targeted Taiwanese websites following a statement by Taiwan's president describing China and Taiwan as two states, an article published by the *PLA Daily* endorsed their actions and encouraged others to join in the future.[22] Similarly, Henderson has reported that when tensions rose again between China and Japan in 2000, "Japanese officials requested that the web sites of known hackers in the

Guangxi, China area be shut down for attacking Japanese web sites. Police responded that they had no intentions of doing so because it was a 'patriotic' web site."[23] The Chinese government had seemed comfortable leveraging the hacktivists' actions for political benefit. But in the early 2000s it was becoming increasingly clear that there was an active group of private citizens ready and willing to serve as proxies, who enjoyed support from the Chinese population and were even revered in some circles as patriotic heroes. The time seemed ripe to shift to a more active stance. A 1999 article in the PLA Daily signaled this more proactive approach, noting that the government called for "developing a computer network warfare capability, training a large number of network fighters in PLA academies, strengthening network defenses in China, and *absorbing a number of civilian computer masters* to take part in future network wars"[24] (emphasis added).

With this more active stance came a more proactive approach to hacker activity. In May 2001, *People's Daily* published an article on its website stating, "We understand the passion of these hackers but we do not endorse their way of expressing it. We do not want to offend patriotic Web surfers but it is important we alert the public to the risk of such acts and prevent further disasters."[25] This statement was paired with government declarations reminding the population that hacking was illegal, and shortly thereafter the leader of the Red Hacker Alliance, Wan Tao, announced that the malicious activity would stop. The incident is another sign of the loose and networked nature of the hacktivist group. If the Red Hacker Alliance had been tightly controlled, there would have been no need for the government to issue such a public statement nor for Wan Tao to respond in kind. Yet, James Mulvenon, a leading US expert on China and cybersecurity, cautioned against "this dynamic be[ing] called control," suggesting instead that it "reflects the population's keen sensitivity to the subtle messages in government propaganda, which continues to create successfully a Leninist climate of self-deterrence and self-censorship that is more powerful than active state repression."[26]

A decade after the 1989 Tiananmen protests, the government was facing a new political force, potentially more challenging to control than a physically constrained street protest.[27] In Henderson's assessment, the Red Hacker Alliance presented Beijing with challenges: "it [was] much better to have a large number of young males protesting foreign incidents outside the country than focusing their sights internally," but the government was well aware that the hacktivists' outward focus might not last.[28] It was already clear that they had a mind of their own and could pose a risk. For example, the patriotic hackers were so patriotic that they wanted to help the government improve its cybersecurity. When the government turned down their offer to help, they grew frustrated and started defacing websites of the Chinese government itself to raise more awareness of the existing vulnerabilities.[29] Facing this new development, officials in Zhongnanhai had to decide which was greater: the potential risk these newly empowered actors posed to domestic stability and potential international escalation, or the potential benefit of using them as additional leverage domestically and abroad.

The government started building its own capabilities around the same time that the patriotic hackers entered the scene. Early references to "information warriors" in the Chinese military and calls for a stand-alone "net force" date back to 1999.[30] The military launched a more systematic effort in 2002, when it created scholarships for students and the Fourth Department of the PLA established a net force combining members of the PLA and information warfare militias.[31] The same year, the Ministry of Public Security took more aggressive steps to maintain domestic stability; around this time, Henderson reported, "dissident groups outside of China complained Chinese hackers attempted to shut down their operations through virus and Trojan attacks focused on the e-mail addresses of the Falun Gong, banned news sites, freenet-china.org, and Xinjiang independence activists."[32]

As the government built up its own internal structures, its ability to mobilize and leverage capabilities beyond the state also grew. As early as 1999, information warfare militias were emerging out of Fujian and Hubei provinces.[33] Another militia was set up two years later at the Institute of Information Engineering at Shihezi University in Xinjiang.[34] In 2003, both defensive and offensive militia units were set up through local telecommunications and cybersecurity companies in the city of Guangzhou, a technology hub in China's south.[35]

The 2004 Chinese defense white paper was the first to formally acknowledge the information warfare militia by referencing the reinforcement of "information-specialized" militia units.[36] That year also marked the point when the number of militias increased significantly. Robert Sheldon and Joe McReynolds, who wrote one of the most detailed analyses of the Chinese militias to date, found that "36% of militias in our sample were formed or first documented" between 2004 and 2006, while acknowledging that it is unclear how representative the sample is.[37] An analysis published several years later found that "Consistent reporting over almost eight years on the establishment of civilian-staffed information warfare militia units leaves little doubt that these units are a permanent addition to the PLA's information warfare force structure... The scope of the recruitment and modernization efforts underway suggests that the PLA is also likely working to develop an employment strategy for these units during wartime."[38]

The government's process to select and monitor these new actors was facilitated by a number of different factors. Even when structures and institutions were still nascent, hacktivists were already reaching out to the government and expressing an interest in supporting the state in a more formal capacity. Such expressions of interest could be easily found in online forums. For example, in 2005, members of the Honker Union of China actively discussed the "need to move toward standardized honker unions. We can't wait until the nation has a crisis to act; we must be prepared to do something meaningful for the motherland. Why can't we become a government-approved network technology security unit?"[39] (A decade later,

Eugene Dokukin would make similar remarks about his desire for support from the Ukrainian government.) To what extent the Chinese government took up such offers is unclear, but they constitute a significant difference from the explicitly anarchist leanings of many early hackers in Europe and North America.[40] In addition to having a pool of willing potential actors among the hacktivist groups, the government could use its various national research programs focusing on information security as a screening mechanism. These included the 863 National High Technology Research and Development Program, established in 1986; the 973 National Key Basic Research Program of 1997; the National 242 Information Security Program; the Information on the Ministry of State Security 115 Program; and the National s219 Information Security Application Demonstration Project (S219).[41] Today, some fifty universities receive funding through these programs, with ten receiving funding from three or more programs, and the following three receiving funding from all five – Harbin Institute of Technology, Southeast University, and Zhejiang University.[42] Significantly, some of the universities and Chinese students engaged in these programs are involved not only in research and development but also in offensive cyber operations.

By the end of Jiang Zemin's tenure in 2003, the relationship between the state and hacktivist groups, like the Red Hacker Alliance, could be best described as an "uneasy truce" balanced between "the alliance's concerns over a possible crackdown on the organization and the government's fear of a hacker-instigated rebellion among its youthful members."[43] Meanwhile, the government's actions were funneling the growing number of hackers in a limited number of directions. Some joined one of the programs set up by the government or created cybersecurity start-ups to profit from the Internet's rapid expansion and increasing value in China. Others became involved in cyber crime. According to Inkster, the government itself developed a stronger interest in cyber espionage around this time, "initially, with little in the way of top-level oversight and control – as the potential of new technology became apparent, driven by the overarching imperative of rapid economic and technological development."[44]

THE CREATION OF MILITIA UNITS AND THE MOVE TOWARDS ORCHESTRATION (2003–13)

By the time Hu Jintao became the president of China in 2003, experts agreed that the hacker groups in China represented independent actors who were "state tolerated" or "state encouraged," and did not have to fear punishment from the government as long as they did not pose a risk to the state.[45] While estimates of their numbers range from a few tens of thousands to over 1 million, Henderson and Taiwanese analysts put the figure at some 300,000 within the decade after China gained access to the Internet.[46] Hackers became popular heroes: a 2005 survey by the Shanghai Academy of Social Sciences found that of the 5,000 elementary school students interviewed,

43 percent "adored" hackers and 33 percent wanted to be one in the future.[47] Meanwhile, the creation of militias around the country was endorsed by the PLA Academy of Military Sciences in 2006 and was again referenced in China's defense white paper that year, marking the culmination of a trend that started in the late 1990s, when the conventional militia system began expanding to include information warfare units.[48] Around this time, the PLA began to incorporate cyber operations in its major exercises[49] and to recruit hackers via competitions and job postings; in addition, the Ministry of Public Security placed job advertisements on hacker forums such as Xfocus and EvilOctal between 2007 and 2008.[50] This is also when the first public reports on hacking by Chinese actors started to emerge.[51] In addition to offering domestic support, the government was reluctant to cooperate with international mutual legal assistance requests[52] and denied that it engaged in any form of sponsorship.[53]

Two illustrative examples of how these university-based and company-based militias operate are the Network Crack Program Hacker group and a company, the Nanhao Group.

The Network Crack Program Hacker (NCPH) group was a hacker group composed of at least seven university students. It was allegedly responsible for intrusions into several US government agencies, including the Pentagon in 2006, according to research by iDefense, a cyber threat intelligence company.[54] NCPH highlights how in China the relationship between the state and the university goes beyond recruiting (which is common in many countries) to actively engaging students in offensive cyber operations. Members of NCPH, including its founder, Tan Dailin, gave interviews to *Time* in 2007, confirming details documented by iDefense and shedding more light on the group's origin and evolution.

Tan, also known as "Wicked Rose" or "Withered Rose," founded the hacker group in 2004 as a 20-year-old student at Sichuan University of Science and Engineering, where he was profiled in the university's newspaper for his hacking skills. That article stated that in July 2005, the "Sichuan Military Command Communication Department located [Tan] through personal information published online and instructed him to participate in the network attack/defense training organized by the provincial military command, in preparation for the coming Chengdu Military Command Network Attack/Defense Competition in September."[55] In its research on NCPH's subsequent activities, iDefense found that

> Wicked Rose implicates himself in his early blog entries and website posts in 2006 and prior. An unknown company or entity reportedly paid Wicked Rose for hacking at the rate of 2,000 RMB a month, about $250 USD... This is a significant amount of money in China, effectively paying hackers a full-time wage for part-time hacking. Throughout the summer of 2006, while Wicked Rose was not in school, over 35 zero-day attacks, proof-of-concept codes, and attacks against un-patched Microsoft Office vulnerabilities are discovered in the wild.[56]

Details from the university newspaper profile suggest that the "unknown entity" paying Tan was the PLA.[57]

In addition to relying on students to project cyber power, the Chinese government also created company-based militia units. One example is the Nanhao Group, a tech company established in 1995 and located in Hengshui, Hebei province. In 2005, in the midst of what Sheldon and McReynolds have identified as the main period when the Chinese government was creating militia units around the country, the PLA set up an information warfare militia at the Nanhao Group. According to a vice president of the company, Bai Gouliang, quoted in an article by *The Financial Times*, "All [Nanhao] staff under the age of 30 belong to the [information warfare] unit."[58] The article described it as consisting of "two groups tasked with cyberattack and cyberdefence," and, according to Bai, it also trained PLA officers.[59] These two examples, NCPH and Nahao, demonstrate that once Beijing started taking a greater interest in offensive cyber operations, its proxy relationships quickly spanned various sectors and actors.

The data theft known as Operation Aurora illustrates the growing scope and sophistication of malicious cyber actions by Chinese actors during that time. McAfee's chief technology officer, George Kurtz, considered the theft the "largest and most sophisticated cyber attack we have seen in years targeted at specific corporations."[60] The intrusion targeted Google in addition to a number of other companies in a variety of sectors. The threat actor is estimated to have consisted of 50–100 hackers for hire.[61] After its detection in 2010, the malicious activity was traced to Shanghai Jiaotong University, which has one of the world's leading computer science departments, and the Lanxiang Vocational School, which offers one of the largest computer classes in the world[62] and has historical ties with the military. Around the world, universities are often used to hide the true origins of malicious cyber attacks because university networks are particularly challenging to secure (as Josephine Wolff has pointed out, this is true in the United States as well).[63] Yet Jiaotong University is not a new name in the annals of hacking: hackers involved in the cyber vandalism targeting US websites in the early 2000s openly acknowledged being students at Jiaotong.

During Jiang Zemin's time in office, the malicious activities of Chinese hackers had been primarily Web defacements and DDoS attacks. Under Hu Jintao's tenure, these escalated to data theft, and the effects of these offensive cyber operations reached a scale and severity that started to cause real headaches to government leaders around the world. In tandem with China's development and its growing riches, corruption grew. In fact, according to Inkster, during the second half of Hu's presidency, "some state-owned enterprises effectively [became] states within the state," due to pervasive corruption.[64] And as the militia system matured and was further institutionalized in the mid-2000s, the government was increasing its domestic control over the Internet by requiring Chinese users to use their actual names and IDs online and cracking down on cybercriminals that did not play by the (implicit) rules.[65] For example, Tan Dailin (aka Withered Rose) had reportedly stated in 2007 that "[t]rue professional hackers don't hack inside [China] because China is too poor and there is no money in it; furthermore, it is also very dangerous."[66] However, he did not stick to this dictum. In 2009, he made news once again, this time because he had been arrested and was facing several years in jail after launching DDoS attacks against fellow hackers at 3800hk, Hackbase, and HackerXFiles, thus violating one of the primary rules among Chinese hackers not to target systems within China.[67]

TIGHTENING CONTROL AND ASPIRATIONAL DELEGATION (2013–TODAY)

When Xi Jinping became China's president, he quickly focused on consolidating his power. It is worth noting that his efforts, such as his anti-corruption campaign, differ from those of his predecessors in that these campaigns continue to this day, whereas in the past such campaigns usually came to an end after a year or two. Moreover, under Xi, even officials at the highest level have been charged with corruption and arrested. In the specific area of cybersecurity, by the time Xi came to power, China had gone through a dramatic evolution. Whereas in 2003, less than 10 percent of China's population had access to the Internet, ten years later nearly half of its more than 1 billion citizens did. As the Internet's importance for the economy and people's daily lives increased, the cybersecurity industry expanded as well, from an estimated USD 527 million in 2003 to USD 2.8 billion in 2011.[68]

Given the Internet's increasing importance, it is not surprising that Xi Jinping decided to create a "leading small group" dedicated to related policy issues in February 2014.[69] These governmental coordinating groups are an instrument for Xi to exercise greater control over the huge Chinese bureaucracy. This particular leading small group, the Leading Small Group for Cybersecurity and Informatization (zhōngyāng wǎngluò ānquán hé xìnxīhuà lǐngdǎo xiǎozǔ), arose out of senior Chinese officials' heightened perception of internal and external threat – in particular the use of social media during the 2011 protests and information about the intelligence activities of the United States and other governments leaked by Edward Snowden in 2013. The fact that Lu Wei, former deputy head of the Communist Party's propaganda department, was appointed head of the leading small group underlines the way that the Chinese government continues to view cybersecurity through the prism of information security and focus on content.

In 2013, the Science of Military Strategy Report for the first time publicly acknowledged that China was building capabilities for information and cyber operations. While the civilian political leadership consolidated power, the PLA also further institutionalized its structures and decision-making processes. Eric Heginbotham, a specialist in Asian security issues at MIT, described Chinese network operations forces as divided into three basic types – professional network warfare forces, authorized forces, and civilian forces:

Professional network warfare forces are armed forces operational units specially employed for carrying out network attack and defense; authorized forces are organized local forces authorized by the armed forces to engage in network warfare, mainly built within the associated government departments, including the Ministry of State Security and the Ministry of Public Security; and the civilian forces are nongovernmental forces which spontaneously carry out network attack and defense, and which can be employed for network operations after mobilization.[70]

Senior officials' desire to have greater control over policies and actions relating to the Internet was certainly fueled by the color revolutions and protests in eastern Europe and the Arab world. A month after the successful revolution in Tunisia in January 2011, pro-democracy protests erupted in China. Although these were much smaller in scale than the protests in the Arab world and eastern Europe and were quickly suppressed through domestic surveillance and censorship, they clearly heightened the concern among China's elite. The government soon further tightened its domestic control by imposing new rules. These included requiring users of microblogs to use their real names instead of pseudonyms and threatening prominent bloggers with arrest if they promoted "disruptive" content that was viewed by more than 5,000 people or shared more than 500 times. These new rules drove significant numbers of Chinese citizens to abandon Sina Weibo, the Chinese equivalent of Twitter (with messages being publicly available for anybody to read), in favor of WeChat, which features a closed system that limits the potential for social media to "go viral."[71] The Chinese Communist Party's 2013 Communiqué on the Current State of the Ideological Sphere, also known as Document 9,[72] listed what became known as the *qige bujiang* ("seven taboo subjects") that were deemed disruptive: universal values, freedom of speech, civil society, civil rights, the historical errors of the CCP, crony capitalism, and judicial independence.[73] The Chinese government has also started to export its best practices for exercising control internally, reportedly assisting Iran with building its National Information Network.[74] And as the Chinese government's confidence in wielding its power on the international stage grew, its more inward-looking intelligence activities turned increasingly towards foreign collection, which had "all but ceased" during the Cultural Revolution.[75]

A few weeks prior to President Xi's visit to Washington in September 2015, the Chinese government responded at last to years of sustained international pressure and arrested several hackers after "U.S. intelligence and law enforcement agencies drew up a list of the hackers the United States wanted arrested."[76] There appears to have been some confusion among Chinese officials over whether the US government's concern was driven by economic espionage. According to *The Washington Post*, the hackers that Beijing had arrested were arrested not for cyber espionage targeting companies but for hacking the US Office of Personnel Management.[77] Apart from this confusion, the Chinese government's willingness to arrest the hackers rather than denying responsibility marked a noticeable change. In fact, the *Xinhua* news agency publicly acknowledged the incident and stated that "[a]mong the cases discussed included the one related to the alleged theft of data of the US Office of Personnel Management by Chinese hackers. Through investigation, the case turned out to be a criminal case rather than a state-sponsored cyber attack as the US side has previously suspected."[78] Jen Weedon, a former threat analyst at the cybersecurity firm FireEye, pointed out that "[c]ertain groups and individuals moonlight on the side and conduct operations for financial gain," making Xinhua's scenario therefore entirely possible.[79] It is another example of the blurry lines that complicate assessments of the Chinese government's behavior. The arrests also raised the question of whether those arrested were the true culprits or other pawns that Beijing was willing to sacrifice for other reasons. In other words, while the arrests served their political purpose, it is unclear whether justice was served, too.[80] What is clear is that the public acknowledgment and arrests themselves were a new development welcomed by commentators.

It is difficult to conclusively determine whether the Chinese government's actions were an isolated event or reflect a shifting policy. The most convincing explanation for the significant decrease in malicious economic cyber espionage activity from China starting in 2013 is that it is due to a confluence of factors. There were powerful domestic drivers to increase control and to counter the piracy of goods and copyright material.[81] In addition, President Xi and President Obama had made an explicit agreement committing both countries not to conduct cyber-enabled theft of intellectual property for competitive advantage, an agreement that was presumably the result of China's larger strategic interest with the United States.[82] It is worth highlighting that the arrests of the hackers following the request by the United States were separate from the mass arrests in China earlier in 2015 as part of "Operation Clean Internet." That campaign targeted 15,000 people accused of cyber crimes, which the Chinese government defined broadly to include not only hacking with unauthorized access but also content deemed harmful by the state.[83]

In November 2015, President Xi announced a major military reform and reorganization of the PLA.[84] It included the creation of the new Strategic Support Force which consolidated Chinese military cyber capabilities and will likely also affect and be a test for Beijing's relationships with cyber proxies.[85] It is the latest step for China towards a monopolist state. China's actions in the coming years will therefore help clarify to what extent China's officials at the top have effective control over the various intelligence agencies, units of the PLA, and the networked system of militias across the country.

CONCLUSION: FROM BROKER STATE TO (ASPIRATIONAL) MONOPOLIST

Overall, the case of China demonstrates how a state can create structures to increase its level of control over non-state actors with offensive cyber capabilities in the short and long term. As China moved from being a broker state towards increasing domestic control, the government's expansion of the militia system created more ties and stronger connections with hacktivists. This effort built on past practices and the use of militias dating back at least to the late Qing dynasty.[86] During the early 2000s, Beijing used these connections not only to issue statements through mainstream media channels but also to reach out to some of the leaders of hacktivist groups in order to spread the government's message. The fact that cyber crime remains a big problem in China suggests a lack of effective law enforcement to limit it, which in turn suggests a lack of capabilities to effectively crack down on a network of thousands of hacktivists. These realities likely contributed to the government's decision to try to co-opt the hacktivists and to establish a militia system.

Like private cybersecurity contractors, China's militias carry out activities that are mostly defensive in nature, including training PLA staff and operational preparation of the environment.[87] However, they are also involved in offensive cyber operations, such as those of the militias at Tianjin Polytechnic University and South China Normal University, both of which focus on network attack.[88] There are no signs that the command and control of these cyber militias differs from those of conventional militias in China. According to Sheldon and McReynolds, the militias "are formal, ongoing groups that operate partially at the behest of the PLA through a dual civil-military command structure"[89]:

> As best we can tell, keeping in mind both the wide range of militia affiliations found in the dataset and the extremely large size of the "primary" militia force (10 million members), it is quite plausible that there are thousands or tens of thousands of information warfare militia units and subunits within China, in which case this dataset would represent less than 1% of that total. . . Of the fifty units, fully eighteen units were associated with educational institutions.[90]

The Chinese militia system differs from the type of contracting found in the United States and other Western nations. Henderson has highlighted that "the Chinese Communist Party will co-opt public use facilities and draft them into military service. Corporations in Western nations may contract to the government on issues of national defense but they are not drafted."[91] At the same time, Beijing, much like Washington, also has an inherent interest in restraining proxies' activities, because they could interfere with ongoing operations carried out by the PLA itself.[92] This suggests that proxies involved in offensive cyber operations are likely to be on a tighter leash than others, and that there will be more active and frequent communications between the government and the proxies to avoid any potential fratricide. At the same time, it is unclear how concepts such as a "people's war," which dates back to the early days of communism and remains relevant, relates to cyber militias and their use. It is also unclear to what extent their use will differ from peacetime to wartime, whether they are viewed as a strategic or auxiliary force, and what levels in the command chain they directly report to.[93]

The Chinese government has been taking more aggressive steps in shutting down hacker forums and arresting high-profile hackers. This process has mirrored actions taken in other areas. For example, once Beijing decided to crack down on piracy and to address corruption at the local level in relevant provinces, "piracy incidents virtually disappeared from the South China Sea."[94] With President Xi's implementation of the 2015 US-China agreement against the cyber-enabled theft of intellectual property for competitive advantage, a similar drop seems to have taken place.[95] According to the executive chairman of the cyber threat intelligence company FireEye, David DeWalt, "The activity stopped after the handshake... It's been dramatic."[96] The government essentially tries to walk a fine line between leveraging actors and capabilities detached from the state and keeping those actors' patriotism in check to avoid unintended escalation. These efforts come with the risk that overly eager and subsequently frustrated proxies might turn against the government rather than focusing their energy externally.

Ultimately, the Chinese leadership views social stability as paramount and sees control over the access and flow of information as a key instrument to achieve this goal. The color revolutions during the first decade of the new century and concerns over Western governments meddling in internal affairs exacerbated these concerns. Therefore, as Inkster has put it, "[t]o feel safe, China needs an international cyber environment that provides assurances in these areas, and it appears unwilling to compromise on the point."[97] Beijing also feels particularly vulnerable because "more than 80 percent of the industrial control systems in China use foreign technologies, and this use is increasing."[98]

President Xi's recent restructuring of the PLA is likely to further increase Beijing's control, as is his system of Leading Small Groups, which has tried to address the lack of a structure similar to the National Security Council in the United States and other countries. However, such efforts may or may not succeed over the long term. Xi's predecessor Hu Jintao tried to create a similar structure twice but failed because he was "unable to overcome entrenched individual and departmental reluctance to cede or share power."[99] Clearly, power struggles continue to present challenges for the Chinese state.

PART III

Implications

8

The Theory: State Responsibility and Cyber Proxies

Machiavelli's disparaging views on mercenaries show the long-standing disdain for proxy actors. There is a broad normative undercurrent in how states organize their coercive power that militates against the use of proxies, as can be seen in the abolition of privateering as an institution. But how does the international community treat proxy relationships today? When is a state responsible for the actions of a non-state actor under existing international law? Can a state be held responsible for proxies held on a tight leash or even a looser one? What about situations where the state is clearly turning a blind eye to the proxies' offensive actions? These are important questions because they pave the way for potential countermeasures and responses. As it stands, international law provides only limited avenues for addressing proxy relationships. Public international law focuses on states not private actors. A state can only be held accountable for the offensive actions of a cyber proxy if that proxy is under tight control of a government and if the effect of the action causes significant harm. It is nevertheless worthwhile to review the existing standards in international law, which are the basis for governments' actions today. This chapter will also discuss the controversy about due diligence and extraterritoriality in the context of cyber proxies.

The 2013 and 2015 UNGGE documents – both of which explicitly reference proxies – provide key insight into how the international community thinks about rules of the road for cyberspace. By specifying that states must not use proxies to "commit internationally wrongful acts using ICTs [information and communications technologies]," and that they must try to ensure that such acts not be undertaken from their territory, the reports made clear that international law applies online as well as offline. Yet, neither of the UNGGE reports actually defines "proxy," nor does the term easily translate into other languages. The 2013 report only describes proxies as "individuals, groups, or organizations, including criminal organizations," that act on behalf of states "in the conduct of malicious ICT actions."[1]

I thank Oxford University Press for granting permission to include material in this chapter from Tim Maurer, "'Proxies' and Cyberspace," *Journal of Conflict & Security Law* 21(3) (2016): 383–403.

The official non-English versions of this report show the challenges of translating the term. The Chinese version uses the term 代 理 人 (*dàilǐ rén*), literally the compound that means "representative" coupled with the word "person," giving the term the notion of an "agent." The Chinese text is at least consistent. The Arabic, French, Spanish, and Russian texts either avoid using the term "proxies" altogether or use a variety of terms, each with its own nuance. The Arabic version uses a term similar to the English word "delegates," whereas the French, Spanish, and Russian texts use the equivalent of "agent" or "intermediary": in French, "leurs agents" and "intermédiaires"; in Spanish, "agentes" and "terceros" (or third parties); in Russian, "посредников" and "представителей," which can be translated as "intermediary" or "middleman." The Russian version goes on to describe a proxy as one who "acts in the interests of states" while the Arabic version can be translated as "entities acting on behalf of states" or "indirect means/ways." There is obviously a spectrum between "acting in the interest of" and "acting on behalf of" – so where do states and international law draw the line?

Dirk Roland Haupt, an international law expert at the German Federal Foreign Office, described the term this way:

> "[P]roxy" is not a technical term in international law as such but based in domestic law, ultimately Roman law. In Roman law, the "procurator" was somebody authorized to act on somebody else's behalf, a meaning it continues to have in Anglo-Saxon corporate and securities law. When it was adopted into international law its meaning shifted and evolved as codified in the *Draft Articles on the Responsibility of States for Internationally Wrongful Acts*.[2]

While there is little public information about how most states interpret the UNGGE language around proxies, some details are available about the US government's understanding of the term. At a 2012 workshop focusing on proxy actors in cyberspace hosted by the ASEAN Regional Forum in Vietnam, Dr. Sharri Clark, a foreign service officer at the US Department of State, defined proxy actors as "groups and individuals who, on behalf of a state (and possibly involving a state unwittingly), take malicious cyber actions against the governments, the private sector, and citizens of other states."[3] Later that year, in a speech at the NSA, Harold Hongju Koh, serving as the 22nd Legal Adviser of the US Department of State at the time, stated:

> States are legally responsible for activities undertaken through "proxy actors," who act on the State's instructions or under its direction or control. The ability to mask one's identity and geography in cyberspace and the resulting difficulties of timely, high-confidence attribution can create significant challenges for States in identifying, evaluating, and accurately responding to threats. But putting attribution problems aside for a moment, established international law does address the question of proxy actors. States are legally responsible for activities undertaken through putatively private actors, who act on the State's instructions or under its direction

or control. If a State exercises a sufficient degree of control over an ostensibly private person or group of persons committing an internationally wrongful act, the State assumes responsibility for the act, just as if official agents of the State itself had committed it. These rules are designed to ensure that States cannot hide behind putatively private actors to engage in conduct that is internationally wrongful.[4]

Interestingly, while Clark allowed the possibility of a state being involved unwittingly in a proxy's activities, Koh's statement was more limited – focusing on actors acting under a state's instruction, direction, or "sufficient degree of control."[5]

In international law, the "control" threshold Koh referenced is essentially where the line of a state's legal responsibility is drawn. This line matters because it determines at what point the targeted state is allowed to take action against another state in response. Meanwhile, whether the targeted state has the right to respond against a non-state actor directly if the host state is unwilling or unable remains highly controversial and limited to effects above the threshold of use of force.[6]

It is therefore worth reviewing the distinctions developed in various international legal regimes.

A FRAMEWORK FOR CYBER PROXY RELATIONSHIPS BASED ON INTERNATIONAL LAW

Table 8.1 offers a comprehensive review of how the activity of a non-state actor can relate to a state. This framework goes beyond the classifications laid out in international law, by adding categories that describe the murkier relationships between a state and non-state actor; many of these details are based on insights from the literature on counterterrorism.[7]

Table 8.1 also highlights two general distinctions when it comes to offensive actions. The first is whether the state responsibility for the proxy's malicious cyber activity is established *ex ante* or *ex post* of the offensive action taking place. It is important to highlight that while the term "cyber attack" is often used in the literature, to date, all effects of offensive cyber operations, with the exception of a handful, have remained below the level considered to constitute use of force or armed attack. Moreover, malicious cyber activity can take place over a prolonged period of time – months if not years – and often goes undetected. For this reason, such activity is therefore better described as "cyber operations" rather than an "attack." Apart from the special case of DDoS attacks targeting the availability of information, intrusions that undermine the availability, confidentiality, or integrity of information often take place over months; they are therefore described here using the descriptors *ex ante* and *in progressu*.

The second distinction is the beneficiary state's choice between the commission and omission of specific acts. Both can occur *ex ante*, *in progressu*, or *ex post*. For example, as long as a state is aware that a particular activity is going to begin or is in

TABLE 8.1 *Framework for state/non-state cyber proxy relationships based on international law*

Time	Counterterrorism literature – Form of sponsorship	Cyber proxies framework (combining counterterrorism, international law, and cybersecurity literature)		Cyber attack literature[8]
		Degrees of detachment	Description of relationship	
	—	State and *de jure* state organ*	Exclusively government actors and state organs recognized as such in domestic law	State-executed (special case: state-rogue-conducted)
		Below are the non-state actors ordered by their degree of detachment from the state starting from low levels to high levels of detachment		
ex ante and *in progressu* · Delegation	Active state sponsorship** (commission)[9]	*de facto* state organ*	Private actors are *de facto* state organs completely dependent on state (can include unauthorized action; e.g., rogue unit)	State-integrated
		Non-state actor exercising "governmental authority"*	Non-state actor exercising elements of government authority* (can include unauthorized action; e.g., rogue unit)	
		Non-state actor under a state's instruction – "auxiliary"*	Non-state actor authorized or acting on instruction of a state usually to supplement a state's activity	State-ordered
		Non-state actor under a state's "direction or control," specifically "effective control"[10]	State involved in control of specific operation, providing guidance through planning, direction, and support with non-state actor as subordinate and dependent on state	
		Non-state actor under a state's "overall control"***[11] (organized groups)	State exercises general influence, namely by – participating in planning and supervision – being involved in organizing, coordinating, or planning – having power or ability to instruct to stop	State-coordinated/State-shaped

	Non-state actor under a state's "overall control"**** (individuals and loose group of individuals)	State issues specific instruction	State-ordered
Orchestration	Non-state actor receiving specific support from state***	State involved in financing, providing equipment, supplying weaponry, training, intelligence support, and/or logistics support	State-coordinated/State-shaped
	Non-state actor receiving general support from state	State provides general encouragement or support	
Sanctioning	Non-prevention ("implied complicity")	State does not prevent activity: state is aware of specific operation and capable of stopping planned activity directly or by warning, yet unwilling	State-ignored
	"Harboring"112	State harbors non-state actor: state is unaware of specific operation but aware and capable of generally denying activities yet willing to provide sanctuary, allow fundraising activity, allow recruiting activity, and/or allow acquisition of weaponry**	
Passive state sponsorship** (omission)	Willful non-termination	State is capable but unwilling to terminate ongoing non-state actor's activity	
	Apologetic non-cooperation	State is willing yet incapable of terminating malicious activity itself but does not allow foreign assistance	State-prohibited-but-inadequate
	Apologetic cooperation	State is willing yet incapable of terminating malicious activity itself but does allow foreign assistance	
	Mitigation and termination following negligence	State is willing and (partially) capable of disrupting or terminating malicious activity but did not harden systems sufficiently to prevent malicious activity in the first place	State-prohibited

Continued

TABLE 8.1 (cont.)

Counterterrorism literature – Form of sponsorship		Cyber proxies framework (combining counterterrorism, international law, and cybersecurity literature)		Cyber attack literature
Time	Form of sponsorship	Degrees of detachment	Description of relationship	
ex post	Sanctioning	Non-state actor's behavior "adopted" by state	State acknowledges and adopts non-state actor's conduct as its own, including taking steps to support or defend beyond mere acknowledgment[3]	State-encouraged
		Non-state actor receives verbal endorsement by state "Condonation"[4]	State endorses non-state actor's activity by expressing verbal support for non-state action*	—
		Non-cooperative investigation	State is capable yet unwilling to punish non-state actor	—
			State does not investigate or cooperate in investigation, and non-state actor remains unknown	—
	—	Apologetic non-punishment	State is willing yet incapable of punishing non-state actor, for example, due to domestic laws protecting privacy or minors	—
	—	Punishment following negligence	State punishes non-state actor but did not harden systems sufficiently to prevent malicious activity in the first place	—

progress, it has a range of choices. It may facilitate the activity or willingly allow it to continue. Or it may do nothing, particularly if it is incapable of stopping the operation or warning the victim. A state also has a range of choices after an activity has started or after it has concluded. It may act to prevent it from recurring – for example, by patching vulnerable infrastructure – or it may provide assistance to, investigate, or punish the actor carrying out the malicious activity. The implications for state responsibility are not a new discussion in international law. For example, J. L. Brierly discussed this topic in an article published in 1928, including the questions of whether failing to punish harmful activity can be considered "implied complicity" or "condonation" of that activity.[15]

In short, the existing international law standards of what constitutes "direction or control"[16] are so high that they are unlikely to be useful for most situations encountered by political decision-makers today. Moreover, what constitutes the kind of "internationally wrongful act" referenced in the UNGGE reports remains undefined and contested. Michael Schmitt and Liis Vihul, who have produced one of the most comprehensive legal analyses of proxies with their 2014 article "Proxy Wars in Cyberspace: The Evolving International Law of Attribution," have noted that states have a lot of latitude in their support of proxies: "the relatively high levels of support that are required before a state can be held responsible for the activities of non-state groups or individuals, as distinct from their own responsibility for being involved, creates a normative safe zone for them."[17] This is not a problem unique to the cyber context; it extends to counterterrorism as well.[18] States' responses to terrorism illustrate that decisions about attribution and when to hold a state responsible are ultimately political.[19] Healey, who has worked at the White House, echoes this assessment with his statement that "[f]or national security policymakers, knowing 'who is to blame?' can be more important than 'who did it?'"[20]

Nevertheless, the nuanced spectrum laid out in Table 8.1 matters because it reflects a deep-rooted sense of justice underlying these relationships, actions, and counteractions. While it is entirely possible to think of a doctrine that would punish a state regardless of its degree of involvement or intent, doing so would upset this shared sense of justice. (The outrage stirred up by some US jurisdictions' willingness to charge accomplices to crimes as principal perpetrators shows that this sense of justice is widespread, and that a more nuanced assessment matters.[21]) While the attribution problem makes the nuanced legal distinctions outlined in Table 8.1 challenging for decision-makers to apply during a crisis, the broader goal of justice makes it important that this framework be available once more data comes to light. Meanwhile, given the challenges of assessing the exact relationship between a state and a proxy at a time of crisis, there is growing interest among scholars in due diligence and a state's responsibility for malicious activity emanating from its territory, independent of whether that activity can be attributed to or is actively sponsored by the state.[22]

DUE DILIGENCE

States not only enjoy rights but also have to fulfill certain obligations under international law. The idea of "due diligence" dates back to the seventeenth century and Hugo Grotius, and it was concretized internationally starting in the nineteenth century with the 1872 *Alabama* Claims Arbitration.[23] US Supreme Court Justice Moore observed in 1927 that "[i]t is well settled that a State is bound to use due diligence to prevent the commission within its dominions of criminal acts against another nation or its people."[24] In the pivotal Corfu Channel case, the International Court of Justice stated that "it is every State's obligation not to knowingly allow its territory to be used for acts contrary to the rights of other States."[25] This finding mirrors the no-harm principle in environmental law dating back to the 1941 Trail smelter dispute, in which a tribunal ruled that a state "owes at all times a duty to protect other states against injurious acts by individuals from within their jurisdictions."[26]

Table 8.1 includes several categories of possible activity that fall below the threshold of "sanctioning" (permitting): these describe situations when a state is willing to take actions against malicious cyber behavior but does not have the capacity to do so. These categories are tied to the ongoing controversy whether or not a state has to request or permit foreign assistance under such circumstances and what kind of due diligence can be reasonably expected from other states.[27] Whatever expectations of appropriate state behavior and due diligence will emerge will in turn determine which of these categories are still considered sanctioning and which fall outside.

The 2015 UNGGE report incorporated several elements related to the discussion about due diligence. First, it posited that under existing international law, (1) "States have jurisdiction over the ICT infrastructure located within their territory," and that (2) "States must not use proxies to commit internationally wrongful acts using ICTs and should seek to ensure that their territory is not used by non-State actors to commit such acts." Yet the report also qualified that claim, stating that (3) "the indication that an ICT activity was launched or otherwise originates from the territory or the ICT infrastructure of a State may be insufficient in itself to attribute the activity to that State" and declaring that accusations of wrongful acts committed by States must be substantiated. In sum, the UNGGE report's reference to proxies and to international law suggests that it focuses on non-state actors operating "under effective control of a state." Haupt took a similar view when he said that "a person or group of people that pretends to act on behalf of a state is not a 'proxy' following this mutual understanding if the state did not issue the instruction or the person or group of people was not under the effective control of the state."[28]

Beyond binding international law, the UNGGE report also discussed "voluntary, non-binding" norms holding that "[s]tates should not knowingly allow their territory to be used for internationally wrongful acts using ICTs." By not specifying the type of actor or degree of control, the report therefore includes a broader range of actors than just those under effective control of a state. The report also adds an expectation that when critical infrastructure is being attacked "[s]tates should respond to appropriate requests for assistance by another State whose critical infrastructure is subject to malicious ICT acts. States should also respond to appropriate requests to mitigate malicious ICT activity aimed at the critical infrastructure of another State emanating from their territory, taking into account due regard for sovereignty." In addition to its section on international law and norms, the UNGGE suggested that states "[c]ooperate, in a manner consistent with national and international law, with requests from other States in investigating ICT-related crime or the use of ICTs for terrorist purposes or to mitigate malicious ICT activity emanating from their territory." This confidence-building measure goes beyond providing assistance at the time a malicious activity occurs to focus on a post-incident investigation and also applies to a broader range of attacks than those on critical infrastructure.

The 2015 UNGGE report is silent on a state's responsibility to take preventive measures. According to Schmitt and Watts, there is as yet no broad agreement on whether due diligence requires states "to prevent cyber infrastructure on a state's territory from being used for purposes that violate obligations owed other states"; instead, they argued, "the better position is that states are only obliged to terminate on-going or imminent cyber operations. In doing so, they need only take those measures that are reasonable in the circumstances."[29] Some governments share the concern that due diligence taken too far would create unreasonable costs and expectations.[30] For example, *The New York Times* recently reported the story of a small company in Wisconsin whose computer was hijacked by Chinese hackers known as the Codoso group.[31] A legal obligation of due diligence could be interpreted to mean that the US government is expected to prevent or terminate such hijacking, and that would likely require a change in existing laws and the government's relationship with ISPs. Adhering to such legal requirements would likely create significant costs. For that reason, the US government has been reluctant to consider due diligence as a legal obligation.[32] Where to draw this line is not a new debate. Edwin Borchard wrote as far back as 1914 that "[w]hat is 'due diligence' in a given case is often difficult to determine."[33]

In addition, some of the systems that would be used to detect and prevent intrusions as part of such due diligence efforts could also be used to monitor people's communication. This is an important difference between cybersecurity monitoring and other monitoring systems of the past (for example, those in place for nuclear tests), and it raises significant human rights concerns. As Healey cautioned, "a push for national responsibility for cyberspace could be manipulated by nations to clamp down on an individual's right to freedom of opinion and expression."[34] This argument, however, does not address causality. Would a push for due diligence be the impetus that drives a state to use a monitoring system for other purposes, or would it serve only as cover to justify surveillance that would happen anyway? And should countries that already have such systems in place for purposes other than cybersecurity be expected to use them to reduce malicious cyber activity?

THIRD COUNTRIES AND EXTRATERRITORIALITY

Due diligence matters not only as an instrument to circumvent the attribution problem. It also matters because of the use of third countries in the conduct of offensive actions. This is not a problem unique to cybersecurity. Scholars of age-old piracy and modern-day terrorism have long debated the role of safe havens and states turning a blind eye to their presence. Al-Qaeda brought to the fore the challenge of hidden terrorist cells across countries worldwide. This problem also exists in the cybersecurity context. However, the UNGGE report does not clarify whether "emanating from their territory" applies to transit states, to states that are the original source of the malicious activity, or to both.

North Korea provides a good example of a government that physically places individuals carrying out offensive cyber operations in third countries instead of operating out of North Korea. This is more out of necessity than choice. North Korea, also known as the "Hermit Kingdom," has very limited connections to the Internet, making it easier to attribute malicious activity coming from the country and creating an incentive for North Korea to launch offensive cyber operations extraterritorially. In order to maintain deniability and avoid sanctions or other retaliation, "North Korea's cyber-espionage, DDoS, and hacking attacks are done by Unit 121 and covert cells around the globe, including in the United States, South Asia, Europe, and South Korea."[35] Reports that the North Korean hackers targeting Sony operated out of a hotel in Thailand and my own interviews with experts support these claims.[36] Seo Sang-ki, the chairman of the intelligence committee of South Korea's National Assembly, said that in addition to physically carrying out offensive cyber operations from third countries, "North Koreans earn foreign money by developing software in China and perform hacking activities to collect national industrial secrets at the same time." Similarly, Kim Hung-kwang, president of the North Korea Intellectuals Solidarity, alleged that "Chinese and North Korean soldiers exchange malicious codes and attack techniques created by Pyongyang."[37]

Governments like North Korea that want to operate from third countries must find countries where their agents can operate without getting detected or arrested. They must identify countries that have not criminalized malicious cyber actions in their domestic laws or whose law enforcement agencies do not have the capacity to effectively enforce such laws. Until recently, Thailand served as such a safe haven. During multiple research interviews, interviewees pointed to migration flows among hackers, from Russia and Belarus to Ukraine as well as from eastern Europe to Thailand and other spots in Southeast Asia. For example, in August 2016, a 44-year-old Russian man and a 25-year-old Uzbek woman were arrested by the FBI in a four-star hotel in Thailand and charged with financial cyber crime. In 2014, Farid Essebar, another Russian hacker, was arrested in Bangkok after Swiss authorities alerted Thai authorities to his presence; a few months later a 26-year-old Moroccan hacker, who had hacked bank accounts in Switzerland, was also arrested following a tip-off by Swiss authorities. In 2013, an Algerian hacker was arrested in Thailand based on information the FBI provided.[38] Criminal hackers from as far away as Lesotho on the southern tip of Africa have ventured to Thailand (and have subsequently been arrested).[39] Thailand is not the only country that has become a hotspot for cybercriminals. In nearby Vietnam, three Russians aged between 30 and 43 are in prison for credit-card fraud.[40] And in July 2015, the Vietnamese police arrested a 34-year-old Chinese hacker who had fled to Vietnam to escape Chinese law enforcement authorities after he and his accomplices had stolen close to USD 5 million from various credit-card accounts.[41] These arrests show that law enforcement agencies in Southeast Asia and elsewhere can be successful at arresting non-state actors operating from their territory. Nonetheless, the fact that citizens from so many different nationalities chose Thailand as the base for their operations suggests it was considered to be a safe haven at least for a while (unless the attraction of Thai beaches trumped usual risk calculations).

These examples again raise the question of what due diligence measures can be expected of a state so that it will be aware when such actors operate from its territory? What actions can be expected of a state if information is shared with its government making it aware of an actor's presence? And specifically, in the context of cybersecurity, what is the probability of anybody noticing such an operation from a third country, especially if the actors' operation and presence in the third country is only short-lived? The latter is a particularly important question considering how long it still takes for an organization in the most advanced countries to detect an intrusion. While the median number of days has dropped from 243 days in 2012 to 205 days in 2014, this is still well over half a year, and in some cases an intruder's presence is not recognized for years.[42]

The more harmful the offensive actions become, the greater the importance of such questions. As the international lawyer Roscini pointed out in his discussion of participation in hostilities, if two states are in an international armed conflict and a state deploys its agents to a third country, "it is the status (combatant, civilian, or civilian taking direct part in hostilities) of the person and not his location that makes him targetable or not under the *jus in bello*."[43] This scenario is more plausible than it might seem at first sight: consider a scenario in which North Korea becomes involved in an international armed conflict with another state and uses hackers based in third countries during such a conflict. Furthermore, can actions be taken in response without the consent of the third country, thereby violating its sovereignty? When it comes to non-state actors operating from a third country, the response to the September 11, 2001, terrorist attacks was an important evolution that enabled actions to be taken against the third country if it was unable or unwilling to address the threat itself. According to Derek Jinks, a law professor at the University of Texas and member of the US Secretary of State's Advisory Committee on International Law, "The emergent 'harboring' or 'supporting' rule represents a substantial relaxation of the traditional attribution regime – one that may signal a shift in the very nature of 'state action.'"[44] However, it remains unclear how to address this problem in the context of offensive cyber operations, whose effects usually remain well below the threshold of use of force or armed attack at which these established legal precedents apply.

A special case of this problem of extraterritoriality is participation in a DDoS attack. Numerous examples indicate that the swarming involved in many DDoS attacks is transnational in terms of both computers hijacked and turned into zombies and of people deciding to join a DDoS attack voluntarily (as in the case of the German and British hackers who lent their support to the Ukrainian Cyber Forces in 2015). Several countries have criminalized such voluntary participation, much as neutrality laws adopted by states centuries ago prohibited citizens from joining foreign armies.[45] However, given law enforcement's limited resources, enforcement of such laws is limited and only likely in the event of a major effect.[46] A state's ability to address such volunteer action in the context of DDoS attacks is limited, especially at scale.

CONCLUSION: INTERNATIONAL COOPERATION UNDER PRESSURE

For offensive cyber actions, whose effects remain well below the threshold of what constitutes use of force – i.e., the vast majority of malicious cyber activity – the phenomenon of non-state actors operating extraterritorially points to increasing challenges for international law enforcement cooperation, including pressure on the existing extradition treaty regime and other jurisdictional nightmares. For example, when the FBI arrested the Russian and the Uzbek in Thailand in 2016, Russia's deputy foreign minister protested the "extrajudicial and illegal abductions [by the United States] of other countries' nationals."[47] The December 2014 arrest of 77 hackers from China in Nairobi, Kenya, led to competing extradition requests.[48] Beijing argued that the cyber crime victims were in China[49] while Taipei protested that eight of the accused hackers were from Taiwan and accused Beijing of abducting them.[50] (Local media in Nairobi reported "military-style dormitories" and suspicions of Chinese engaging in "high tech espionage and Internet fraud";[51] however, the reporter Lily Kuo described a haphazard cyber crime network and local Sinophobia.[52]) Such controversies and discussions about reforming mutual legal assistance treaties are a symptom of what will likely continue to be a growing international problem.

There is certainly no shortage of potential safe havens. Mapping the bilateral extradition as well as mutual legal assistance treaties and agreements of the United States alone, which has one of the most extensive regimes worldwide, clearly illustrates the existing patchwork, as shown in Figures 8.1 and 8.2.

Ultimately, a key question for the coming years is whether the international community will consider due diligence in the context of cybersecurity a legal

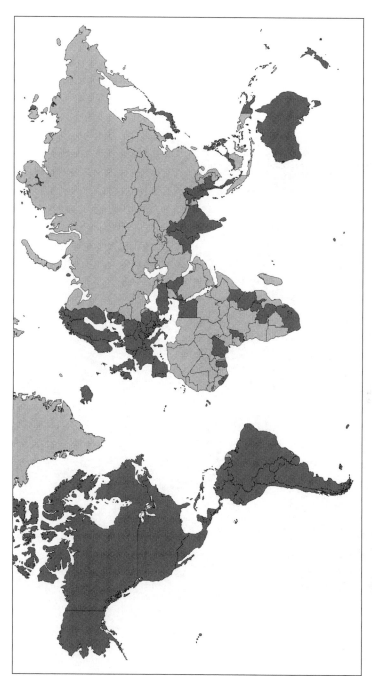

FIGURE 8.1 Countries with bilateral extradition treaties and agreements with the United States.[53]

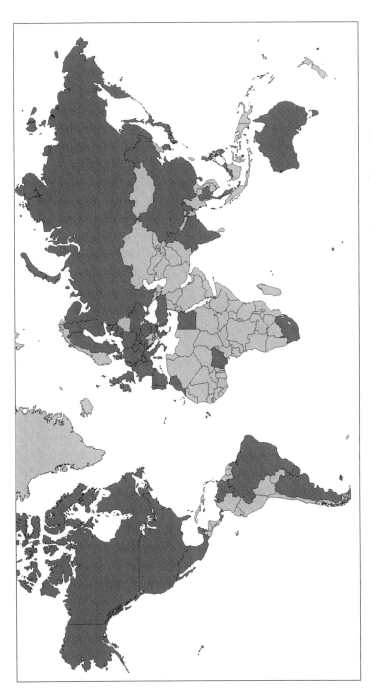

FIGURE 8.2 Mutual legal assistance treaties and agreements with the United States.[54]

obligation and arrive at a common understanding of what type of measures a state would be expected to implement. Schmitt argues in favor of applying the due diligence concept to cyberspace.[55] Doing so would create a new set of expectations a state can bring to bear *vis-à-vis* the state (or states) that the malicious activity transits through or originates from. If a state fails to meet these expectations, this could be used to justify more robust actions. In addition, failure to establish due diligence would have an escalatory effect. As Schmitt has noted, "Unless the due diligence principle is extended to cyberspace, target states may find themselves permitted to respond only through law enforcement or by using diplomacy or retorsion to encourage the state from which hostile cyber operations are being launched (or where the cyber infrastructure being used is located, as in cases of remote control) to take action to end them."[56] What such actions might look like – and why it is in states' self-interest to manage their proxy relationships carefully – is the focus of the following chapter.

9

The Practice: Shaping Cyber Proxy Relationships

States that wish to shape relationships with cyber proxies – either their own or those of other states – can build on lessons learned about why states change their approach to non-state actors.[1] Generally, the effort to shape proxy relationships occurs along one of two dimensions: either a state wishes to shape another state's proxy relationships, or it wishes to shape its own proxy relationships. This chapter explores both of these dimensions. First, it discusses the DIME(LE) framework as a model for how states can shape another state's proxy relationships. Then it examines three specific aspects of how a state can keep its own house in order: by determining what it considers to be inherently governmental functions; by establishing the role and responsibilities of its private sector; and by developing mechanisms to keep hacktivism, at bay.

States interested in trying to shape another state's proxy relationships can try to influence these various factors by (1) working to change that state's awareness of the threat posed by these non-state actors; (2) building up that state's capacity to prevent, stop, or punish a non-state actor's malicious activity (when the state is aware and willing but unable to take action); or (3) exerting coercive power through naming and shaming, sanctions, and military or law enforcement punishment (the latter options being available only to a limited number of states).[2]

In the cybersecurity context, many of these steps have already been taken or are currently underway. There is no doubt that awareness of cyber threats has increased significantly in recent years, reaching all the way up to heads of state and the G20.[3] Some governments are also trying to raise other governments' awareness. For example, the US Department of State has carried out workshops in African countries aimed at raising awareness.[4] In addition, capacity-building has become a buzzword at international cybersecurity conferences. The Global Forum on Cyber Expertise, launched at the Global Conference on Cyberspace in The Hague in April 2015, provides expertise to those in need, including working with governments to develop national cybersecurity frameworks and laws.[5] The Convention on Cyber Crime, adopted in 2001 and entering into force in 2004, was an early international attempt to increase the capacity for international law enforcement (capacity which remains woefully inadequate in many countries, poor and rich alike). The convention required parties to create a minimum set of procedures for computer crime investigations pertaining to data storage and search and seizure, as well as measures governing international cooperation, including extradition and mutual assistance. The International Telecommunication Union, a specialized agency of the UN, launched its Global Cybersecurity Agenda in 2007 following the mandate it was given at the 2005 World Summit on the Information Society.[6] And regional organizations have also been a catalyst for capacity-building; for example, ASEAN focused on creating a national computer emergency response team in each of its ten member states – a goal that was achieved by 2012.[7]

Projecting coercive power to influence other states' proxy relationships, the third element in the toolbox, is worth highlighting. One useful, if limited, framework for describing such efforts is the DIME(LE) model that outlines the various instruments of statecraft – diplomacy, information, military, economy, and (in the expanded version) law enforcement – that can be used for this purpose. The goal of using these instruments can be distinguished along a short-term and long-term time horizon. In the short term, the DIME(LE) toolbox can be used to change a beneficiary's risk calculus in the hope that it will lead states to seek greater restraint when it comes to risk. In the long term, continued pressure through DIME(LE) can aim to change a state's systematic approach to proxy relationships and shift the state's position from that of a broker to that of a monopolist state with more control over its proxies. Both are illustrated in Figure 9.1.

The first element of the DIME(LE) model is classic diplomacy. The operation of diplomacy in recent years can be seen in several governments that have issued public and private statements urging the Chinese government to take action against cyber-enabled economic espionage. These calls have ranged from German Chancellor Merkel's complaints to Chinese Premier Wen Jiabao in 2007 to US Secretary of State Clinton's demarche following the hack of Google in 2009 and US President Obama's raising the issue quietly during his meetings with Chinese President Xi.[8] (For its part, Beijing has also been engaged in similar long-standing diplomatic efforts to convey China's view on information security and the threat it perceives from content sponsored by foreign actors.)

The second element, information, has been used to name and shame actors for offensive actions originating from their territories. This practice takes place with varying degrees of explicitness. According to Segal, for many years US government officials would name and shame the Chinese government indirectly through anonymous news reports out of concern that more aggressive steps could hurt the broader bilateral relationship. The pressure became more overt in 2013, when "the calculus on public disclosure changed … [and] government officials began calling out the Chinese government and military." This shift in policy coincided with a report from the cybersecurity firm Mandiant suggesting that Unit 61398 of the PLA was in fact "APT1" – the advanced persistent threat (APT[9]) responsible for attacks on more than

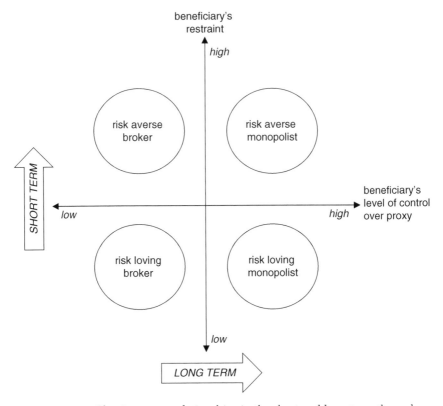

FIGURE 9.1 Shaping proxy relationships in the short and long term through DIME(LE).

one hundred US companies.[10] Even then, the Mandiant report did not accuse Beijing definitively; instead they left a narrow window for deniability:

> We believe the totality of the evidence we provide in this document bolsters the claim that APT1 is Unit 61398. However, we admit there is one other unlikely possibility: A secret, resourced organization full of mainland Chinese speakers with direct access to Shanghai-based telecommunications infrastructure is engaged in a multi-year, enterprise scale computer espionage campaign right outside of Unit 61398's gates, performing tasks similar to Unit 61398's known mission.[11]

Couching this conclusion in probabilistic terms and assessing the likelihood of alternative explanations, the Mandiant report confirmed Inkster's assessment that while establishing proof to the standard of "beyond a reasonable doubt" is difficult, "if one looks at this phenomenon in probabilistic terms the case for China's culpability becomes far more compelling."[12] (Meanwhile, Beijing's diplomatic efforts were also complemented by its own shaming campaign based on the information that Edward Snowden passed to the press.)

The third element of DIME(LE) – military action – can be employed either covertly or overtly to change a state's proxy relationships, as occurs in the context of nuclear proliferation[13] and counterterrorism, respectively.[14] More specifically, a state may try to undermine trust between the proxy and the beneficiary by exploiting vulnerabilities in the relationship such as divergent interests and information asymmetries. Such efforts can disrupt the relationship and can potentially lead to the state abandoning the proxy, either partially or fully.[15] The same approach, which is often used in counterterrorism efforts, can be applied to a state's relationship with hacktivists or cybercriminals.[16] In the context of criminal networks, effectively exploiting such weaknesses also requires in-depth knowledge of the network's internal norms.[17]

An example of a government using disinformation operations to disrupt a non-state actor's internal trust is when the Abu Nidal Organization "effectively destroyed itself after the CIA fed information into the organization that it was penetrated by United States and other intelligence agencies."[18] This is similar to how the hacktivist group Anonymous was severely disrupted after the British equivalent of the NSA, GCHQ, targeted the network's communication channel in 2011, and one of its members was arrested and became a law enforcement informant.[19] A few years later, the US military also stepped up its use of offensive cyber operations to disrupt the terrorist activities of the Islamic State. US officials have remained tight-lipped about this operation, except to say that "the attacks include efforts to prevent the group from distributing propaganda, videos, or other types of recruiting and messaging on social media sites such as Twitter, and across the Internet in general."[20] To date, very few studies have shed light on the trust structures of cyber proxy actors and criminal networks, an area ripe for more research.[21]

Economic measures are another element of the DIME(LE) statecraft toolkit. The US government laid the groundwork for punitive action against proxy attacks through a 2015 executive order that enabled the US president to block the property of individuals engaged in significant malicious cyber-enabled activities.[22] Economic sanctions have been used repeatedly to impose economic costs on a country in order to change its behavior. At the same time, comprehensive economic sanctions have become highly controversial and are often viewed as counterproductive, leading to the rise of more targeted sanctions.[23] The executive order allowing individuals (rather than entire countries) to be sanctioned for taking part in significant malicious cyber-enabled activities is an example of this shift. (Meanwhile, Beijing has also employed economic measures, denying access to its market and blocking Facebook, Twitter, and other US-based companies to underline its position.[24])

The final element of the expanded DIME(LE) model is law enforcement. Historically confined to a state's own borders, law enforcement agencies have since expanded their activities internationally – for example, to combat transnational organized crime. In the search for effective tools to counter the new cybersecurity threats from abroad, some governments turned to law enforcement agencies for another reason. Like intelligence agencies, law enforcement agencies conduct rigorous investigations, but, unlike intelligence agencies, law enforcement agencies must produce mostly public evidence to prosecute an actor. The US government has therefore started to use indictments by US law enforcement agencies as part of its toolkit to counter malicious cyber threats. While the arrest and prosecution of hackers living abroad is highly unlikely, especially if they are in countries such as Russia, Iran, and China, the indictments nevertheless serve the function of information published as part of a naming and shaming strategy.

The first example of a government using its law enforcement agencies for this purpose is the indictment of five Chinese military officers that the US government made public in April 2015.[25] Unsealing the indictment and directly accusing members of a foreign military marked a serious escalation of the Obama administration's naming and shaming efforts, which has continued to the present. The next year, the US government also unsealed the indictments against the three members of the Syrian Electronic Army and the seven Iranian hackers; this was followed by the indictment of the Russian and Canadian hackers that was made public in March 2017.

Ultimately, attempting to influence another state's use of proxies is risky. Some of the more aggressive steps in the DIME(LE) framework could escalate the situation and trigger more aggressive actions by the proxy, the beneficiary, or both. Such attempts could also backfire by increasing domestic support for a non-state actor, or by pushing the state from passive into active sponsorship.[26] Another challenge is that the use of proxies may need to be weighed against other important issues in the bilateral relationship. Moreover, Arvid Bell, a scholar at Harvard University focusing on crisis negotiations, noted that, paradoxically, "Parties usually overestimate the other party's control over proxies while underestimating their own level of control."[27] In short, a strategy based on DIME(LE) alone is not a silver bullet and given the overall evolution of capabilities and threats, focusing on these issues domestically is just as important (and provides greater legitimacy when encouraging others to follow suit).

KEEPING ONE'S OWN HOUSE IN ORDER: DETERMINING INHERENTLY GOVERNMENTAL FUNCTIONS

Even without external actors trying to shape a state's proxy relationships, it is in a state's self-interest to manage its proxy relationships carefully. A state's projection of power depends on its ability to strike a balance between leveraging and controlling its proxies. A key question for any state is therefore what constitute "inherently governmental functions" – in other words, what functions should not be entrusted to a proxy? This is not a settled issue, particularly in the context of offensive cyber operations. (In democratic systems, the state's relationship with proxies is under the public's scrutiny. The government is ultimately held accountable by its citizens;

proxies add a level of separation between the citizenry and its sovereign and chosen representatives.)

The US government provides a rare insight into a government's deliberations about this issue. In the United States, the FAIR Act of 1998 defined "inherently governmental functions" as "function[s] so intimately related to the public interest as to require performance by Federal Government employees."[28] Government officials often highlight that acts of war fall under this heading: performing them is reserved for military personnel.[29] However, the effects of most offensive cyber operations remain below the threshold of the use of force and armed attack but might nevertheless carry significant escalatory risk. How should the concept of inherently governmental functions be applied to such operations?[30] The only explicit public reference to cyber in the relevant Pentagon document, instruction DoDI 1100.22, is in a parenthetical phrase:

> Manpower shall be designated military ... if the planned use of destructive combat capabilities is part of the mission assigned to this manpower (including destructive capabilities involved in offensive cyber operations, electronic attack, missile defense, and air defense). ... This does not include technical advice on the operation of weapon systems or other support of a non-discretionary nature performed in direct support of combat operations.[31]

Cyber operations raise specific issues in this regard. First, the modularity and prolonged duration of offensive cyber operations – outlined in the adapted tip-of-the-spear framework presented in Chapter 1 (see Figure 1.2) – raise questions regarding which activities constitute "inherently governmental functions" and which are "closely associated functions" that can be delegated to contractors. Drawing this distinction is a challenge not only for the US government but for all states, democratic or not. In their discussion of lawful targets for counterattacks, Yale Law professor Oona Hathaway and her co-authors noted that

> The civilian designer of a weapons system has traditionally not been treated as a direct participant in hostilities. However, the programmer who works with military intelligence may tweak the code to enable the attack, right up until the moment of the attack. The actions of such a civilian – particularly of a civilian who regularly engages in such activity – could be considered a "continuous function [that] involves the preparation, execution, or command of acts or operations amounting to direct participation in hostilities."[32]

How these categories apply to offensive cyber operations has been discussed publicly only recently. James R. Lisher II, a US Air Force Judge Advocate General, and author of one of the rare articles on the topic, argued that "[n]ow is the time for the DoD to determine what functions are [inherently governmental functions] that may not be outsourced in cyberspace operations."[33] Lisher suggested that contractors could be used for weaponization, reconnaissance, and training. He also pointed to actions taken to enable a potential future attack, which are known as "cyber operational preparation of the environment" and could be said to fall into the "closely associated functions" category.[34] However, he pointed out that how cyber operational preparation of the environment "is defined is critical to the analysis of whether this function is one that crosses over into the [inherently governmental functions] domain or one that is merely "closely associated" with [inherently governmental functions]."[35]

Other countries have or can be expected to have similar internal deliberations about what types of functions can be delegated to their respective proxies (like militias). Those likely include discussions for how best to ensure that proxies' behavior remains aligned with the government's priorities. Information about offensive cyber operations will likely be classified and compartmentalized on a need-to-know level. This has not changed since the days when Captain MacFall kept details about his collaboration with the mafia from his superiors during World War II. However, such classification presents unique challenges for effective monitoring and oversight, especially as this field expands into what the military considers to be an entirely new operational domain. In addition to introducing multiple categories requiring different levels of review, a government can also consider increasing the reporting requirements for the proxy. For example, in October 2009, the US Director for National Intelligence established a requirement that the intelligence community share information about its core contract personnel annually.[36] The United States' detailed discussions and its policies governing inherently governmental functions are a model other countries could adopt as they expand their activities into cyberspace.

KEEPING ONE'S OWN HOUSE IN ORDER: DETERMINING THE ROLE OF THE PRIVATE SECTOR

As the security environment deteriorates and states remain unable to effectively protect companies (as well as NGOs, human rights activists, and think tanks) from hackers, governments may be facing increasing domestic pressure to allow non-state actors, namely companies, to take more aggressive steps to defend themselves. If this occurs, it will be crucial for governments to clearly identify the boundaries of what is considered appropriate behavior. The extraterritorial nature of the publicly known examples also suggests that any such changes require international coordination and harmonization. In any case, it is crucial for any state to be transparent about how it views the role and responsibilities of private companies in the context of cybersecurity and what authorities are granted to them.

The self-protection techniques adopted by companies are often described as "active cyber defense," "private sector countermeasures," or "hacking back." For example, Stewart Baker at the law firm Steptoe & Johnson LLP and former US Assistant Secretary of Homeland Security for Policy, as well as former general counsel of the NSA, argues that "the US government should encourage responsible private sector countermeasures."[37] A 2012 survey among Black Hat USA conference participants found that 36 percent of "information security professionals have engaged in retaliatory hacking."[38] Such activity includes launching DDoS attacks but also extends to tracing intruders and accessing other computers to assess what data might have been stolen or to disrupt the attacker's infrastructure. (More often than not, this includes accessing computers of innocent third parties unaware that their system has been hijacked.) Reporters at Bloomberg revealed that "[s]ome companies are enlisting cybersecurity firms, many with military or government security ties," for this purpose.[39] Active cyber defense by the private sector – in other words, a company hiring another company for this purpose – fits into the framework of a non-state beneficiary using a non-state proxy and could create new escalatory risks.

A few media reports shed more light on this issue. For example, following the massive DDoS attacks by Iranian hackers against US financial institutions, a JPMorgan Chase & Co. employee proposed in a closed-door meeting in February 2013 "that the banks hit back from offshore locations, disabling the servers from which the attacks were being launched."[40] Harris quotes a former military intelligence officer explaining that "[b]anks have an appetite now to strike back because they're sick of taking it in the shorts . . . if the government can't act, or won't, it's only logical they'll do it themselves."[41] But it is not just banks. After it was hacked in 2014, Sony reportedly hired a firm to launch DDoS attacks against websites where its stolen data was available, apparently using Amazon Web Services as the platform for doing so (in violation of its terms and conditions agreement).[42] During the same time period, media reports emerged that the FBI was investigating whether any US financial institutions had hired hackers to disable servers used by Iranian hackers against them.[43] A smaller-scale demand for hacking-for-hire services comes from private investigators, who pay hackers USD 50–250 to gain access to email accounts.[44]

Extraterritoriality again comes into play. In the United States, the Computer Fraud and Abuse Act criminalizes unauthorized access to computers, and the Department of Justice manual for prosecuting computer crimes makes clear that, "[a]lthough it may be tempting to do so (especially if the attack is ongoing), the company should not take any offensive measures on its own, such as 'hacking back' into the attacker's computer – even if such measures could in theory be characterized as 'defensive.' Doing so may be illegal, regardless of the motive."[45] That is why there is an incentive to launch such operations from other jurisdictions.[46] The Bloomberg report illustrates this with the following example:

> RSA, the security division of Hopkinton, Massachusetts-based EMC Corp. that generated $987 million in revenue last year and whose clients include government agencies, banks and defense contractors, has insulated its Israeli division so that its

analysts could engage in activities they might not be able to do in the US, according to a former employee, who asked not to be named discussing internal company matters. RSA experts in Israel send malware into online forums where stolen data is swapped, or the experts hack directly into these computers, the person said. This allows them to recover stolen bank passwords and other data on behalf of financial institutions through methods the banks can't use themselves, the person said, adding that no US-based employees of RSA are allowed to engage in the activities or handle the data... The growing arsenal of unconventional services is often provided by consultants who formerly worked at intelligence agencies or the Pentagon.[47]

As the previous examples from India and South Korea illustrate, it is not only US companies that appear to be engaged in "hacking back." The Dutch researcher Dennis Broeders also wrote in 2015 about "firms operating on the Dutch market" that offer take-down services, and that "[s]ome of these are Israeli companies that operate very effectively and largely under the radar of public attention, but do seem to be able to find their clients."[48]

While this activity has been isolated so far and takes place mostly in the shadows, this might change in the future. In 2011, General Hayden, former director of the CIA and the NSA under President George W. Bush, suggested, "We may come to a point where defense is more actively and aggressively defined even for the private sector and what is permitted there is something that we would never let the private sector do in physical space... Let me really throw a bumper sticker for you: how about a digital Blackwater?"[49] In the US, advocates for such active cyber defense have mostly been experts affiliated with or close to the Republican Party. With the Republican Party controlling both houses of Congress following the November 2016 elections, such an amendment to the Computer Fraud and Abuse Act could happen relatively quickly.

KEEPING ONE'S OWN HOUSE IN ORDER: NATIONALISM AND HACKTIVISM

Nationalism remains a powerful driver in many states, monopolist and broker states alike, and it is a source for existing or potential future proxy relationships. For example, after the 1989 Tiananmen Square protest, the Chinese government launched its Patriotic Education Program, which was designed to inculcate students with a sense of nationalism.[50] Barry R. Posen, director of MIT's Security Studies Program, highlighted nationalism as the instrument that connects otherwise dispersed individuals for the projection of power, defining nationalism "as the propensity of individuals to identify their personal interest with that of a group that is too large to meet together; to identify that interest on the basis both of a 'culture' that the group shares, and a purported history that the group purportedly shares; and to believe that this group must have a state structure of its own in order to thrive."[51]

Nationalism is a particularly powerful force in the digital age since the Internet's many-to-many communication facilitates mobilization of dispersed individuals across geographic distances, including across borders transnationally.

Hacktivist networks and DDoS attacks illustrate this phenomenon. They also highlight how such campaigns can take on a life of their own – which is why countries with particularly strong manifestations of nationalism need to be able to manage the behavior of patriotic hacktivists both in peacetime and (especially) in times of conflict. The emergence of the Honker Union is representative of a broader global trend starting in the late 1990s of hacktivists becoming involved in international disputes. According to the FBI, by 2001, several hacktivist groups had already emerged and were engaging each other around the globe, including inter-actions between Israelis and Palestinians, Indians and Pakistanis, and Chinese and Japanese.[52]

These interactions both reflect and complicate the relations between the respective states. The Chinese and US governments have both faced challenges in managing hacktivists, for example, and their actions provide a template for how states can approach this issue. In 2001, when Chinese patriotic hacktivists were targeting the United States, the Chinese government eventually decided to intervene and stop the hacktivists' attacks. The Chinese government started by using its official media outlets to publish statements from the head of the People's Daily Online editorial staff that while they understood the hackers' "passion," they discouraged the attacks and warned the public against taking similar action. This was followed by Ministry for Public Security statements made online, in phone text messages, and in traditional media outlets declaring the activity illegal. Not long after, Wan Tao, one of the hacktivists' leaders, also urged an end to the malicious activity.[53] According to Henderson, "The ability to ensure compliance with these directives seems tenuous at best and may be aimed at keeping the situation under control rather than 100% observance. When authorities in Beijing decided that the hacker war between China and the United States had gone on long enough, they began issuing public statements and contacting leaders of the alliance telling them that it was time to stop."[54] Interestingly, a year later, a joint statement by five Chinese hacker forums discouraged potential malicious activity timed for the anniversary of the 2001 incident. The Chinese government's actions demonstrate a state's ability to shape hacktivists' actions during a campaign.

The US government has also demonstrated the preventative capacity of such statements. In 2003, the FBI's National Infrastructure Protection Center (NIPC) issued an advisory "to heighten the awareness of an increase in global hacking activities as a result of the increasing tensions between the United States and Iraq... Regardless of the motivation, the NIPC reiterates such activity is illegal and punishable as a felony. The US government does not condone so-called 'patriotic hacking' on its behalf."[55] Over a decade later, in the wake of the Sony hack, North Korea's Internet went offline for several hours. Seeing this, Healey speculated, "It is entirely possible this is good ol' American patriotic hackers, mimicking the Jester, looking to strike back against North Korea" – and if so, "then the Department of Justice must do like they did at the time of the Iraq invasion in 2003 and warn them that it does not condone so-called 'patriotic hacking' on its behalf."[56]

These actions by the Chinese and US governments can serve as blueprints for other governments seeking to influence hacktivists' activity. Such actions can be taken preventatively, pre-emptively, or during a campaign. The advantage of taking these steps preventatively and pre-emptively is that it minimizes the risk of hacktivist operations taking on a life of their own. Scholars of conventional proxies also persuasively argue for such action to be taken at the very outset of conflict to avoid an escalatory dynamic, in which one party's use of proxies leads others to follow suit.[57] Herman J. Cohen, former US Assistant Secretary of State for African Affairs, for example, wrote that "[f]irm action should take place at the very outset of such wars when there is still a possibility of pulling proxy forces back."[58] The devil is also in the detail when a government issues such statements. For example, a 2001 FBI statement about the patriotic Chinese hackers' attack on US websites highlighted that "Pro United States hackers responded with similar defacements, messages, and damage on 300 Chinese web sites." The statement went on to note that in the course of the incident "some pro-Chinese hackers violated hacker etiquette by wiping some compromised servers. The rule of thumb is to deface or crash a web site but to leave the information intact, otherwise it is considered bad form."[59] In other words, governments can also clearly specify what type of behavior they consider appropriate and what behavior they consider inappropriate.

While some states might be willing to proactively issue statements opposing malicious actions online, those that are more reluctant might at least be willing to ask hacktivists to adhere to a "no first use" type policy; and the most reluctant governments might agree to issue preventative statements tied to a specific level of severity, thereby drawing clear red lines hacktivists should not cross and identifying which types of activity will no longer be considered legitimate political protest. Governments that are willing to control hacktivists but are as yet unable to do so could demonstrate such willingness not just by issuing statements such as those discussed above – they could also accept offers of outside assistance in investigations or efforts to mitigate malicious activity, as well as issuing statements of regret and, potentially, offers of reparations. At the same time, it is clear that not all states will take any such action. Indeed, some have encouraged freewheeling hacktivist activity and will likely continue to do so. For example, when students in Tomsk launched a DDoS attack against the website of Chechen separatists in 2002, "the local FSB branch was fully aware of the attack, putting out a press release that defended the students' actions as a legitimate 'expression of their position as citizens, one worthy of respect'" (this response helps explain the Russian government's position *vis-à-vis* the DDoS attack against Estonia five years later).[60]

CONCLUSION: NUDGING AND MANAGING INSTEAD
OF DICTATING AND PROHIBITING

Trying to reduce the escalatory risk associated with cyber proxies and to limit the proliferation of cyber capabilities will be a major challenge for governments in the coming years and decades. If recent history and conventional proxies are any indication, one must temper expectations of what can realistically be achieved in the short term. Even in the long term, powerful drivers stand in the way of such efforts, trends such as the increasing number of states expressing a desire to acquire capabilities for this domain or the broader changes to states' relationships with private actors. It is difficult to see how, for example, calls for emulating the process leading to the prohibition of privateering could result in a similar outcome for certain cyber proxies today. Treaties, such as the one abolishing privateering in 1856, as an instrument of international statecraft are increasingly falling out of favor. Hacker safe havens are not limited to the coast, at the boundary of a state's sovereignty, but are found inland within a country's territory further removed from outsiders eager to arrest them. And the incentive structures for states to rely on non-state actors to project cyber power are unlikely to change in the foreseeable future.

While the US government has successfully used the tools of the DIME(LE) framework to make progress on some specific issues, namely the dispute with China over the cyber-enabled theft of intellectual property for competitive advantages to companies, their effect will likely be limited in affecting broader change. For example, despite the front-page media coverage of the various indictments, when those accused will stand trial in a court remains uncertain. Such efforts will have less impact when used against governments that care less than the Chinese about being named and shamed. Relatedly, the use of cyberspace for political and military purposes is still a comparatively new phenomenon. States are reluctant to take actions that could restrict their capabilities and perceived advantages in this area without a mature understanding of the consequences of such actions.

How to keep one's own house in order in and of itself will be a challenge for any state. The controversy over the new export controls for cyber tools agreed to by members of the Wassenaar Arrangement on Export Controls for dual-use goods and technologies illustrated the lack of established best practices and mature policy solutions to many of these emerging questions, including those about the spread of capabilities and growing threat. The efforts by the Chinese and US governments to actively shape hacktivists' behavior are among the early signs that such practices are beginning to emerge, as is the discussion about how to define inherently governmental functions. The flipside of more and more states becoming active in this space is that more and more variation and experimentation is likely to occur, shedding light on what approaches work better than others. Finally, some of the staunchest defenders of the classic Westphalian notion of sovereignty are also among those states with comparatively loose relationships to proxies. Tightening those relationships at home would lend greater weight to calls on the international stage to respect sovereignty or otherwise expose a certain amount of hypocrisy.

All taken together, though, the nature of cyberspace and international relations at the beginning of the twenty-first century suggests that realistic expectations are best summed up as being able to nudge rather than to dictate to others, and expecting to manage instead of to prohibit the development and spread of cyber capabilities.

Conclusion: Cyber Proxies, the Future, and Suggestions for Further Research

Interstate war has been continuously declining since World War II, and states have repeatedly used proxies in the past to avoid conflicts from escalating to war.[1] Cyber proxies can be used for the same purpose, especially since cyberspace has enabled a new set of effects below the threshold of use of force and armed attack. However, they also inject new escalatory dynamics into the mix.

Against this background, several key findings emerge. First, projecting coercive power through cyberspace is not only a state-centric affair. It is often a dynamic interplay between the state and proxy actors detached from the state, raising important questions over control, authority, and the legitimate use of cyber capabilities. This, in and of itself, is nothing new. However, unlike most weaponry used by militaries, offensive cyber operations are low-cost. The cost of a hacking operation lasting months or even years does not compare with that of a single F-35 fighter jet (which can run to more than USD 250 million).[2] For this reason, Nye has convincingly argued, the Internet is contributing to a diffusion of power from state to non-state actors. Usually, when a new technology with military utility emerges on the scene, states are its first adopters, if not its inventors, and it only later becomes accessible to non-state actors. However, non-state hackers started emerging before some of the most technologically advanced states had even started to realize the potential of hacking, and most states only began investing in this area during the past decade. In other words, states have never enjoyed a monopoly on cyber tools. Non-state actors with cyber capabilities have been available for states to use as proxies from the day that states themselves became interested in projecting power through this new technology. So, while the Internet certainly leads to a diffusion of power generally, cyber power itself was diffuse from the start.

Second, states have been using proxies for a wide variety of purposes not limited to projecting power abroad. For example, in both Russia and Iran, reports about government-supported hackers targeting dissidents predated reports about such proxies hitting targets abroad. Similarly, companies like Gamma International offer their tools and services to law enforcement agencies for internal purposes and to intelligence agencies and militaries for external purposes. Some proxies purposefully develop tools for more explicit military purposes, such as targeting critical infrastructure systems. When it comes to data collection, it is noteworthy that, for a significant share of proxies, the line between domestic and foreign is blurred. Furthermore, states' use of proxies depends on their specific threat perception. How much this threat perception varies among states is illustrated by the differences in their terminology.[3] The member states of the Shanghai Cooperation Organization use the term *information* security and see a threat in "the dissemination of information that … undermines other countries' political, economic and social stability, as well as their spiritual and cultural environment."[4] Their use of proxies reflects their underlying information security doctrines. Countries protecting content as a human right, on the other hand, have been careful to speak in terms of *cyber*security, and their proxy relationships similarly reflect their laws and policies.

A third finding is that categorizing proxies based on intent is not particularly helpful. Not only do proxies' motives change over time – as demonstrated by the hacktivists in China, whose actions shifted from political to profit-driven over time – but proxies can have mixed motives at any given moment. For example, the indictment of the three members of the Syrian Electronic Army, usually considered a politically motivated hacktivist group, explicitly referenced their personal profit-driven as well as their political ambitions. Similarly, cyber criminals can be politically motivated. For example, Vladislav Horohorin, also known as "BadB" and one of the most wanted cyber criminals in the late 2000s, had a video embedded on his website depicting him as a hero combating US imperialism. It revealed the strong political undertone to his criminal behavior and that of his collaborators even as they raked in millions of dollars in credit-card fraud. That is why proposed typologies of proxies based on motivation[5] quickly face limitations when applied to real-world examples, and risk distorting analyses of the phenomenon. The same is true for typologies of proxies based on whether their targets are perceived as internal or external threats. Proxy actors in a number of different countries have engaged in malicious cyber activity targeting both perceived internal and external threats, creating a methodological challenge for such typologies.

Fourth, a review of how states have used cyber proxies to date suggests three main types of proxy relationships: (1) delegation, (2) orchestration, and (3) sanctioning (approving or permitting). *Delegation* describes proxies on a tight leash with the state and under the state's effective control. Private security contractors, such as the contractors hired by the US Cyber Command are the best illustrations of this relationship. *Orchestration* applies to proxies on a somewhat looser leash with the state, those who receive funding or tools but no specific instructions. The orchestration bond is often based not on a contract but on a shared ideological bond, thereby minimizing the agency problem. The relationship between the Iranian government and students described in Chapter 5 illustrates this category.[6] The concept of *sanctioning* builds on the framework of passive support developed by counterterrorism scholars to describe the phenomenon in which a state is aware of the activity of a non-state actor and indirectly benefits from its actions and turns a blind eye. In the context of cybersecurity, sanctioning can be seen in the case of Russian hackers committing cyber crime without having to fear punishment from Russian security agencies, as long as their targets lie beyond the borders of Mother Russia.

Any state may pursue any of these three relationships or "mix" them; nonetheless, states systematically tend to favor one approach over the others and exhibit a significant degree of path dependence. Given the global private market of cyber contractors and the ease of transferring intangible code, it made sense initially to hypothesize that states would exhibit new types of behavior; for example, Iran might simply hire a company in Argentina to carry out some operation. However, it quickly became clear that states so far have relied on and expanded their existing model for proxy relationships, whatever that may be. The good news is that this suggests that cyber proxies are not an entirely new animal – a great deal can be learned from existing scholarship on proxies. The bad news is that those trying to get states to tighten the leash on some of their proxies may encounter old challenges: the existing scholarship suggests that states change their systematic approach for engaging with proxies only very slowly, usually in the span not of years but of decades.[7]

Last but not least, while countries pursue different models for proxy relationships and have different doctrines for the use of coercive cyber power, they also face a common challenge. Ultimately, they all use cyber proxies to project power and to achieve their objectives in international politics, including, occasionally, as part of warfare. As a result, they all have an interest in balancing the benefits of proxy relationships with the cost and increased risk of escalation. In addition, democratic states must ensure proxy relationships are subject to their accountability mechanisms and system of checks and balances. For example, what should be considered "inherently governmental functions" in the context of offensive cyber operations remains an unsettled question. When states wish to disable an adversary's system, can this be carried out by a cybersecurity contractor or would that cross a line? Should the line be drawn at planting a destructive implant in another system or only when a disruptive effect is launched? How can such actors be effectively monitored and, if necessary, sanctioned (restrained)? What if the actor is a student at a university in another country? States also face the long-term challenge that offensive cyber capabilities are, by and large, not costly hardware but simply knowledge. How do you manage the spread of this knowledge to an increasing number of non-state actors in the long run if states have an incentive to actively forge proxy relationships in the short run?

Often when someone is asked how to manage cyber proxies, the first response is about building a normative regime and taboo of unacceptable practices. From the perspective of those in democratic countries, it would certainly be desirable for more countries to move in the direction of greater control and accountability. However, a normative taboo similar to that against privateering is unlikely in the foreseeable future. The current shortage of cyber expertise and capabilities within governments around the world is fueling a dependence on non-state actors. In fact, many countries are extending their existing models for leveraging non-state actors to project coercive power in cyberspace. Even some of the states best described as monopolists are moving towards what Bobbitt described as the market state and are increasingly intertwined with private actors.

The current flagship project of the Israeli government in Be'er Sheva is one of the best examples of this trend.[8] Together with Ben Gurion University and a group of companies, the government is essentially trying to build the Israeli version of Silicon Valley. The government's decision to move its intelligence unit, Unit 8200 – Israel's equivalent of the NSA or the Government Communications Headquarters of the UK – to the Negev, shows how serious it is about this project.[9] But it is more than that. It is one of the most ambitious attempts to realize what Klimburg suggested in his article "Mobilizing Cyber Power": the integration of the government's capabilities with that of the private sector and academia. The president of Ben Gurion University, Rivka Carmi, painted the project's vision this way: "[Y]ou won't be able to differentiate buildings of the park and buildings of the army unit. We want to establish 'co-opetition', collaboration and competition among the various players for the brightest people."[10] This trend raises new questions about the long-term viability of existing norms based on existing distinctions of public/private and the expectation that new regimes will be built along similar lines.

Those seeking to shape other states' proxy relationships can draw on the lessons learned about conventional proxies. However, these lessons suggest that external actors have only limited ability to significantly influence proxy relationships over the short to medium term. As Byman argued in the context of passive support, ending or changing such relationships is "straightforward conceptually but difficult in practice."[11] The relationships are embedded in, and a function of, a state's political system and broader approach to projecting power. An external actor has only limited levers to shift systemically the nature of another actor's proxy relationships. A state may face significant challenges in affecting the proxy relationships built into another state's DNA, but it can often exercise greater control over cybersecurity companies, hacktivists, and those breaking the law at home. States have a shared self-interest in managing their proxy relationships carefully for two primary reasons: first, to be in control of escalation and, second, because of the potential proliferation of capabilities.

The Internet enables a new spectrum of harmful effects that, in turn, introduce a new set of escalatory dynamics. The latter are increasingly on the minds of government officials and cybersecurity experts around the world. For example, when the Russian participants in a 2011 conference (hosted by the Institute for Information Security Issues of Lomonosov Moscow State University together with the Russian Security Council) were asked to rank ten different issues relating to cybersecurity, they placed escalation at the top of the list. According to Thomas, this "demonstrates that even unofficially the Russians are very interested in containing the outbreak of a cyber incident."[12] Such concerns have led the Organization for Security and Co-operation in Europe, which consists of fifty-seven participating states, to adopt two agreements outlining confidence-building measures around cyber activity. These measures include the establishment of hotlines to be used by states at times of international crisis to avoid miscalculation due to accidents or rogue activity. Trivial as it may sound, establishing such hotlines is actually a major accomplishment in international affairs.[13]

Additional challenges arise in the specific context of cybersecurity. In the past, militaries were important drivers and incubators for anti-escalatory agreements. Thomas Schelling, nuclear theorist and Nobel Laureate, noted that when a phone line was set up by Israeli and Arab military commanders during the 1948 cease-fire in Jerusalem, it was military commanders, not "civilian arms-control enthusiasts,"[14] who had the idea. His account is a reminder of the long military tradition of communicating with the adversary, be it for the exchange of prisoners of war or to handle emergencies. The challenge of offensive cyber operations is that many countries' cyber capabilities are concentrated within intelligence agencies whose bureaucracies do not have this tradition reflected in their institutional cultures, raising the question of how mechanisms like hotlines can be effectively implemented in an environment where not only the military but also intelligence agencies are involved.

A separate category of escalatory risk directly relates to the potential unintended consequences of using proxies – including rogue action – that are described in principal–agent theory. But there is also a more subtle, piecemeal, long-term dimension to escalation, which Schelling described as "salami tactics":

> Tell a child not to go in the water and he'll sit on the bank and submerge his bare feet; he is not yet "in" the water. Acquiesce, and he'll stand up; no more of him is in the water than before. Think it over, and he'll start wading, not going any deeper; take a moment to decide whether this is different and he'll go a little deeper, arguing that since he goes back and forth it all averages out. Pretty soon we are calling to him not to swim out of sight, wondering whatever happened to all our discipline.[15]

In addition to the erosion of control that Schelling describes, the child is also setting a precedent for others to follow. The slippery slope dimension of this picture is therefore an important illustration of how norms and actors' behavior can change incrementally over time. Using proxies for increasingly aggressive types of offensive cyber operations could have a similar effect. In other words, the actions of non-state proxies still shape state behavior and consequently international norms.

A third source of escalatory risk is the diffusion of reach. Because the Internet makes it possible to cause effects remotely over great distances, a proxy no longer needs to be confined to the territory of the conventional conflict; this creates additional escalatory risk *vis-à-vis* third countries. A proxy can operate from a beneficiary's territory, or from the territory of a third, neutral country. This differs from earlier models of "safe havens" in that hackers' smaller footprint makes it more likely that the third country will be unaware of the hackers' presence on its soil. In their study of the role of African nations, Jan Kallberg and Steven Rowlen suggested that it might be possible for a beneficiary to "fly its operatives into a country in the developing world to carry out the attack using Internet access gained under the false pretense of conducting business or any other lawful purpose."[16] While there is no publicly known case where this has happened, it is not far-fetched, as the recent arrest of 77 cyber criminals from China living in Kenya illustrates.[17]

For this reason, the new UNGGE's language with regard to due diligence is of great import. As a 2016 report by the UN Institute for Disarmament Research prepared for the new UNGGE pointed out,

> Due diligence requires States to ensure that their territory is not used for harmful actions directed against other States. A State is obliged to "take all available measures" and "do all that could be reasonably expected of it" in a specific circumstance. If a State takes all feasible and reasonable measures but is unable to prevent an internationally wrongful act, then there is no violation of principles, but there may still be an obligation to notify and cooperate.[18]

States will need to agree (or agree to disagree) on whether taking "all available measures" extends to protecting infrastructure or only applies in the context of an ongoing operation and countermeasures. (At the same time, a growing number of skeptics doubt that the UNGGE process and the aspirational, voluntary norms outlined in the 2015 UNGGE report will lead to the emergence of actual norms and expectations of appropriate behavior by a majority of states.[19])

A separate challenge is the proliferation of capabilities, which raises the broader question of what states, whether brokers or monopolists, can do to manage the growing market for coercive cyber power and slow the spread of capabilities. The traditional methods of arms control have limited utility. Cyber weapons are made of code. Code is intangible, written – rather, typed – knowledge, and can easily be moved across large geographic distances. Cyber weapons are usually composed of different modules. "To be a world-class hacker, you have to be able to effectively use code and exploits created by others just as much as create your own," David Brumley wrote in an email (May 1, 2017) to me. He and his colleagues won DARPA's Cyber Grand Challenge in 2016 as well as repeatedly winning first place at DefCon's Capture the Flag competition over the past few years. In addition, most cyber tools can be used in both offensive and innocuous ways, further complicating attempts to apply conventional arms control mechanisms. In fact, the notion of control is itself somewhat misleading as there are too many avenues to share capabilities to effectively control any such flows. However, if we move beyond binary notions of non-proliferation and arms control, there are certainly possibilities for slowing the spread of cyber capabilities. Proxies are an important factor in this equation, as proxy relationships often involve a transfer of expertise, which, in the context of offensive cyber operations, could include sharing knowledge of a zero-day vulnerability, blueprints for packaging modules of code into more sophisticated malware that makes the sum larger than its parts, or more sophisticated malware itself.

Ultimately, proxies are here to stay. They are the pawns in the greater strategic chess game. Cyber proxies are simply the newest kids on the block. Meanwhile, the international discussions about how to effectively control them and related escalatory dynamics, much like the broader discussion about cybersecurity, will remain challenging in the foreseeable future. As with disputes over the meaning of "terrorism," governments don't even agree on what they mean by "cybersecurity" or "information security," let alone "proxies." Proxy activity cannot be ignored, though, because unlike states whose relations are strongly interdependent, proxies, as actors detached from the state, have fewer incentives to adhere to international norms.

Future Research

This book has tried to outline a general framework for thinking about cyber proxies based on inductive analysis and case study research. The hope is that it will be used for future empirical research on cyber proxies as more data becomes available. This includes closely tracking developments in the countries examined in this book and studying proxy relationships in other countries.

The existing literature on militias, terrorist groups, and pirates outlines several hypotheses applicable to cyber proxies; these are worth testing in the future as more empirical data becomes available.[1] For example, Hasting's analysis of piracy syndicates suggests that the internal structure of piracy syndicates depends on whether they focus on seizing ships and cargo or kidnapping for ransom. In the case of seizing ships and cargo, the degree of secrecy between the beneficiary hiring the pirates as agents and the pirates is much higher: pirates sometimes learn what ship to target only on the day of the action itself, and they may not know the end destination of the cargo they seize until the deed is done. Pirates focusing on kidnapping for ransom, on the other hand, operate more publicly, and sometimes even have spokespersons engaging with the media. Such a trade-off between control and secrecy has also been found in studies of terrorist networks.[2] Similar analysis of cyber proxies would be very valuable once more empirical data is available. As Robert Axelrod and Rumen Iliev have argued in their analysis on the timing of cyber conflict,

> What is most needed is a sophisticated understanding of how to estimate the potential Gains (and loses [*sic*]) from actually using the resource in a particular setting. As we saw, these Gains (and losses) arise not only from the direct effects of the intrusion, but also the indirect effects such as increased vigilance if the news gets out, and also the political effects if an emerging international norm is violated or reinforced.[3]

The same argument applies to proxy actors and the factors that come into play through proxy relationships.

With regard to other countries that stand out for future case studies, India is certainly one of the top contenders. In 2010, *The Times of India* reported that, "[b]orrowing a page from China's art of cyber war," the [Indian] government was planning to create a "small army of software professionals to spy on the classified data of hostile nations by hacking into their computer systems. IT workers and ethical hackers who sign up for the ambitious project will be protected by law."[4] Senior officials including National Security Adviser Shiv Shankar Menon discussed such a plan at a meeting in July 2010. The proposal envisioned that the National Technical Research Organization (NTRO) and the Defense Intelligence Agency would be the lead agencies and that NTRO would also develop the legal protection, given that under the Indian IT act the punishment for hacking is usually imprisonment for up to three years, a fine, or both. The following year, the Indian government was trying to recruit hackers for this endeavor on websites.[5]

India also makes for an interesting case study due to its growing market in teaching hacking skills. Pavan Duggel, a lawyer focusing on cyber crime in India, pointed out to me that "All over India, hacking schools are offering ethical hacker courses for a few hundred dollars with the promise of a rosy job afterward. However, the jobs usually don't follow, creating an increasing number of people with at least a basic level of skills."[6] Jiten Jain, another Indian cybersecurity expert, underscored this point, adding that these students "are drawn to unethical hacking for lack of opportunities [upon completing the courses]," and arguing that "[i]t is important to bring them into the loop."[7] It will be interesting to study how the Indian government will manage this growing supply of hackers.

Another area ripe for additional research is the ongoing discussion in several countries about allowing private companies to employ a broader set of techniques for their defense.[8] If governments change their laws to enable the private sector to use more of these techniques, this will be an important additional area to analyze, especially the question of how governments might shape this private market of cyber capabilities. Wyatt Hoffman and Ariel Levite from the Carnegie Endowment for International Peace studied two possible mechanisms governments might use. The first one is an international code of conduct, emulating the one established for conventional private military and security companies in 2008.[9] The second is having insurance companies play a key role (as they did in the effective tackling of the piracy problem in the 2000s), including a licensing regime under which companies can only offer augmented defensive services to other companies if they have a license to do so, which would be available only after meeting certain criteria.

A special type of proxy that requires further research is that of informants and law enforcement agencies. Because of the diffusion of reach, the actions of informants are no longer easily bound by geographic distances and borders, but can have remote effects. Take Hector Xavier Monsegur, also known by his hacker alias "Sabu." In 2011, Monsegur was caught by the FBI and turned into an informant. In his late twenties at the time, Monsegur had been a hacker for a little over a decade and had been part of LulzSec, an Anonymous splinter group.[10] As an FBI informant, he encouraged other hackers to hack foreign government websites. According to a document filed in the US District Court for the Southern District of New York, "Monsegur also engaged in a significant undercover operation in an existing investigation through which, acting at the direction of law enforcement, Monsegur gathered evidence that exposed a particular subject's role in soliciting cyber attacks on a foreign government."[11] This apparently included targeting websites of the governments of Iran, Brazil, and Pakistan, and the specific request to transfer data from Syrian government websites to a server monitored by the FBI.[12]

This example raises important questions about the distinction between domestic and foreign, as well as between civilian and military, spheres in the digital age. For example, whether a foreign government that was hacked perceives Hector Xavier Monsegur to be an informant or a privateer will determine whether the response will be channeled through existing law enforcement cooperation mechanisms or through military escalation. This case also raises questions under US law. (One could ask if Monsegur needed a letter of marque and reprisal under Article 1, Section 8, of the US Constitution.) A more practical question is whether the guidelines for informants' actions have been updated to take into account the potential implications for foreign relations in the digital age. For understandable reasons, the court documents deliberately limited the information about the types of websites and countries targeted as part of Monsegur's activities. However, this omission leaves unresolved whether the hacks abroad were part of a law enforcement operation or an intelligence one – and whether Monsegur was intentionally or unintentionally used as a proxy. Was this an exception or is this practice more common? Are other countries using informants in a similar fashion?

Another issue that remains under-studied is the empowerment of the individual generally. As Nazli Choucri, a political science professor at MIT, argued, "Cyberspace empowers and enables individuals in ways that were previously not possible."[13] This again highlights the importance of expertise and skills in this area – raising the question of whether such individuals require special treatment. The empowerment of a single individual deserves further attention, even as it illustrates the broader trend of the diffusion of power that is challenging existing norms and changing thinking about the status of individuals.[14] In terms of potential policy options, the International Science and Technology Centre, established in 1992 after the collapse of the Soviet Union, is an interesting case study. The center was set up to "create opportunities for weapons scientists and engineers in the former Soviet Union to work on nonmilitary projects" because they had lost their jobs.[15] Given the state of the Russian economy, there was concern that without such support they would offer their expertise for hire elsewhere, thereby posing a threat to nuclear non-proliferation. This multilateral effort includes the European Union, Norway, the US, Canada, Japan, and South Korea, and focuses on Russia, Ukraine, Armenia, Belarus, Georgia, Kazakhstan, Kyrgyzstan, and Tajikistan as recipient states. Some 75,000 scientists have benefited from the program with funding totaling nearly USD 1 billion.[16]

The centre is a good example that economic measures are useful not only because they can impose a cost on undesirable behavior; they can also be used to create a positive incentive for changing behavior – a lever that may be especially effective in the case of cybercriminals driven by profit. This kind of positive incentive is one of the most neglected instruments for changing a proxy's behavior. For example, one could imagine a program tailored to countries that have a pool of highly skilled technical labor but limited ability to absorb it all. Given that sophisticated cyber capabilities are tied to expertise and that quality matters more than quantity, such a program could focus on improving local business opportunities through foreign direct investments or, where corruption is rife, offer opportunities elsewhere through visa sponsor programs. Clearly, such incentives would work only for profit-driven actors, not the politically driven, and national security concerns would need to be addressed depending on the country's history and relations. Nevertheless, anecdotal evidence suggests that many participants in the black market would consider options that would allow them to avoid the challenges of fluctuating income and an uncertain future. As a former black-hat hacker told me in Kiev, "I eventually realized that I was even better as a manager than as a hacker. Now, I employ several former black hats who, as they grew older, were looking for a job with steady income especially once they got married and had kids."[7] However effective such strategies may be practically, they are also among the least feasible politically, as they usually require long-term rather than short-term investment and do not necessarily satisfy the demand for justice. Related strategies to combat poverty and corruption take years if not decades to show lasting impact.

More work is required on how to conceptualize sophistication in the context of offensive cyber operations. For example, one trend is that offensive cyber operations are reaching further down the stack and being buried deeper inside the targeted systems.[18] In addition, there seems to be a trend of an increasing number of offensive cyber operations relying on a mix of malware such as malware developed for criminal purposes and subsequently incorporated in political campaigns. (This also makes distinctions between criminal and military malware – "crimeware" versus "milware" – less meaningful.[19]) For example, the malware called BlackEnergy, which initially appeared on cyber-crime markets in 2007, was subsequently used for the DDoS attack against Georgia and was also adapted for political espionage with additional tailored code.[20] In 2014, the Finnish firm F-Secure published a report describing BlackEnergy being deployed against government organizations in Ukraine. The report concluded by stating that "the use of BlackEnergy for a politically-oriented attack is an intriguing convergence of criminal activity and espionage. As the kit is being used by multiple groups, it provides a greater measure of plausible deniability than is afforded by a custom-made piece of code."[21] And Kaspersky Lab found BlackEnergy being used in combination with SCADA-related plugins to target industrial control systems.[22] The combination of existing malware with new customized code illustrates the increasing modularity and commoditization of offensive cyber operations and the increasing separation between malware developers and malware deployers.

Information about vulnerable SCADA systems and how to exploit industrial control systems is available for purchase on the underground. The fact that we have not yet seen more serious incidents involving these systems suggests that although the supply exists, demand has thus far been low.[23] But there are signs that more actors are showing an interest in acquiring such capabilities and an intent to use them. For example, in March 2016, news emerged that a hacktivist group linked to Syria gained access to a water utility's control system in an unspecified country. Reports said that "In at least two instances, they managed to manipulate the system to alter the amount of chemicals that went into the water supply and thus handicap water treatment and production capabilities so that the recovery time to replenish water supplies increased."[24] It is therefore an issue to watch.

An additional line of research will need to focus on attribution capabilities (which are highly asymmetric), their evolution, and the effect of such asymmetries. Importantly, attribution capabilities are not static. Some researchers are actively trying to solve the attribution "problem." For example, the "Enhanced Attribution Program" of DARPA, the Defense Advanced Research Projects Agency in the United States, aims to enable the government not only to "characterize the attacker but also share the attacker's *modus operandi* with prospective victims and predict where he or she will strike next."[25] At the same time, other researchers have been trying to strengthen pseudonymity and anonymity online after reading the material Edward Snowden had exposed. Attribution capabilities are also not limited to states – as Microsoft's proposal for an attribution council composed of government and non-governmental actors demonstrates.[26] Cyber threat intelligence companies like Mandiant play an increasingly important role in naming and shaming. For example, iSight, a company bought by FireEye in 2016 (FireEye also acquired Mandiant in 2014), has a staff of over 200 cyber threat intelligence analysts, which would place iSight, "if it were a government-run cyber intelligence agency, among the 10 largest in the world."[27] Studying these non-governmental attribution capabilities and their implications for international relations is an important stand-alone line of research.

A top priority must be the study of offensive cyber operations and the use of social media in the context of elections. The incidents in eastern Europe during the 2016 US elections, and the 2017 European elections, show the urgency of this issue. A March 2016 Bloomberg portrait of the hacker Andres Sepulveda provides a rare insight into the inner workings of such campaigns. Sepulveda is a hacker currently serving a ten-year prison sentence in Colombia on various cyber-crime charges related to the Colombian presidential election in 2014. (He is not to be confused with Daniel Sepulveda, US ambassador and Deputy Assistant Secretary of State and US Coordinator for International Communications and Information Policy.[28]) According to Sepulveda, "[m]y job was to do actions of dirty war and psychological operations, black propaganda, rumors – the whole dark side of politics that nobody knows exists but everyone can see," and he allegedly traveled to over half a dozen countries over the span of eight years to influence elections. The cost of his services varied: "For $12,000 a month, a customer hired a crew that could hack smartphones, spoof and clone Web pages, and send mass e-mails and texts. The premium package, at $20,000 a month, also included a full range of digital interception, attack, decryption, and defense." The money was channeled through middlemen and, according to Sepulveda, some of the targeted candidates might not have been aware of his work.[29] His claims suggest that this phenomenon is not limited to North America or Europe but extends to Latin America, and that it is not only the Russian government that is conducting such operations. In short, apparently, we have only seen the tip of the iceberg so far.

The last area to highlight for future research is cyber terrorism. To start, there is the important analytical distinction between the terrorist use of the Internet and cyber terrorism.[30] A terrorist using the Internet is like any other Internet user – using search engines, social media, etc., except for a terrorist purpose. Cyber terrorism, however, is a terrorist act carried out through hacking. Peter Singer and Allan Friedman pointed out that while tens of thousands of articles on cyber terrorism had been written in magazines and journals when they wrote their book, not a single person had been physically hurt by cyber terrorism.[31] However, that does not mean that terrorists have not been interested in causing harm through offensive cyber operations.[32] The Islamic State, for example, has shown an interest in hacking the US electrical grid.[33]

So far, these efforts have remained at a very low level of sophistication, but there are signs that they are evolving. In 2015, for the first time, the US Department of Justice charged a terrorist suspect with hacking. The Kosovo citizen Ardit Ferizi was arrested in Malaysia on a US provisional arrest warrant, accused of having "provided material support to the Islamic State of Iraq and the Levant" by hacking and copying personal data of US service members and passing it to Junaid Hussain, a British citizen and member of the Islamic State.[34] Hussain subsequently posted the data – including names, phone numbers, and locations – online, encouraging supporters to attack the service members so exposed.[35] In another striking development, Hussain was targeted and killed by a drone strike in Raqqa, Syria, only a few weeks later.[36] In other words, there are now empirical examples not only of terrorists engaged in offensive cyber operations of growing consequence but also of a state actively killing such actors because of such activity and connected threats of violence. Cyber terrorism is therefore an issue not to be neglected in the years to come.

Notes

PREFACE

1. Vitaly Shevchenko, "'Little Green Men' or 'Russian Invaders'?", *BBC News*, March 11, 2014, www.bbc.com/news/world-europe-26532154.
2. "Ukraine crisis: Deadly Anti-Autonomy Protest Outside Parliament," *BBC News*, August 31, 2015, www.bbc.com/news/world-europe-34105925.
3. "Cyber Warrior Steps Up Effort to Help in War with Russia," *KyivPost*, February 10, 2015, www.kyivpost.com/content/kyiv-post-plus/cyber-warrior-steps-up-effort-to-help-in-war-with-russia-380184.html.
4. Peter Rollberg, *Historical Dictionary of Russian and Soviet Cinema* (Lanham, MD: Scarecrow Press, 2009), 199–200.
5. "Cyber Warrior Steps Up Effort."
6. Aric Toler, "Ukrainian Hackers Leak Russian Interior Ministry Docs with 'Evidence' of Russian Invasion," *Global Voices*, December 13, 2014, https://globalvoices.org/2014/12/13/ukrainian-hackers-leak-russian-interior-ministry-docs-with-evidence-of-russian-invasion/; Vijai Maheshwari, "Ukraine's Lonely Cyberwarrior vs. Russia," *Daily Beast*, February 18, 2015, www.thedailybeast.com/articles/2015/02/18/ukraine-s-lonely-cyber-warrior.html.
7. Nadiya Kostyuk and Yuri M. Zhukov, "Invisible Digital Front: Physical Violence and Cyber Warfare in Ukraine," unpublished paper dated March 15, 2016, 21–22.
8. Toler, "Ukrainian Hackers Leak Russian Interior Ministry Docs."
9. Andrei Soldatov and Irina Borogan, *The Red Web: The Struggle Between Russia's Digital Dictators and the New Online Revolutionaries* (New York: Public Affairs, 2015), 288.
10. Richard A. Clarke and Robert K. Knake, *Cyber War: The Next Threat to National Security and What to Do About It* (New York: Ecco, 2011); Thomas Rid, *Cyber War Will Not Take Place* (New York: Oxford University Press, 2013); Erik Gartzke, "The Myth of Cyberwar: Bringing War in Cyberspace Back Down to Earth," *International Security* 38(2) (Fall 2013).
11. Lucian Constantin, "Researcher Finds Over 20 Vulnerabilities in SCADA Software," *CIO*, November 26, 2012, www.cio.com/article/2390147/securityo/

researcher-finds-over-20-vulnerabilities-in-scada-software.html; David Kushner, "Fear This Man," *Foreign Policy*, April 26, 2016, http://foreignpolicy.com/2016/04/26/fear-this-man-cyber-warfare-hacking-team-david-vincenzetti/; Gabriella Coleman, *Hacker, Hoaxer, Whistleblower, Spy: The Many Faces of Anonymous* (New York: Verso, 2014); Max Fisher, "Syrian Hackers Claim AP Hack That Tipped Stock Market by \$136 Billion. Is It Terrorism?" *Washington Post*, April 23, 2013, www.washingtonpost.com/news/worldviews/wp/2013/04/23/syrian-hackers-claim-ap-hack-that-tipped-stock-market-by-136-billion-is-it-terrorism/.

12. Nicole Perlroth and David E. Sanger, "Nations Buying as Hackers Sell Flaws in Computer Code," *New York Times*, July 14, 2013, www.nytimes.com/2013/07/14/world/europe/nations-buying-as-hackers-sell-computer-flaws.html.

13. Kevin Cirilli, "Hackers Have Powers Beyond Most Countries, Expert Says," *The Hill*, October 20, 2014, http://thehill.com/policy/cybersecurity/221287-hackers-have-powers-beyond-most-countries-says-expert.

14. This question mirrors the opening line of Janice Thomson's seminal work on privateers published in 1994: "Why Are Global Coercive Capabilities Organized the Way They Are?" (Janice E. Thomson, *Mercenaries, Pirates, and Sovereigns: State-Building and Extraterritorial Violence in Early Modern Europe* (Princeton University Press, 1994), 3.)

15. An important word of caution: the indictment of the Iranian hackers makes clear that "the entirety of the text of the Indictment, and the description of the Indictment set forth herein, constitute only allegations, and every fact described should be treated as an allegation." The same applies to all other indictments referenced in this text.
    "Manhattan U.S. Attorney Announces Charges Against Seven Iranians for Conducting Coordinated Campaign of Cyber Attacks Against U.S. Financial Sector on Behalf of Islamic Revolutionary Guard Corps-Sponsored Entities," US Department of Justice, US Attorney's Office for the Southern District of New York, March 24, 2016, www.justice.gov/usao-sdny/pr/manhattan-us-attorney-announces-charges-against-seven-iranians-conducting-coordinated; "Computer Hacking Conspiracy Charges Unsealed Against Members of Syrian Electronic Army," US Department of Justice, March 22, 2016, www.justice.gov/opa/pr/computer-hacking-conspiracy-charges-unsealed-against-members-syrian-electronic-army.

16. "U.S. Charges Russian FSB Officers and Their Criminal Conspirators for Hacking Yahoo and Millions of Email Accounts," Department of Justice press release (March 15, 2017), www.justice.gov/opa/pr/us-charges-russian-fsb-officers-and-their-criminal-conspirators-hacking-yahoo-and-millions.

17. Aliya Sternstein, "Here Are the Companies That Won a Spot on \$460m Cyber Command Deal," *Nextgov*, May 23, 2016, www.nextgov.com/cybersecurity/2016/05/cybercom-inks-460m-operations-support-deal-booz-saic-others/128523/; United States Cyber Command (USCYBERCOM) Omnibus Contract, Solicitation No. HC1028-15-R-0026 (2015), 18.

18. Robert Sheldon and Joe McReynolds, "Civil Military Integration and Cybersecurity: A Study of Chinese Information Warfare Militias," in *China*

and Cybersecurity: Espionage, Strategy, and Politics in the Digital Domain, ed.
Jon R. Lindsay, Tai Ming Cheung, and Derek S. Reveron (New York: Oxford
University Press, 2015), 188–224.

19. Eneken Tikk, Kadri Kaska, and Liis Vihul, *International Cyber Incidents: Legal
Considerations* (Tallinn: Cooperative Cyber Defence Centre of Excellence,
2010), 23–24.

20. Jordan Robertson, Michael Riley, and Andrew Willis, "How to Hack an
Election," *Bloomberg Businessweek*, March 31, 2016, www.bloomberg.com/fea
tures/2016-how-to-hack-an-election/.

21. David Kushner, "Fear This Man," *Foreign Policy*, April 26, 2016, http://
foreignpolicy.com/2016/04/26/fear-this-man-cyber-warfare-hacking-team
-david-vincenzetti/.

22. Daniel Byman, "Passive Sponsors of Terrorism," *Survival* 47(4) (2005).

23. In-person conversation in May 2016. The employee preferred to remain
anonymous.

24. "Helsinki Accords," *Encyclopaedia Britannica Online*, last updated April 10,
2012, www.britannica.com/event/Helsinki-Accords.

25. This facet of the cybersecurity discussion lends itself to further research focus-
ing on the potential "securitization" of the human rights debate; see
Barry Buzan, Ole Wæver, and Jaap de Wilde, *Security: A New Framework for
Analysis* (Boulder, CO: Lynne Rienner, 1998); Myriam Dunn Cavelty, "From
Cyber-Bombs to Political Fallout," *International Studies Review* 15(1) (2013);
Myriam Dunn Cavelty, *Cyber-Security and Threat Politics* (New York:
Routledge, 2008).

26. Erica D. Borghard and Shawn W. Lonergan, "Can States Calculate the Risks of
Using Cyber Proxies?", *Orbis* 60(3) (2016).

27. James T. Areddy, "Xinjiang Arrests Nearly Doubled in '14, Year of 'Strike-Hard'
Campaign," *Wall Street Journal*, January 23, 2015, http://blogs.wsj.com/chinar
ealtime/2015/01/23/xinjiang-arrests-nearly-doubled-in-14-year-of-strike-hard-cam
paign/.

1 CYBER PROXIES: AN INTRODUCTION

1. Niccolò Machiavelli, *The Prince* (first published 1532, Dover Publications, 1992);
Janice E. Thomson, *Mercenaries, Pirates, and Sovereigns: State-Building and
Extraterritorial Violence in Early Modern Europe* (Princeton University Press,
1994); Max Weber, "Politik als Beruf," *Gesammelte Politische Schriften* (Munich,
1921).

2. "Who Controls Cyberspace? A Puzzle for National Security and International
Relations" (conference, Explorations in Cyber International Relations,
Cambridge, MA, November 6–7, 2012), http://ecir.mit.edu/index.php/events/
ecir-workshops/263-who-controls-cyberspace.

3. Michael Mann, *The Sources of Social Power, Vol. I: A History of Power from the
Beginning to AD 1760* (New York: Cambridge University Press, 1986), 11.

4. Ariel Ahram uses the term "broker" in Ariel Ahram, "Origins and Persistence of State-Sponsored Militias: Path Dependent Processes in Third World Military Development," *Journal of Strategic Studies* 34(4) (2011): 551.

5. Philip Bobbitt describes the "market state" in Philip Bobbitt, *The Shield of Achilles: War, Peace, and the Course of History* (New York: Anchor Books, 2003).

6. See Avant and Chayes for a good discussion; Deborah D. Avant, *The Market for Force: The Consequences of Privatizing Security* (New York: Cambridge University Press, 2005); Sarah Chayes, *Thieves of State: Why Corruption Threatens Global Security* (New York: W.W. Norton & Company, 2016).

7. Weber, "Politik als Beruf."

8. Richard A. Clarke and Robert K. Knake, *Cyber War: The Next Threat to National Security and What to Do About It* (New York: Ecco, 2011); Thomas Rid, *Cyber War Will Not Take Place* (New York: Oxford University Press, 2013).

9. Nicole Perlroth and Michael Corkery, "North Korea Linked to Digital Attacks on Global Banks," DealBook (blog), *New York Times*, May 26, 2016, www .nytimes.com/2016/05/27/business/dealbook/north-korea-linked-to-digital-thefts-from-global-banks.html.

10. In the Bangladeshi case, the hackers "only" stole USD 81 million. "Bangladesh Probes 2013 Hack for Links to Swift-Linked Central Bank Heist," Reuters, May 25, 2016, www.cnbc.com/2016/05/25/bangladesh-probes-2013-hack-for-links-to-swift-linked-central-bank-heist.html.

11. "Cyber Crime Ring Steals up to $1 Billion from Banks: Kaspersky," *Reuters*, February 14, 2015, www.reuters.com/article/us-cybersecurity-banks-idUSKBN0LJ02E20150215.

12. "Motor Vehicles Increasingly Vulnerable to Remote Exploits" (Public Service Announcement, Alert No. I-031716-PSA), Federal Bureau of Investigation, March 17, 2016, www.ic3.gov/media/2016/160317.aspx.

13. William J. Lynn III, "Defending a New Domain: The Pentagon's Cyber Strategy," *Foreign Affairs* (September 2010), www.foreignaffairs.com/articles/ united-states/2010–09-01/defending-new-domain.

14. Jason Healey, "Introduction," in *A Fierce Domain: Conflict in Cyberspace, 1986 to 2012*, ed. Jason Healey (Vienna, VA: Cyber Conflict Studies Association, 2013).

15. Joseph S. Nye, Jr, *The Future of Power* (New York: Public Affairs, 2011); Alexander Klimburg, "Mobilising Cyber Power," *Survival* 53 (2011): 43, 56.

16. Machiavelli, *The Prince*, 31.

17. United Nations, "Report of the Group of Governmental Experts on Developments in the Field of Information and Telecommunications in the Context of International Security," June 24, 2013, UN Doc. A/68/98.

18. Ibid., July 22, 2015, UN Doc. A/70/174.

19. Avant, *The Market for Force*, 24. I will follow and adopt Avant's persuasive reasoning and approach: "In keeping with the most common usage, I will use 'private' to refer to non-governmental actors. Commercial entities and NGOs

fall into this category – however, so do vigilantes, paramilitaries, and organized crime bosses. Though I will use public to denote governmental institutions of whatever sort, because the meaning of public is associated with the pursuit of collective ends, my analysis will distinguish between governments that have the capacity and legitimacy to claim to work toward collective ends and those that do not."

20. Daniel Kuehl, "From Cyberspace to Cyber Power: Defining the Problem," in *Cyberpower and National Security*, ed. Franklin D. Kramer, Stuart H. Starr, and Larry K. Wentz (Dulles, VA: Potomac Books, 2009), 38.

21. Nye, *The Future of Power*, 123; see also David J. Betz and Tim Stevens, "Chapter One: Power and Cyberspace," *Adelphi Series* 51 (2011); Kuehl, "From Cyberspace to Cyber Power"; John B. Sheldon, "Deciphering Cyber Power: Strategic Purpose in Peace and War," *Strategic Studies Quarterly* (Summer 2011): 95–112; and, for a Chinese perspective, Li Zhang, "A Chinese Perspective on Cyber War," *International Review of the Red Cross* 94 (2012). What these definitions have in common is that they are agency-oriented and actor-centric and do not focus on institutions or structures. See Michael Barnett and Raymond Duvall, "Power in International Politics," *International Organization* 59(1) (2005) for comprehensive discussion of power.

22. Nye, *The Future of Power*, 128.

23. Rid, *Cyber War Will Not Take Place*.

24. See, for example, Jon R. Lindsay and Erik Gartzke, "Coercion Through Cyberspace: The Stability–Instability Paradox Revisited," forthcoming in Kelly Greenhill and Peter Krause, eds., *The Power to Hurt: Coercion in the Modern World* (2017), 17.

25. Robert Jervis, "Force in Our Times," *International Relations* 25(4) (2011): 406.

26. Herman Kahn, *On Escalation: Metaphors and Scenarios* (New York: Fredrick A. Praeger, 1965), 15.

27. Thomas Schelling, *Arms and Influence* (New Haven, CT: Yale University Press, 2008), 3.

28. Ibid., 32.

29. K. J. Holsti, "The Concept of Power in the Study of International Relations," *Background* 7(3) (1964): 190.

30. Robert Belk and Matthew Noyes, *On the Use of Offensive Cyber Capabilities: A Policy Analysis on Offensive US Cyber Policy* (Cambridge, MA: Harvard University Belfer Center for Science and International Affairs, 2012).

31. Ibid.

32. Noyes and Belk limit the use of the term "offensive" to cyber operations with disruptive or damaging effects, excluding "the broader set of cyber activity that produces no significant effect or is benign in nature." They consider offensive objectives to be "those seeking to coerce rival action, impose harm, or degrade rival capabilities," while "informational objectives seek either to access or to expose information that is not generally, or publicly, available." However, in the international context, countries will disagree as to whether an effect is significant or benign, and indeed this question lies at the center of the geopolitical

debate. As noted earlier, China and Russia consider information dissemination a potential threat to their regimes' stability. Meanwhile, Germany and Brazil have been leading the charge to delegitimize offensive cyber operations for collection purposes – in other words political espionage. Even the US government uses different approaches for what it considers to be legitimate depending on the context. In the international context, the US government has been very careful to exclude content from its definition of threats to cybersecurity and to exclude political espionage from its calls for international cybersecurity norms. Yet, domestically, the US government has criminalized, through the Computer Fraud and Abuse Act, all intentional "external cyber actions," outlawing any unauthorized access to computer systems except those lawfully conducted by US government agencies. Belk and Noyes, *On the Use of Offensive Cyber Capabilities*, 18, 21; 18 U.S.C. § 1030.

33. Confidentiality, integrity, and availability of information are the three main elements specified in the International Organization for Standardization (ISO) Standard 27000. "ISO/IEC 27000:2012(en)," ISO, www.iso.org/obp/ui/#iso:std: iso-iec:27000:ed-2:v1:en.

34. This book will also use the terms "cyber action" and "cyber operation" interchangeably; the latter is the more common term in the cybersecurity literature (though one could technically draw a distinction that an operation consists of multiple actions). See, for example, Presidential Policy Directive 20 and Marco Roscini, *Cyber Operations and the Use of Force in International Law* (New York: Oxford University Press, 2014).

35. Herbert Lin, "Escalation Dynamics and Conflict Termination in Cyberspace," *Strategic Studies Quarterly* (Fall 2012): 46–47; Trey Herr builds on this framework with his PrEP (propagation method, exploit and payload) model which adds a useful list of different propagation methods from compromised website and certificate authorities to email attachments and removable devices: Trey Herr, *PrEP: A Framework for Malware and Cyber Weapons* (Washington, DC: George Washington University Cyber Security Policy and Research Institute, 2014).

36. Belk and Noyes, *On the Use of Offensive Cyber Capabilities*, 18; similarly, Heather Harrison Dinniss distinguishes between "content-level data" and "operational-level data – also known as logical-level data." Heather A Harrison Dinniss, "The Nature of Objects: Targeting Networks and the Challenge of Defining Cyber Military Objectives," *Israel Law Review* 48(1) (2015): 41.

37. Barack Obama, "Presidential Policy Directive 41," Office of the Press Secretary, the White House, July 26, 2016, https://web.archive.org/web/20160729134917/ https://www.whitehouse.gov/sites/whitehouse.gov/files/documents/Cyber%2BIncident%2BSeverity%2BSchema.pdf.

38. This book's definition differs from those of authors who define cyber proxies as "non-state actor(s) that conduct offensive cyber operations to achieve political objectives on behalf of a patron state. A patron state may provide training, equipment, and logistical support to a cyber proxy, enabling them to fight

indirectly on its behalf. This definition excludes operations conducted for the sole purpose of espionage, although it can be difficult for targets of these operations to differentiate between offense and espionage, given that the latter is a necessary component of the former." (Erica D. Borghard and Shawn W. Lonergan, "Can States Calculate the Risks of Using Cyber Proxies?", *Orbis* 60 (3) (2016): 406.) Borghard and Lonergan's definition is not used for the reasons discussed, including the desire not to limit the definition to disruptive or destructive effects due to the potentially changing nature of a proxy's activities and to include effects such as those of the DNC hack or cyber-enabled theft of intellectual property for commercial purposes.

39. Email correspondence with Beau Woods dated March 21, 2017.

40. Leo Kelion, "Fatal A400M Crash Linked to Data-Wipe Mistake," *BBC News*, June 10, 2015, www.bbc.com/news/technology-33078767.

41. Brian Krebs, "Cyber Incident Blamed for Nuclear Power Plant Shutdown," *Washington Post*, June 5, 2008, www.washingtonpost.com/wp-dyn/content/article/2008/06/05/AR2008060501958.html.

42. *Air Traffic Control: FAA Needs a More Comprehensive Approach to Address Cybersecurity As Agency Transitions to NextGen*, GAO-15-360 (Washington, DC: Government Accountability Office, 2015), www.gao.gov/products/GAO-15-370.

43. Patrik Maldre, *Global Connections, Regional Implications: An Overview of the Baltic Cyber Threat Landscape* (Tallinn: International Centre for Defence and Security, 2015), 21.

44. Andrey Nikishin, "ICS Threats. A Kaspersky Lab View, Predictions and Reality," presentation at RSA Conference, Moscone Center, San Francisco, CA, February 29 – March 4, 2016.

45. Krebs, "Cyber Incident Blamed for Nuclear Power Plant Shutdown."

46. "Analysis of the Cyber Attack on the Ukrainian Power Grid," E-ISAC and SANS, March 18, 2016, https://ics.sans.org/media/E-ISAC_SANS_Ukraine_DUC_5.pdf.

47. John Leyden, "Water Treatment Plant Hacked, Chemical Mix Changed for Tap Supplies," *The Register*, March 24, 2016, www.theregister.co.uk/2016/03/24/water_utility_hacked/.

48. Ibid.

49. "Hacktivists Mess with Chemicals in Water Treatment Plant," *Nextgov*, http://www.nextgov.com/cybersecurity/threatwatch/2016/03/software-vulnerability-social-engineering-scada/2624/.

50. Jose Pagliery, "The Inside Story of the Biggest Hack in History," *CNN*, August 5, 2015, http://money.cnn.com/2015/08/05/technology/aramco-hack/.

51. Ibid.

52. Kim Zetter, "Hacker Lexicon: What Is a Zero Day?", *Wired*, November 11, 2014, www.wired.com/2014/11/what-is-a-zero-day/.

53. Adam Meyers, "VICEROY TIGER Delivers New Zero-Day Exploit," CrowdStrike Blog, November 6, 2013, www.crowdstrike.com/blog/viceroy-tiger-delivers-new-zero-day-exploit/.

54. Nicole Perlroth, "Report Says Cyberattacks Originated Inside Iran," *New York Times*, December 2, 2014, www.nytimes.com/2014/12/03/world/middleeast/report-says-cyberattacks-originated-inside-iran.html.

55. Jon R. Lindsay and Lucas Kello, "Correspondence: A Cyber Disagreement," *International Security* 39(2) (2014): 184.

56. Brian Krebs, "Story-Driven Résumé: My Best Work 2005–2009," Krebs on Security (blog), December 29, 2009, https://krebsonsecurity.com/2009/12/story-driven-resume-my-best-work-2005–2009-3/.

57. I thank Morgan Marquis-Boire and a former government official who preferred to remain anonymous for their input to this section.

58. Thomas Rid and Peter McBurney, "Cyber-Weapons," *RUSI Journal* 157(1) (2012): 11.

59. Jon R. Lindsay, "The Impact of China on Cybersecurity: Fiction and Friction," *International Security* 39(3) (Winter 2014/15): 34.

60. Michael J. Assante and Robert M. Lee, *The Industrial Control System Cyber Kill Chain* (SANS Institute Reading Room, 2015), 1.

61. Dale Peterson, "Offensive Cyber Weapons: Construction, Development, and Employment," *Journal of Strategic Studies* 36(1) (2013).

62. Andrea Peterson, "The NSA Has Its Own Team of Elite Hackers," *Washington Post*, August 29, 2013, www.washingtonpost.com/news/the-switch/wp/2013/08/29/the-nsa-has-its-own-team-of-elite-hackers/.

63. James C. Mulvenon, "Chinese Cyber Espionage," Testimony before the Congressional-Executive Commission on China, June 25, 2013. Gary Brown and Owen Tullos (respectively the former first Staff Judge Advocate and deputy Staff Judge Advocate at US Cyber Command) have also highlighted stealth as a key distinguishing variable in their spectrum of cyber operations, ranging from more stealthy to less stealthy corresponding with ranging from enabling operations (more stealthy) to cyber disruption and cyber attack (less stealthy): Gary D. Brown and Owen W. Tullos, "On the Spectrum of Cyberspace Operations," *Small Wars Journal*, December 11, 2012, http://smallwarsjournal.com/print/13595.

64. "About Us," GLEG, http://gleg.net/about.shtml.

65. "GLEG," GLEG, http://gleg.net/.

66. "Scada+ Pack," GLEG, http://gleg.net/agora_scada.shtml.

67. Michael N. Schmitt and Sean Watts, "Beyond State-Centrism: International Law and Non-state Actors in Cyberspace," *Journal of Conflict & Security Law* (published online, August 13, 2016), 2.

68. Nye, *The Future of Power*.

69. Tony Smith, "Hacker Jailed for Revenge Sewage Attacks," *The Register*, October 31, 2001, www.theregister.co.uk/2001/10/31/hacker_jailed_for_revenge_sewage/.

70. Juan C. Zarate, *The Cyber Financial Wars on the Horizon: The Convergence of Financial and Cyber Warfare and the Need for a 21st Century National Security Response* (Washington, DC: FDD Press, 2015), 6, 10.

71. "Cyber Leaders: A Discussion with the Honorable Eric Rosenbach" (panel discussion, Center for Strategic and International Studies, Washington, DC, October 2, 2014), http://csis.org/event/cyber-leaders. Gary Brown and Owen Tullos, the former Staff Judge Advocate and Deputy Staff Judge Advocate at US Cyber Command, have also done some excellent thinking about the spectrum of cyber operations, complementing how cyber operations fit into the broader spectrum of political activity: see Brown and Tullos, "On the Spectrum of Cyberspace Operations."

72. Teng Jianqun and Xu Longdi, *Cyber War Preparedness, Cyberspace Arms Control and the United States* (Beijing: China Institute of International Studies, 2014), 11.

73. Nigel Inkster, *China's Cyber Power* (New York: Routledge, 2016), 71.

74. Based on the cyber kill chain and the industrial control system cyber kill chain models; Lockheed Martin, "Gaining the Advantage: Applying Cyber Kill Chain Methodology to Network Defense," www.lockheedmartin.com/content/dam/lockheed/data/corporate/documents/Gaining_the_Advantage_Cyber_Kill_Chain.pdf; Assante and Lee, *The Industrial Control System Cyber Kill Chain.*

75. US Defense Science Board, *Resilient Military Systems and the Advanced Cyber Threat* (Washington, DC: Office of the Under Secretary of Defense for Acquisition, Technology and Logistics, 2013), 21–23.

76. Figure 1.3 differs from the Defense Science Board's taxonomy in that tier V is not limited to a state actor and by clarifying the distinction between tiers III and IV based on effects. See also this RAND study on the underground malware market considering botnet owners as in between unsophisticated and sophisticated actors while exploit developers, zero-day researchers, and malware writers represent subject matter experts falling into the highly skilled category. Penetration testers also fall into this category whereas reverse engineers have a special skill. Lillian Ablon, Martin C. Libicki, and Andrea A. Golay, *Markets for Cyber Crime Tools and Stolen Data: Hackers' Bazaar* (Santa Monica, CA: RAND Corporation, 2014), 6.

77. US Defense Science Board, *Resilient Military Systems and the Advanced Cyber Threat,* 21–23.

78. The fact that the Jester has been able to remain anonymous supports the assumption that he or she is an individual since communication between two or more people significantly increases the chance of detection.

79. Ashlee Vance, "WikiLeaks Struggles to Stay Online After Attacks," *New York Times,* December 3, 2010, www.nytimes.com/2010/12/04/world/europe/04domain.html.

80. Tammy Leitner and Lisa Capitanini, "'Patriotic Hackers' Claim to Fight Cyber War Against Terrorists," *NBC Chicago,* February 19, 2015, www.nbcchicago.com/news/local/Patriotic-Hackers-Cyber-War-Against-Terrorists-292825571.html.

81. Ibid.

82. John Leyden, "Patriot Hacker 'The Jester' Attacks Nations Offering Snowden Help," *The Register*, July 4, 2013, www.theregister.co.uk/2013/07/04/patri ot_hacker_takes_aim_snowden_asylum_candidates/.

83. T. J. O'Connor, *The Jester Dynamic: A Lesson in Asymmetric Unmanaged Cyber Warfare* (SANS Institute, 2011), www.sans.org/reading-room/whitepapers/attack ing/jester-dynamic-lesson-asymmetric-unmanaged-cyber-warfare-33889, 6, 18.

84. Ibid., 19–20.

85. Ibid., 25.

86. For example, the Jester encouraged over 80,000 Twitter followers to contribute to the Wounded Warrior Project, an organization supporting injured veterans. O'Connor, *The Jester Dynamic*, 3, 7.

87. In-person interview with Katie Moussouris in Washington, DC, on July 25, 2015.

88. Walter W. Powell, "Neither Market nor Hierarchy," *Research in Organizational Behavior* 12 (1990).

89. Jonathan Lusthaus, "Honour Among (Cyber)Thieves?", Extra Legal Governance Institute, University of Oxford, working paper no. 2016–1, www.exlegi.ox.ac.uk/images/Papers/HonourAmongCyberThieves.pdf, 31.

90. Kurt Thomas et al., "Framing Dependencies Introduced by Underground Commoditization," paper presented at the 2015 Workshop on the Economics of Information Security, Delft University of Technology, The Hague, The Netherlands, June 22–23, 2015.

91. Ablon et al., *Markets for Cyber Crime Tools*, 8–9.

92. Li Zhang, "A Chinese Perspective on Cyber War," *International Review of the Red Cross* 94 (2012): 805.

93. "India's Spy Agencies Explored 'Sypware' [*sic*] from Hacking Team: Leaked Mails on WikiLeaks," *Business Standard*, July 10, 2015, www.business-standard .com/article/current-affairs/india-s-spy-agencies-explored-sypware-from-hack ing-team-leaked-mails-on-wikileaks-115071001148_1.html.

94. CrowdStrike, *CrowdStrike Global Threat Report – 2013 Year in Review* (January 2014), 26; see also, Snorre Fagerland, Morten Kråkvik, and Jonathan Camp, *Operation Hangover – Unveiling an Indian Cyberattack Infrastructure* (San Diego, CA: Norman Shark, May 2013); Ellen Messmer, "Peculiar Malware Trail Raises Questions About Security Firm in India," *Network World*, May 20, 2013, www.networkworld.com/article/2167354/malware-cybercrime/peculiar- malware-trail-raises-questions-about-security-firm-in-india.html.

95. *The Information Security Specialist* (New Delhi, India: Appin Security Group), www.appincoimbatore.com/images/appin_profile.pdf.

96. Kaspersky Lab, *The "Icefog" APT: A Tale of Cloak and Three Daggers*, http://kasperskycontenthub.com/wp-content/uploads/sites/43/vlpdfs/icefog.pdf, 49–50.

97. Andrew Nusca, "Hayden: 'Digital Blackwater' May Be Necessary for Private Sector to Fight Cyber Threats," Between the Lines (blog), ZDNet, August 1, 2011, www.zdnet.com/blog/btl/hayden-digital-blackwater-may-be-necessary-for- private-sector-to-fight-cyber-threats/53639.

98. Peter Singer, *Corporate Warriors: The Rise of the Privatized Military Industry* (Ithaca, NY: Cornell University Press, 2003), 48.

99. Jenny Jun, Scott LaFoy, and Ethan Sohn, *North Korea's Cyber Operations: Strategy and Responses* (New York: Rowman & Littlefield, 2015), 55.

100. Cylance, *Operation Cleaver* (2015), https://cdn2.hubspot.net/hubfs/270968/ 2015_cylance_website/images/cleaver_page/Cylance_Operation_Cleaver_ Report.pdf?t=1475096805700, 63.

101. "Estonian Defence League's Cyber Unit," Estonian Defence League, www .kaitseliit.ee/en/cyber-unit.

102. Estonian Defence Forces," Estonian Defence Forces, www.mil.ee/en/ defence-forces.

103. "militia," Oxford Dictionaries, https://en.oxforddictionaries.com/definition/ militia.

104. Tom Gjelten, "Volunteer Cyber Army Emerges in Estonia," *NPR*, January 4, 2011, www.npr.org/2011/01/04/132634099/in-estonia-volunteer-cyber-army- defends-nation.

105. Karen Alter points out that principal–agent theory allows us to "locate different Agents along a continuum of highly 'controlled' Agents to highly 'autono- mous' Agents." However, this spectrum is still confined to the notion of delegation and arguably excludes looser relationships, notably the concept of sanctioning. Moreover, self-appointed proxies and sanctioning differ from other independent actors discussed in the scholarship, such as trustees, in that such trustees are chosen for their authority in order to strengthen the legiti- macy of a specific process. See Karen J. Alter, "Agents or Trustees? International Courts in Their Political Context." *European Journal of International Relations* 14.1 (2008): 36.

106. Richard Joseph, *Democracy and Prebendal Politics in Nigeria* (New York: Cambridge University Press, 1987).

107. Ariel Ahram, "Origins and Persistence of State-Sponsored Militias: Path Dependent Processes in Third World Military Development," *Journal of Strategic Studies* 34(4) (2011): 551.

108. Ibid., 537.

109. Rod Hague and Martin Harrop, *Comparative Government and Politics: An Introduction*, 9th ed. (New York: Palgrave MacMillan, 2013), 363.

110. North Korea is an example of an emerging cyber power that initially appeared to be a good candidate for a case study, especially considering reports of North Korean hackers conducting the Sony hack from a hotel in Thailand, the plausible deniability that the North Korean government would gain by using proxies, and the history of actors supporting North Korea from foreign terri- tories such as Japan. However, North Korea proved not to be a typical case of proxy use. During several in-person interviews, experts in Washington, DC, focusing on North Korea, officials in law enforcement and close to the intelligence services in South Korea, and security researchers in the region (including in countries with friendly ties to North Korea) agreed that these hackers were most likely not just loosely tied to the North Korean government

but were part of it. The North Korean government's obsession with control was one key reason for this assessment, and experts argued that the hackers operated from third countries because of North Korea's limited access to the Internet, which would make any malicious activity emanating directly from North Korean territory much easier to attribute directly. For these reasons, North Korea was excluded from the selected case studies. (It arguably represents a deviant case given its exceptional behavior and is certainly worth further research.)

For related literature, see HP Security Research, "Profiling an Enigma: The Mystery of North Korea's Cyber Threat Landscape," August 2014, https://community.hpe.com/hpeb/attachments/hpeb/off-by-on-software-security-blog/388/2/HPSR%20SecurityBriefing_Episode16_NorthKorea.pdf; see also James A. Lewis et al., "North Korea's Cyber Operations: Strategy and Responses," Center for Strategic and International Studies, Office of the Korea Chair, November 23, 2015, https://csis-prod.s3.amazonaws.com/s3fs-public/legacy_files/files/publication/151123_Cha_NorthKoreaCyber_handout_final.pdf; in-person interview with Jenny Jun in Washington, DC, on March 25, 2015; in-person interview with a South Korean cybersecurity expert in Seoul, South Korea, on May 8, 2015, and with a South Korean law enforcement officer in Seoul, South Korea, on May 9, 2015 (both the last two preferred to be listed anonymously); in-person interview with a Mongolian cybersecurity researcher, who also preferred to be listed anonymously, in Ulan Bator, Mongolia, on May 5, 2015.

111. Senate Committee on Armed Services, *Hearing to Receive Testimony on U.S. Strategic Command, U.S. Transportation Command, and U.S. Cyber Command in Review of the Defense Authorization Request for Fiscal Year 2016 and the Future Years' Defense Program*, 114th Congress, 1st session, March 19, 2015, transcript (Washington, DC: Alderson Reporting Company, 2015), 61.

112. Jason Healey, "The Spectrum of National Responsibility for Cyber Attacks," *Brown Journal of World Affairs* 18(1) (2011). While it is possible to argue that this level of nuance is too granular for policymaking and that there ought to be an agreement that the day job determines the person's status generally, it seems likely that governmental lawyers apply existing tests at this more granular level.

113. Erica D. Borghard and Shawn W. Lonergan, "Can States Calculate the Risks of Using Cyber Proxies?", *Orbis* 60(3) (2016): 408.

114. Ibid., 414.

115. See also Avant, who equates the provision of external security with "protecting borders" and internal security with "keeping order within borders." Avant, *The Market for Force*, 16.

116. According to the US Department of Defense, "a clandestine operation differs from a covert operation in that emphasis is placed on concealment of the operation rather than on concealment of the identity of the sponsor." William Safire, "Spookspeak," *New York Times*, February 13, 2005, www.nytimes.com/2005/02/13/magazine/spookspeak.html?_r=0.

117. The law of agency uses the terminology *disclosed/undisclosed*. "Agency (law)," *Encyclopaedia Britannica*, www.britannica.com/topic/agency-law; William

Draper Lewis, "The Liability of the Undisclosed Principal in Contract," *Columbia Law Review* 9(2) (1909): 116–135.

118. I thank Beau Woods for this point.
119. See, for example, Geraint Hughes's shedding new light on a joint covert operation by the UK and Oman in South Yemen in the 1970s after new material became available to the public. Hughes, "A Proxy War in Arabia."
120. Thomas Rid and Ben Buchanan, "Attributing Cyber Attacks," *Journal of Strategic Studies* 38(1–2) (2015): 4.
121. Eric Grosse, "Security Warnings for Suspected State-Sponsored Attacks," Google Security Blog, June 5, 2012, https://security.googleblog.com/2012/06/security-warnings-for-suspected-state.html.
122. Alex Stamos, "Notifications for Targeted Attacks," Facebook Security, October 16, 2016, www.facebook.com/notes/facebook-security/notifications-for-targeted-attacks/10153092994615766/.
123. Scott Charney, "Additional Steps to Help Keep Your Personal Information Secure," Microsoft on the Issues (official blog), December 30, 2015, http://blogs.microsoft.com/on-the-issues/2015/12/30/additional-steps-to-help-keep-your-personal-information-secure/.
124. Bob Lord, "Notifying Our Users of Attacks by Suspected State-Sponsored Actors," Yahoo!: The Paranoid (official blog), December 21, 2015, https://yahoo-security.tumblr.com/post/135674131435/notifying-our-users-of-attacks-by-suspected.
125. Rid and Buchanan, "Attributing Cyber Attacks," 4.
126. Krebs, "Story-Driven Résumé: My Best Work 2005–2009."
127. "Conversations with a Hacker: What Guccifer 2.0 Told Me," *BBC News*, January 14, 2017, www.bbc.com/news/blogs-trending-38610402.
128. The US intelligence agencies highlight that "[h]igh confidence generally indicates that judgments are based on high-quality information from multiple sources. High confidence in a judgment does not imply that the assessment is a fact or a certainty; such judgments might be wrong." See Office of the Director of National Intelligence, *Background to "Assessing Russian Activities and Intentions in Recent US Elections": The Analytic Process and Cyber Incident Attribution* (McLean, VA: Office of the Director of National Intelligence, January 2017).
129. Ibid., ii–iii.
130. Jeff Stone, "Meet Fancy Bear and Cozy Bear, Russian Groups Blamed for DNC Hack," Passcode (blog), *Christian Science Monitor*, June 15, 2016, www.csmonitor.com/World/Passcode/2016/0615/Meet-Fancy-Bear-and-Cozy-Bear-Russian-groups-blamed-for-DNC-hack.
131. Sheera Frenkel, "Meet the Mysterious New Hacker Army Freaking Out the Middle East," *BuzzFeed*, June 23, 2015, www.buzzfeed.com/sheerafrenkel/who-is-the-yemen-cyber-army; Lorenzo Franceschi-Bicchierai, "There's Evidence the 'Yemen Cyber Army' Is Actually Iranian," Motherboard, *Vice*, June 26, 2015, http://motherboard.vice.com/read/theres-evidence-the-yemen-cyber-army-is-actually-iranian; "Google Teams Up with CIA to Fund

'Recorded Future' Startup Monitoring Websites, Blogs & Twitter Accounts," *Democracy Now!*, July 30, 2010, www.democracynow.org/2010/7/30/google_teams_up_with_cia_to; Gili, "The Iranian-Saudi Conflict and Its Cyber Outlet," Recorded Future (blog), June 26, 2015, www.recordedfuture.com/iranian-saudi-cyber-conflict/.

132. Brian Bartholomew and Juan Andres Guerrero-Saade, "Wave Your False Flags! Deception Tactics Muddying Attribution in Targeted Attacks," paper presented at Virus Bulletin Conference, Denver, CO, October 5–7, 2016, https://securelist.com/files/2016/10/Bartholomew-GuerreroSaade-VB2016.pdf.

133. Angelos Keromytis, "Enhanced Attribution," Defense Advanced Research Projects Agency, www.darpa.mil/program/enhanced-attribution.

134. "David Sanger; Richard Haas; Jimmy Walker," *Charlie Rose*, August 1, 2016, https://charlierose.com/videos/28536.

135. Greg Austin offers an interesting discussion of the implications of cybersecurity from a middle power perspective; see Greg Austin, *Middle Powers and Cyber-Enabled Warfare: The Imperative of Collective Security* (Canberra: Australian Centre for Cyber Security, University of New South Wales Canberra, 2016), www.unsw.adfa.edu.au/australian-centre-for-cyber-security/sites/accs/files/uploads/DISCUSSION%20PAPER%20Middle%20Powers%20REARMED%2027%20Jan%202016.pdf.

136. Koh's speech remains the most up-to-date, detailed outline of the U.S. government's thinking on these issues by the time this book was being finalized in July of 2016; see Harold Hongju Koh, "International Law in Cyberspace" (USCYBERCOM Inter-Agency Legal Conference, Fort Meade, MD, September 18, 2012), www.state.gov/s/l/releases/remarks/197924.html.

137. John Kerry, Remarks at the Virtuous Circle Conference, Palo Alto, CA, October 10, 2016, www.state.gov/secretary/remarks/2016/10/262958.html.

138. John Gerring, "The Case Study: What It Is and What It Does," in *The Oxford Handbook of Comparative Politics*, ed. Carles Boix and Susan C. Stokes (New York: Oxford University Press, 2009), 10, 26.

139. Ibid., 26.

140. Ibid., 10.

141. Jack S. Levy, "Case Studies: Types, Designs, and Logics of Inference," *Conflict Management and Peace Science* 25 (2008): 6.

142. "Evolution of the Cyber Domain: The Implications for National and Global Security," International Institute for Strategic Studies, December 2, 2015, 54.

143. Nigel Inkster, *China's Cyber Power* (New York: Routledge, 2016), 124.

144. Lynn, "Defending a New Domain."

145. Nye, *The Future of Power*.

146. David E. Sanger, Michael S. Schmidt, and Nicole Perlroth, "Obama Vows a Response to Cyberattack on Sony," *New York Times*, December 19, 2014, http://www.nytimes.com/2014/12/20/world/fbi-accuses-north-korean-government-in-cyberattack-on-sony-pictures.html; Peter Elkind, "Inside the Hack of the Century," *Fortune*, July 1, 2015, http://fortune.com/sony-hack-part-1/;

Amanda Hess, "Inside the Sony Hack," *Slate*, November 22, 2015, http://www.slate.com/articles/technology/users/2015/11/sony_employee s_on_the_hack_one_year_later.html.

147. "Manhattan U.S. Attorney Announces Charges Against Seven Iranians for Conducting Coordinated Campaign of Cyber Attacks Against U.S. Financial Sector on Behalf of Islamic Revolutionary Guard Corps-Sponsored Entities," US Department of Justice, US Attorney's Office for the Southern District of New York, March 24, 2016, www.justice.gov/usao-sdny/pr/manhattan-us-attor ney-announces-charges-against-seven-iranians-conducting-coordinated.

148. Zachary Cohen, "The F-35: Is the World's Most Expensive Weapons Program Worth It?", *CNN*, July 16, 2015, www.cnn.com/2015/07/16/politics/f-35-jsf-operational-costs/.

149. Lindsay and Gartzke, "Coercion Through Cyberspace."

150. Tim Maurer, "SOLAR SUNRISE: Cyber Attack from Iraq?", in *A Fierce Domain: Conflict in Cyberspace, 1986 to 2012*, ed. Jason Healey (Vienna, VA: Cyber Conflict Studies Association, 2013).

151. Robert O. Keohane, "The Globalization of Informal Violence, Theories of World Politics, and 'The Liberalism of Fear,'" paper presented at the annual meeting of the American Political Science Association, Boston, MA, August 28, 2002.

152. Ibid.

153. James A. Lewis, "Cybersecurity and Stability in the Gulf," Center for Strategic and International Studies, January 2014, https://csis-prod.s3.amazo naws.com/s3fs-public/legacy_files/files/publication/140106_Lewis _GulfCybersecurity_Web_0.pdf; Michael Corkery, Jessica Silver-Greenberg, and David E. Sanger, "Obama Had Security Fears on JPMorgan Data Breach," *Dealbook* (blog), *New York Times*, October 8, 2014, http://dealbook .nytimes.com/2014/10/08/cyberattack-on-jpmorgan-raises-alarms-at-white-house-and-on-wall-street/; Matthew Goldstein, "U.S. Extends Investigation of JPMorgan Chase Hacking," Dealbook (blog), *New York Times*, July 28, 2015, www.nytimes.com/2015/07/29/business/us-extends-bank-breach-investigation .html?_r=0; Kim Zetter, "Four Indicted in Massive JPMorgan Chase Hack," *Wired*, November 10, 2015, www.wired.com/2015/11/four-indicted-in-massive-jp-morgan-chase-hack/.

154. Adam Segal, *The Hacked World Order: How Nations Fight, Trade, Maneuver, and Manipulate in the Digital Age* (New York: Public Affairs, 2016), 11.

155. Brian Krebs, "The Democratization of Censorship," Krebs on Security (blog), September 25, 2016, https://krebsonsecurity.com/2016/09/the-democratization-of-censorship/.

156. Kim Zetter, "NSA Acknowledges What We All Feared: Iran Learns from US Cyber Attacks," *Wired*, February 10, 2105, www.wired.com/2015/02/nsa-acknowledges-feared-iran-learns-us-cyberattacks/.

157. Singer, *Corporate Warriors*, 76.

158. Scott Henderson, "China Starting to Worry About Its Own Hackers," The Dark Visitor (blog), August 5, 2009, www.thedarkvisitor.com/category/hackers-talking/.

2 PROXIES: AN INSTRUMENT OF POWER SINCE ANCIENT TIMES

1. Thucydides, *History of the Peloponnesian War*, http://classics.mit.edu/Thucydides/pelopwar.html.
2. Geraint Hughes, *My Enemy's Enemy: Proxy Warfare in International Politics* (Portland, OR: Sussex Academic Press, 2014).
3. Harro von Senger, *The Book of Stratagems* (New York: Penguin Books, 1991); Timothy Thomas, "Nation-State Cyber Strategies: Examples from China and Russia," in *Cyber Power and National Security*, ed. Franklin D. Kramer, Stuart H. Starr, and Larry K. Wentz (Dulles, VA: Potomac Books, 2009).
4. "Thirty-Six Stratagems: Ancient Ruses Can Still Be Useful," *Shanghai Daily*, July 7, 2013, www.shanghaidaily.com/Vibe/now-and-then/%E4%B8%89%E5%8D%81%E5%85%AD%E8%AE%A1-ThirtySix-Stratagems-Ancient-ruses-can-still-be-useful/shdaily.shtml.
5. Deborah Avant, "The Implications of Marketized Security for IR Theory: The Democratic Peace, Late State Building, and the Nature and Frequency of Conflict," *Perspectives on Politics* 4(3) (2006): 509.
6. Cecily G. Brewer, "Peril by Proxy: Negotiating Conflicts in East Africa," *International Negotiation* 16(1) (2011); for a critique arguing that the Cold War connotation is too limited, see Mumford, *Proxy Warfare*, 97; *The Compact Edition of the Oxford English Dictionary: Complete Text Reproduced Micrographically – Vol. II, P–Z* (New York: Oxford University Press, 1971), 2342–2343.
7. "Proxy," *Merriam-Webster*, www.merriam-webster.com/dictionary/proxy.
8. Ariel Ahram, *Proxy Warriors: The Rise and Fall of State-Sponsored Militias* (Stanford University Press, 2011).
9. Idean Salehyan, "The Delegation of War to Rebel Organizations," *Journal of Conflict Resolution* 54 (2010): 496.
10. Chris Mark Wyatt, "Princes, Patriots, and Proxies: Great Power, Politics and the Assertion of Afghan Sovereignty," *Fletcher Security Review* I(II) (2014); Bertil Dunér, "Proxy Intervention in Civil Wars," *Journal of Peace Research* 18 (1981).
11. R. Kim Cragin, "Semi-Proxy Wars and U.S. Counterterrorism Strategy," *Studies in Conflict & Terrorism* 38 (2015); Michael A. Newton, "War by Proxy: Legal and Moral Duties of 'Other Actors' Derived from Government," *Case Western Reserve Journal of International Law* 23(2/3) (2006); Geraint Hughes, "A Proxy War in Arabia: The Dhofar Insurgency and Cross-Border Raids into South Yemen," *Middle East Journal* 69 (2015).
12. Dunér, "Proxy Intervention in Civil Wars."

13. To list a few definitions by other scholars, according to Mumford, proxy wars are "indirect engagement in a conflict by third parties wishing to influence its strategic outcome. They are constitutive of a relationship between a benefactor, who is a state or non-state actor external to the dynamic of an existing conflict, and their chosen proxies who are the conduit for weapons, training and funding from the benefactor." Mumford, *Proxy Warfare*, 11. According to Klare, "a proxy can be defined as a nation-state or political entity that conducts military activities on behalf of (and at the behest of) the U.S. government, usually under circumstances that preclude direct involvement by the United States itself. Proxies are similar to mercenaries in that they expect a consideration or quid pro quo of some sort in return for their cooperation; they are dissimilar, however, in that they may harbor strategic or ideological reasons of their own for carrying out the requested activity." Michael T. Klare, "Subterranean Alliances: America's Global Proxy Network," *Journal of International Affairs* 43(1) (1989). He and Mumford are among the few scholars who include both state and non-state actors in their definition of a proxy. Hughes in his article on Syria suggests that "a proxy war is defined here as one in which states (or sponsors) aid and abet non-state proxies involved in a conflict against a common adversary, or a target." Geraint Hughes, "Syria and the Perils of Proxy Warfare," *Small Wars & Insurgencies* 25(3) (2014): 523. Brewer defines a proxy war as "a conflict in which one party fights its adversary via another party rather than engaging that party in direct conflict," adding that "[t]he term 'proxy war' is typically associated with Cold War power struggles of the past. It connotes the United States and Union of Soviet Socialist Republics taking sides in third-country conflicts ... Superpower proxy support in these wars wreaked havoc across Africa, Asia, including Afghanistan, the Middle East and Latin America ... Proxy wars are inter-state conflicts fought via intra-state means." Brewer, "Peril by Proxy," 137–138. Herman J. Cohen, former US Assistant Secretary of State for African Affairs, argued that "a proxy war cab [*sic*] be defined as an internal conflict that has been orchestrated and supported almost entirely from the outside." Herman J. Cohen, "US-Africa Policy as Conflict Management," *SAIS Review* 21(1) (2001): 241. Abbink defines "proxy wars as being secondary, often 'low intensity' armed conflicts, pursued in the context of a major geopolitical power struggle or an outright war between states, carried out by subsidiary or co-opted insurgent movements, usually of an ethno-regional nature." Jon Abbink, "Ethiopia–Eritrea: Proxy Wars and Prospects of Peace in the Horn of Africa," *Journal of Contemporary African Studies* 21(3) (2003): 409.
14. Ahram, *Proxy Warriors*; Hughes, *My Enemy's Enemy*; Mumford, *Proxy Warfare*.
15. Philip Bobbitt, *The Shield of Achilles: War, Peace, and the Course of History* (New York: Anchor Books, 2003), 331.
16. Alex S. Wilner, "Apocalypse Soon? Deterring Nuclear Iran and Its Terrorist Proxies," *Comparative Strategy* 31(1) (2012): 22.
17. Hughes, "Syria and the Perils of Proxy Warfare," 522.
18. Klare, "Subterranean Alliances," 104; Brewer, "Peril by Proxy."

19. Karl W. Deutsch, "External Involvement in Internal Wars," in *Internal War: Problems and Approaches*, ed. Harry Eckstein (New York: Free Press of Glencoe, 1964), 102; Yaacov Bar-Siman-Tov, "The Strategy of War by Proxy," *Cooperation and Conflict* 19(4) (1984); Gérard Prunier, "Rebel Movements and Proxy Warfare: Uganda, Sudan and the Congo (1986–99)," *African Affairs* 103 (412) (2004): 359–383; Mumford, *Proxy Warfare*; Ariel Ahram, "Origins and Persistence of State-Sponsored Militias: Path Dependent Processes in Third World Military Development," *Journal of Strategic Studies* 34(4) (2011); Hughes, *My Enemy's Enemy*; Daniel Byman and Sarah Kreps, "Agents of Destruction? Applying Principal–Agent Analysis to State-Sponsored Terrorism," *International Studies Perspectives* 11(1) (2010).

20. Ariel Ahram's scholarship is worth highlighting for its focus on the organization of force in developing countries (which stands in contrast to the implicit geographic bias underlying other related scholarship). He explained how some states in the Third World that have not faced strong external threats did not only act as brokers indifferent to pursuing a monopoly over the legitimate use of force but also actually advanced the opposite by relying on state-sponsored militias to address internal threats. He conceptualized "violence devolution as a mode of military development rather than as a defective mode of state formation" and provided "an empirically grounded view of the contingent and varied pathways that lead some LDSs [late-developing states] to militias and others to conventional, centralized, and bureaucratic armies." Ahram, *Proxy Warriors*, 130.

21. In spite of Machiavelli's disparaging views, many states, including the world's major powers, continue to rely on mercenaries. The 2015 *Law of War Manual* released by the US Department of Defense highlights on p. 170 that "[t]he act of being a mercenary is not a crime in customary international law nor in any treaty to which the United States is a Party... Mercenaries are often nationals of States that are not parties to a conflict," adding that "[t]he United States has not accepted any such provision because these efforts are not consistent with fundamental principles of the law of war." The 2004 *Campaign Dictionary of Military Terms* states in the entry on "private military company" that "[t]his is an emotive subject, and many critics, including journalists and government officials, have dismissed PMCs as *mercenaries*, using the term in a derogatory context. PMCs which operate within the constraints of international law and the Geneva Convention would argue that they provide a legitimate service, especially to the governments of the poorer nations, whose own military assets are inadequate and who, for political or strategic reasons, have been unable to obtain military assistance from the international community (e.g. UN peacekeeping forces)." In recent academic scholarship, Malcolm Patterson's 2008 *Privatising Peace* is in many ways a defense of the use of mercenaries, whereas Sarah Percy's 2007 *Mercenaries: The History of a Norm in International Relations* is an analysis of the normative argument against it.

22. Deborah Avant, *The Market for Force: The Consequences of Privatizing Security* (Cambridge University Press, 2005): 23.

23. For a fascinating account and one of the earliest comprehensive discussions, see Francis R. Stark, *The Abolition of Privateering and the Declaration of Paris* (New York: AMS Press, 1967; originally published, 1897) (including quips about Great Britain from the perspective of a nineteenth-century American).

24. Janice E. Thomson, *Mercenaries, Pirates, and Sovereigns: State-Building and Extraterritorial Violence in Early Modern Europe* (Princeton University Press, 1994), 24. Thomson also mentions on pp. 21–22 that the definition of privateers is enshrined in international law as "vessels belonging to private owners, and sailing under a commission of war empowering the person to whom it is granted to carry on all forms of hostility which are permissible at seas by the usages of war." This definition is so intimately connected and specific to the experience of naval warfare and its history that it does not lend itself to use as a more generic analytical category. It also does not mention the profit-making aspect of the enterprise that is so often mentioned when the analogy is made to cybersecurity. For example, whereas much of the discussion about how to define mercenaries has focused on whether or not they fight for economic gain, privateering also had a strong economic impetus.

25. Michael Schmitt and Liis Vihul, "Proxy Wars in Cyber Space: The Evolving International Law of Attribution," *Fletcher Security Review* I(II) (2014): 55, 59–60.

26. Wyatt, "Princes, Patriots, and Proxies," 126.

27. Salehyan, "The Delegation of War to Rebel Organizations"; Stephen J. Majeski and David J. Sylvan, "Institutionalizing the ad Hoc: New Military Aid Programs" (American Political Science Association 2013 Annual Meeting, Chicago, August 29–September 1, 2013), http://papers.ssrn.com/sol3/papers .cfm?abstract_id=2300093; Ahram, "Origins and Persistence of State-Sponsored Militias," 543.

28. Brewer, "Peril by Proxy," 138.

29. Bar-Siman-Tov sees a proxy's activation by an activator as a crucial condition; see Bar-Siman-Tov, "The Strategy of War by Proxy," 266.

30. Mumford, *Proxy Warfare*, 56.

31. Wyatt, "Princes, Patriots, and Proxies," 126.

32. Dunér, "Proxy Intervention in Civil Wars," 354.

33. Thucydides, *History of the Peloponnesian War*; Machiavelli, *The Prince*.

34. Justin Bernier, "Asia's Shifting Strategic Landscape: China's Strategic Proxies," *Orbis* 47(4) (2003): 634; Klare, "Subterranean Alliances," 97–98.

35. Deborah D. Avant, Martha Finnemore, and Susan K. Sell, eds., *Who Governs the Globe?* (New York: Cambridge University Press, 2010).

36. A few additional comments explaining the choice for this definition. First, using the term "intermediary," instead of "third party," "client," or "agent," highlights not only a relationship between the beneficiary and the proxy but between the beneficiary and the targeted actor as well as the proxy's instrumental nature. Second, it also does not include a reference to the proxy being directly or indirectly involved, which is not a very useful distinction analytically, especially in the context of offensive cyber operations where geography and the

location of the proxy actors are significantly less relevant. Some academic definitions, for example, Andrew Mumford's, rely on geography to determine whether the proxy is directly or indirectly involved, arguing that this distinction sets proxy warfare (no presence on the ground) apart from a covert operation (some presence on the ground). However, the 2006 US Quadrennial Defense Review directly contradicts this approach, referencing covert operations as the "indirect approach." Moreover, geography is no longer a differentiating factor for direct and indirect interventions when it comes to proxy activity in cyberspace, also making the distinction internal/external less useful from the perspective of a more universal definition. See, for example, Dan Miodownik and Oren Barak, "Introduction," in *Non-state Actors in Intrastate Conflicts*, ed. Dan Miodownik and Oren Barak (Philadelphia: University of Pennsylvania Press, 2013), 4. Meanwhile, using the term "intermediary" captures the dimension of indirect referring to an additional actor being involved. Third, nationality is also excluded as it quickly loses its analytical utility in light of empirical realities, as powerfully explained by Malcolm Hugh Patterson, author of the 2009 book *Privatising Peace: A Corporate Adjunct to United Nations Peacekeeping and Humanitarian Operations*. (Nationality, however, obviously does matter especially when it comes to questions of jurisdictions, as illustrated by Taiwan's protests in 2016 over Kenya's extradition of arrested cybercriminals to China, to name a particularly complicated example.)

Last but not least, the definition excludes a chronological limitation, namely whether the relationship was established *ex ante* or *ex post* of the action.

37. Phillip Towle, "The Strategy of War by Proxy," *RUSI Journal* 126(1) (1981).
38. An earlier version of this section used the term "unequal" instead of "asymmetric"; see Tim Maurer, "'Proxies' and Cyberspace," *Journal of Conflict and Security Law* (published online, October 19, 2016). The terminology was changed to align with Dunér's insightful discussion of this issue: Dunér, "Proxy Intervention in Civil Wars," 357.
39. Dunér, "Proxy Intervention in Civil Wars," 357.
40. Ibid., 359.
41. Jan Kellberg and Steven Rowlen present a different approach in writing about "African nations as proxies in covert cyber operations." They state that "[d]eveloping countries could be used as proxies, without their knowledge and consent, through the unauthorised usage of these countries' information systems in an attempt to attack a third country by a state-sponsored offensive cyber operation. If the purpose of the cyber attack is to destabilize a targeted society and the attack succeeds, the used proxies are likely to face consequences in their relations with foreign countries, even if the proxy was unaware of the covert activity." Yet, reminiscent of Deutsch's definition, they neglect the important distinction between the state as an actor and the state's infrastructure, the former implying a degree of autonomy whereas the latter is passive and therefore excluded from this book's definition. Jan Kallberg and Steven Rowlen, "African Nations as Proxies in Covert Cyber Operations," *African Security Review* 23(3) (2014): 307.

42. For examples of this concept in the counterterrorism literature, see Wilner, "Apocalypse Soon?"; Daniel Byman, "Passive Sponsors of Terrorism," *Survival* 47(4) (2005).

43. Mumford, *Proxy Warfare*, 11.

44. In an excellent analysis, Yaacov Bar-Siman-Tov demonstrated that a party simply benefiting is not enough to qualify as constituting a proxy relationship, which is why the combination of benefiting while knowingly not stopping is an important one, which Bar-Siman-Tov does not address, as he focuses solely on active support. Bar-Siman-Tov, "The Strategy of War by Proxy," 265.

45. Figure 2.1 is a synthesis of several models developed by other scholars. Imposition of cost was added to Dahl's traditional definition of power to better reflect actions such as the cyber-enabled theft of intellectual property that is not designed to change actor c's behavior *per se* but can result in a relative gain in power for actor a *vis-à-vis* actor c. Figure 2.1 also builds on the O-I-T model by Abbott et al. Finally, a fully comprehensive framework could include a few additional actors such as intergovernmental organizations. Given the increasingly robust mandates of UN peace operations, for example, that do take sides under certain conditions, I disagree with Mumford that international organizations should be excluded *per se*. See Mumford, *Proxy Warfare*, 45–46; Robert Dahl, "The Concept of Power," *Behavioral Science*, 2 (1957): 202–203; K. J. Holsti, "The Concept of Power in the Study of International Relations," *Background* 7(4) (1964): 181; Kenneth W. Abbott et al., eds., *International Organizations as Orchestrators* (New York: Cambridge University Press, 2015), 4.

46. Stephen Krasner used the term "domestic sovereignty" to describe domestic control. See Stephen D. Krasner, *Sovereignty: Organized Hypocrisy* (Princeton University Press, 1999).

47. Barack Obama, "Executive Order – Blocking the Property of Certain Persons Engaging in Significant Malicious Cyber-Enabled Activities," Office of the Press Secretary, the White House, April 1, 2015, www.whitehouse.gov/the-press-office/2015/04/01/executive-order-blocking-property-certain-persons-engaging-significant-m.

48. Malcolm Hugh Patterson, *Privatising Peace: A Corporate Adjunct to United Nations Peacekeeping and Humanitarian Operations* (New York: Palgrave Macmillan, 2009), 48–49, presents another argument why it is relevant to include intergovernmental organizations in a broader framework conceptualizing all potential proxy relationships including niche actors.

49. Senger, *The Book of Stratagems*, 51; Shawn Conners, ed., *Military Strategy Classics of Ancient China – English & Chinese: The Art of War, Methods of War, 36 Stratagems & Selected Teachings* (Special Edition Books, 2013), 302–303. Stephen Majeski and David Sylvan present a more recent picture in their study on client states and military aid programs: Majeski and Sylvan, "Institutionalizing the ad Hoc."

50. Nick Hopkins and Julian Borger, "Exclusive: NSA pays £100m in secret funding for GCHQ," *The Guardian*, August 1, 2013, www.theguardian.com/uk-news/2013/aug/01/nsa-paid-gchq-spying-edward-snowden.

51. For example, while Hughes chose the phrase "my enemy's enemy" as the title for his book on proxy warfare, Stephen Walt referenced the excerpt from the *Arthashastra* in his 1985 International Security article on alliance formation. Hughes, *My Enemy's Enemy*; Stephen Walt, "Alliance Formation and the Balance of Power," International Security 9(4) (1985), 3; Bar-Siman-Tov, "The Strategy of War by Proxy"; Mumford, *Proxy Warfare*, 16.

52. This is similar to Michael T. Klare's stating "[f]ormal alliances have always been acknowledged publicly and have almost always been cemented by a treaty entailing specific, ongoing military obligations... Proxy relationships, on the other hand, are usually unacknowledged (as such) and normally entail an informal agreement or quid pro quo." Meanwhile, Bar-Siman-Tov considers a proxy relationship between states to be a subset of alliance relations. Klare, "Subterranean Alliances," 98; Bar-Siman-Tov, "The Strategy of War by Proxy," 265. It is also worth mentioning that there is an international law literature focusing specifically on the nature of unequal treaties; Elena Conde Pérez and Zhaklin Valerieva Yaneva, "Unequal Treaties in International Law," *Oxford Bibliographies*, last updated August 30, 2016, http://www.oxford bibliographies.com/view/document/obo-9780199796953/obo-9780199796953-0131.xml.

53. Francis R. Stark, "The Abolition of Privateering and the Declaration of Paris" in *Studies in History, Economics and Public Law*, ed. Faculty of Political Science of Columbia University (New York: Columbia University, 1897); Thomson, *Mercenaries, Pirates, and Sovereigns*; Christopher Ford, "Here Come the Cyber Privateers" (Hudson Institute, 2010), http://www.hudson.org/research/9112-here-come-the-cyber-privateers; Bruce Hallas, "Are Nation States Resorting to Cybersecurity Privateering?" (2012), http://www.brucehallas.co.uk/are-nation-states-resorting-to-cybersecurity-privateering/; Joseph Roger Clark, "Arghh ... Cyber-Pirates" (2013), http://josephrogerclark.com/2013/05/28/arghh-cyber-pirates/; Jordan Chandler Hirsch and Sam Adelsberg, "An Elizabethan Cyberwar," *New York Times*, May 31, 2013, http://www.nytimes.com/2013/06/01/opinion/an-elizabethan-cyberwar.html?_r=0; P. W. Singer and Allan Friedman, *Cybersecurity and Cyberwar: What Everyone Needs to Know* (New York: Oxford University Press, 2014); Thomas E. Ricks, "Cyber-Privateers," *Foreign Policy*, April 29, 2014, http://foreignpolicy.com/2014/04/29/cyber-priva teers/; Florian Egloff, "Cybersecurity and the Age of Privateering: A Historical Analogy" (Oxford: Cyber Studies Working Papers, 2015), http://www.politics.ox .ac.uk/materials/centres/cyber-studies/Working_Paper_No.1_Egloff.pdf.

54. Avant, *The Market for Force*; Peter Singer, *Corporate Warriors: The Rise of the Privatized Military Industry* (Ithaca, NY: Cornell University Press, 2003); Željko Branović and Sven Chojnacki, "The Logic of Security Markets: Security Governance in Failed States," *Security Dialogue* 42 (2011).

55. Cragin, "Semi-Proxy Wars and U.S. Counterterrorism Strategy"; Newton, "War by Proxy"; Hughes, "A Proxy War in Arabia."

56. Mumford, *Proxy Warfare*, 56.

57. Singer, *Corporate Warriors*; Avant, *The Market for Force*; Sean McFate, *The Modern Mercenary: Private Armies and What They Mean for World Order* (New York: Oxford University Press, 2014).

58. Cecily Brewer in her analysis of conflicts in Africa offers an additional useful distinction between proxies fighting each other and proxies not targeting each other but each other's patron (which she calls reciprocated type I vs. type II proxy warfare). Brewer, "Peril by Proxy," 141–142.

59. Thomson, *Mercenaries, Pirates, and Sovereigns*, 27; Bobbitt, *The Shield of Achilles*, 91.

60. I thank Bob Axelrod for this additional historical example; for more details, see "Jean Laffite," *Encyclopaedia Britannica*, www.britannica.com/biography/Jean-Laffite.

61. Antony Beever quoted in Mumford, *Proxy Warfare*, 26.

62. Hughes, "A Proxy War in Arabia," 62.

63. Tyrone Groh offers a systematic list of non-state proxy wars since World War II in his dissertation, counting twenty-eight such conflicts in Asia, Africa, the Middle East, and South and Central America in 1945–2001. Tyrone Groh, "War on the Cheap? Assessing the Costs and Benefits of Proxy War" (dissertation submitted to the Faculty of the Graduate School of Arts and Sciences of Georgetown University, February 23, 2010), vi. This list is still not comprehensive as more information gets declassified; for example, Hughes, "A Proxy War in Arabia."

64. Raiu in an interview with Reuters on September 26, 2013 about hacking activity against Japanese and South Korean institutions; see Joseph Menn, "Hacker 'Mercenaries' Linked to Japan, South Korea Spying: Researchers," *Reuters*, September 26, 2013, www.reuters.com/article/2013/09/26/net-us-cyberattacks-china-idUSBRE98O13V20130926.

65. Christopher Ford, "Here Come the Cyber Privateers" (Hudson Institute, 2010), www.hudson.org/research/9112-here-come-the-cyber-privateers; Jordan Chandler Hirsch and Sam Adelsberg, "An Elizabethan Cyberwar," *New York Times*, May 31, 2013, www.nytimes.com/2013/06/01/opinion/an-elizabethan-cyberwar.html?_r=0; Bruce Hallas, "Are Nation States Resorting to Cybersecurity Privateering?" (2012), www.brucehallas.co.uk/are-nation-states-resorting-to-cybersecurity-privateering/; Clark, "Arghh ... Cyber-Pirates"; Thomas E. Ricks, "Cyber-Privateers," *Foreign Policy*, April 29, 2014, http://foreignpolicy.com/2014/04/29/cyber-privateers/; Egloff, "Cybersecurity and the Age of Privateering"; Singer and Friedman, *Cybersecurity and Cyberwar*; Peter W. Singer and Allan Friedman, "Shiver My Interwebs: What Can (Real) Pirates Teach Us About Cybersecurity?", *Future Tense* (blog), *Slate*, January 1, 2014, www.slate.com/articles/technology/future_tense/2014/01/cybersecurity_and_cyberwar_excerpt_what_real_pirates_can_teach_us.html.

66. Captain Edwin Grohe of the US Navy, wrote one of the most comprehensive analyses of the cyber dimensions and proxies involved in the ongoing Syrian conflict: Edwin Grohe, "The Cyber Dimensions of the Syrian Civil War: Implications for Future Conflict," *Comparative Strategy* 34(2) (2015). Meanwhile, Robert Sheldon and Joe McReynolds provide the most comprehensive analysis of Chinese information warfare militias to date: Robert Sheldon and Joe McReynolds, "Civil Military Integration and Cybersecurity: A Study of Chinese Information Warfare Militias," in *China and Cybersecurity: Espionage, Strategy, and Politics in the Digital Domain*, ed. Jon R. Lindsay, Tai Ming Cheung, and Derek S. Reveron (New York: Oxford University Press, 2015).

67. Shane Harris, *@War: The Rise of the Military-Internet Complex* (New York: Eamon Dolan/Mariner Books, 2014), 121; Irv Lachow, Principal Cyber Researcher at MITRE Corporation is analyzing this industry in greater depth in his forthcoming "Cyber Contractors" article.

68. Avant, *The Market for Force*, 24.

69. Kimberley Thachuk, "Corruption and International Security," *SAIS Review of International Affairs* 25(1) (2005): 143–146.

70. Moisés Naím, "Mafia States: Organized Crime Takes Office," *Foreign Affairs* 91 (3) (2012).

71. Alexander Klimburg, "Mobilising Cyber Power," *Survival* 53 (2011): 49.

72. In-person interview with expert, who preferred to be listed anonymously, in September 2015.

73. Mumford, *Proxy Warfare*, 8. This category obviously includes a much greater universe of actors, such as hitmen in the drug trade of New York, and is beyond the scope of this book. Benjamin Weiser, "Two Men Indicted in Conspiracy That Involved Hired Killings," *New York Times*, June 7, 2003, www.nytimes .com/2003/06/07/nyregion/2-men-indicted-in-conspiracy-that-involved-hired-killings.html; "Lovers Top Contract Killing Hit List," *Reuters*, February 5, 2004, www.cnn.com/2004/WORLD/asiapcf/02/05/australia.killings.offbeat.reut /index.html.

74. David Kravets, "Exclusive: I Was a Hacker for the MPAA," *Wired*, October 22, 2007, http://archive.wired.com/politics/onlinerights/news/2007/10/p2p_hacker? currentPage=all.

75. Ben Grubb, "Film Industry Hires Cyber Hitmen to Take Down Internet Pirates," *Sydney Morning Herald*, September 8, 2010, www.smh.com.au/tech nology/technology-news/film-industry-hires-cyber-hitmen-to-take-down-inter net-pirates-20100907-14ypv.html; Singh, "Bollywood Hiring Cyber Hitmen to Combat Piracy"; Gabriella Coleman, *Hacker, Hoaxer, Whistleblower, Spy: The Many Faces of Anonymous* (New York: Verso, 2014), 97–99.

76. Cho Jin-seo, "Ban on Cyber Asset Trading Clouds Game Industry," *Korea Times*, May 10, 2007, www.koreatimes.co.kr/www/news/biz/2016/02/326_2660 .html.

77. Cho Jin-seo, "Hackers Paralyze Web Sites of Game Money Trading Firms," *Korea Times*, October 12, 2007, www.koreatimes.co.kr/www/news/biz/2016/02/

123_11821.html; Kim Kyeong-won, "ItemMania Responds to DDoS Attack," *Money Today*, December 17, 2008, www.mt.co.kr/view/mtview.php? type=1&no=2008121708584755122&outlink=1.

78. Park Yeong-tae, "ItemBay Hacker Caught," *Korea Economic Daily*, June 1, 2009, www.hankyung.com/news/app/newsview.php?aid=2009060154331;   Kwak Kyeong-bae, "This Disgrace to the Chinese Hacking Attack Competitors … the Industry 'Shock,'" *Daily Game*, October 8, 2010, www.dailygame.co.kr/view .php?ud=33149.

79. Émile El-Hokayem, "Hezbollah and Syria Outgrowing the Proxy Relationship," *Washington Quarterly* 30(2) (2007): 44; for additional studies focusing on Hizballah, Syria, and Iran, see Hughes, "Syria and the Perils of Proxy Warfare," 522–538; Sargon Hadaya, "A Proxy War in Syria," *International Affairs: A Russian Journal of World Politics, Diplomacy & International Relations* 59(6) (2013): 176; for an additional analysis focusing particularly on Iran's role in this context, see Shannon W. Caudill, "Hizballah Rising: Iran's Proxy Warriors," *Joint Force Quarterly* 49 (2008): 130–133.

80. Thomson, *Mercenaries, Pirates, and Sovereigns*, 32.

81. Geraint Hughes's analysis of a joint covert operation by the UK and Oman in South Yemen in the 1970s. Calling it a "proxy war" is an illustration of not just one but two states acting as principals, using exiled Mahra tribesmen for cross-border raids into Yemen. Hughes, "A Proxy War in Arabia."

82. See, for example, Ora Szekely's analysis of different forms of principals, ranging from cohesive single principals to multiple and divided collective principals. She finds the single principal to be the most effective at exercising control over the agent whereas a collective principal consisting of multiple veto players and multiple principals increases the potential for diverging interests and the agent's autonomy. Ora Szekely, "A Friend in Need: The Impact of the Syrian Civil War on Syria's Clients (A Principal–Agent Approach)," *Foreign Policy Analysis* 12 (2016): 452–453.

83. This builds on the general hypotheses identified by Abbott et al. in their work on orchestration.

84. Building on Abbott et al., *International Organizations as Orchestrators*, 20; Salehyan, "The Delegation of War to Rebel Organizations," 508.

85. Peter Apps, "Analysis: In Cyber Era, Militaries Scramble for New Skills," Reuters, February 9, 2012, www.reuters.com/article/us-defence-cyber-idUSTRE8182HI20120209.

86. US News Best Global Universities Ranking 2016 for computer science, math, and engineering; Shanghai Ranking's Academic Ranking of World Universities 2016 for computer science and math as well as the field of engineering; *Times Higher Education* World University Rankings 2016–2017; *Freedom in the World: 2016* (Washington, DC: Freedom House, 2016), https://freedomhouse.org/sites/ default/files/FH_FITW_Report_2016.pdf; "Corruption Perceptions Index 2015," Transparency International, www.transparency.org/cpi2015.

87. Alissa de Carbonnel, "Hackers for Hire: Ex-Soviet Tech Geeks Play Outsized Role in Global Cyber Crime," *NBC News*, August 22, 2013, www.nbcnews.com

/technology/hackers-hire-ex-soviet-tech-geeks-play-outsized-role-global-6C10981346.

88. Singer, *Corporate Warriors*, 175.

89. Steve Morgan, "Worldwide Cybersecurity Market Continues Its Upward Trend," *CSO*, July 9, 2015, www.csoonline.com/article/2946017/security-lea dership/worldwide-cybersecurity-market-sizing-and-projections.html.

90. "Israel Turns Self-Defence into Industry Boom for Cyber Techs," Reuters, September 23, 2014, http://in.reuters.com/article/2014/09/23/israel-cybersecur ity-companies-idINKCN0HI0YB20140923.

91. Department for International Trade Defence and Security Organisation and Home Office, *Increasing Our Security Exports: A New Government Approach* (London, 2014), www.gov.uk/government/publications/increasing-our-secur ity-exports-a-new-government-approach.

92. See also the discussion of creating new intermediaries in the context of orchestration: Abbott et al., *International Organizations as Orchestrators*, 367.

93. Building on Abbott et al., *International Organizations as Orchestrators*, 20; Salehyan, "The Delegation of War to Rebel Organizations," 509.

94. See, for example, Wilner, "Apocalypse Soon?", 21.

95. See, for example, Salehyan, "The Delegation of War to Rebel Organizations," 504; Allison Stanger, *One Nation Under Contract: The Outsourcing of American Power and the Future of Foreign Policy* (New Haven, CT: Yale University Press, 2009), 93.

96. Byman and Kreps, "Agents of Destruction?", 2.

97. Abbott et al., *International Organizations as Orchestrators*, 6.

98. *Cybersecurity and Cyberwarfare: Preliminary Assessment of National Doctrine and Organization* (Geneva: UNIDIR, 2011), http://unidir.org/files/publica tions/pdfs/cybersecurity-and-cyberwarfare-preliminary-assessment-of-national-doctrine-and-organization-380.pdf.

99. Stanger, *One Nation Under Contract*, 93.

100. Apps, "Analysis: In Cyber Era."

101. *The Cyber Index: International Security Trends and Realities* (Geneva: United Nations Institute for Disarmament Research, 2013).

102. "Unit 8200 and Israel's High-Tech Whiz Kids," *UPI*, June 4, 2012, http://www .upi.com/Unit-8200-and-Israels-high-tech-whiz-kids/43661338833765/; Matthew S. Cohen, Charles D. Freilich, and Gabi Siboni, "Israel and Cyberspace: Unique Threat and Response," *International Studies Perspectives* (2015): 10; Apps, "Analysis: In Cyber Era."

103. Irving Lachow, "The Private Sector Role in Offensive Cyber Operations: Benefits, Issues and Challenges" (June 15, 2016), papers.ssrn.com/ abstract=2836201, 10.

104. Ibid., 11.

105. Some evidence also suggests that the likelihood of the use of proxies increases if states are engaged in protracted conflicts; see Stanger, *One Nation Under Contract*, 93; Szekely, "A Friend in Need," 451.

106. Hughes, *My Enemy's Enemy*, 26; Salehyan, "The Delegation of War to Rebel Organizations," 494.

107. Hughes, *My Enemy's Enemy*, 25.

108. Christopher Gelpi, Peter D. Feaver, and Jason Reifler, "Success Matters: Casualty Sensitivity and the War in Iraq," *International Security* 30(3) (Winter 2005/06).

109. Thomas Groves and Maria Tsvetkova, "Special Report: Moscow Stifles Dissent as Soldiers Return in Coffins," Reuters, September 12, 2014, www.reuters.com/article/us-ukraine-crisis-russians-special-repor-idUSKBN0H70S920140912.

110. Bar-Siman-Tov, "The Strategy of War by Proxy," 263; Mumford, *Proxy Warfare* 5, 38.

111. Byman and Kreps, "Agents of Destruction?", 1–2; Wilner, "Apocalypse Soon,?" 22.

112. Byman and Kreps, "Agents of Destruction?", 6.

113. For a discussion of the logic of consequences and the logic of appropriateness, see James G. March and Johan P. Olsen, "The Institutional Dynamics of International Political Orders," *International Organization* 52 (4) (1998): 943–969.

114. Mumford, *Proxy Warfare*, 87.

115. Bobbitt, *The Shield of Achilles*, 322.

116. T. J. O'Connor, *The Jester Dynamic: A Lesson in Asymmetric Unmanaged Cyber Warfare* (SANS Institute, 2011), www.sans.org/reading-room/whitepapers/attacking/jester-dynamic-lesson-asymmetric-unmanaged-cyber-warfare-33889, 23–24.

117. Tammy Leitner and Lisa Capitanini, "'Patriotic Hackers' Claim to Fight Cyber War Against Terrorists," *NBC Chicago*, February 19, 2015, www.nbcchicago.com/news/local/Patriotic-Hackers-Cyber-War-Against-Terrorists-292825571.html.

118. Byman, "Passive Sponsors of Terrorism," 129–131.

119. Ibid., 120–123.

120. Misha Glenny, *McMafia: A Journey Through the Global Criminal Underworld* (New York Vintage 2008), 48.

121. Holsti, "The Concept of Power," 185.

122. Klimburg, "Mobilising Cyber Power."

123. Although it is a central theme in the literature on power, Abbott et al. omit the condition of the orchestrator having the capacity and appropriate mechanism to act as an orchestrator in the first place, and to use an intermediary when available. Abbott et al.'s orchestrator capabilities hypothesis also does not focus on the orchestrator's ability to orchestrate but rather on their lack of certain capabilities.

124. Building on Abbott et al., *International Organizations as Orchestrators*, 20.

125. Byman and Kreps, "Agents of Destruction?", 13.

126. Salehyan, "The Delegation of War to Rebel Organizations," 507.

127. Ibid.

128. Holsti, "The Concept of Power," 182.

129. Abbott et al., *International Organizations as Orchestrators*, 17; Byman and Kreps, "Agents of Destruction?", 3.

130. Barry M. Mitnick, "Origin of the Theory of Agency: An Account by One of the Theory's Originators," University of Pittsburgh, www.pitt.edu/~mitnick/agen cytheory/agencytheoryoriginrev11806r.htm.

131. Byman and Kreps, "Agents of Destruction?"; Salehyan, "The Delegation of War to Rebel Organizations"; Justin V. Hastings, "Understanding Maritime Piracy Syndicate Operations," *Security Studies* 21(4) (2012): 683–721.

132. Tine Hanrieder, "Gradual Change in International Organisations: Agency Theory and Historical Institutionalism," *Politics* 34(4) (2014); Salehyan, "The Delegation of War to Rebel Organizations," 502–503.

133. For a good review of agency theory, see Susan P. Shapiro, "Agency Theory," *Annual Review of Sociology* 31 (2005): 272.

134. Hughes, *My Enemy's Enemy*, 49.

135. Patrick Malone, "Pentagon Farmed Out Its Coding to Russia," *Daily Beast*, November 4, 2015, www.thedailybeast.com/articles/2015/11/04/pentagon-farmed-out-its-coding-to-russia.html.

136. Salehyan, "The Delegation of War to Rebel Organizations," 505.

137. Hughes, "A Proxy War in Arabia," 104.

138. "MH17 Crash: Big Buk Missile Part Found in Ukraine," *BBC News*, June 6, 2016, www.bbc.com/news/world-europe-36462853.

139. Salehyan, "The Delegation of War to Rebel Organizations," 506; for a similar point, see also Byman and Kreps, "Agents of Destruction?", 8.

140. One could add the caveat that this only applies to an actor acting under conventional rational constraints and not facing an existential threat or driven by radical ideology.

141. Byman and Kreps, "Agents of Destruction?", 11; Salehyan, "The Delegation of War to Rebel Organizations," 502; Hastings, "Understanding Maritime Piracy Syndicate Operations," 700.

142. Byman and Kreps, "Agents of Destruction?", 11.

143. Salehyan, "The Delegation of War to Rebel Organizations," 505–506.

144. Ibid., 506; Byman and Kreps, "Agents of Destruction?", 10, 14.

145. Byman and Kreps, "Agents of Destruction?", 9, 14.

146. Department of Defense, *Quadrennial Defense Review 2014* (Washington, DC: Office of the Secretary of Defense, 2014), http://archive.defense.gov/pubs/ 2014_Quadrennial_Defense_Review.pdf, 47.

147. Wesley Bruer and Michael Pearson, "Ex-Blackwater Contractors Sentenced in Nusoor Square Shooting in Iraq," *CNN*, April 14, 2015, www.cnn.com/2015/ 04/13/us/blackwater-contractors-iraq-sentencing/.

148. Abbott et al., *International Organizations as Orchestrators*, 17.

149. While Byman and Kreps use the principal–agent model in their study of state-sponsored terrorists, it is worth pointing out that the orchestration framework by Abbott et al. was not published until six years after their article appeared. Given their criticism of the principal–agent model, Byman and Krebs may

well have used the concept of orchestration if it had been available as an alternative model at the time. Byman and Kreps, "Agents of Destruction?", 12.

150. This definition is directly paraphrased and based on the definition of orchestration by Abbott et al. but revised to be more generally applicable, including to proxy relationships. Abbott et al., *International Organizations as Orchestrators*, 3–4.

151. Ibid., 18.

152. Ibid., 17; Byman and Kreps, "Agents of Destruction?", 5.

153. Abbott et al., *International Organizations as Orchestrators*, 17.

154. Ibid., 19.

155. Ibid., 22.

156. Byman and Kreps, "Agents of Destruction?", 10–11; Barry Posen, "Nationalism, the Mass Army, and Military Power," *International Security* 18(2) (1993).

157. See also Walter W. Powell, "Neither Market nor Hierarchy," *Research in Organizational Behavior* 12 (1990).

158. Ronald J. Deibert, Rafal Rohozinski, and Masashi Crete-Nishihata, "Cyclones in Cyberspace: Information Shaping and Denial in the 2008 Russia-Georgia War," *Security Dialogue* 43(1) (2012): 18.

159. The definition by Byman differs slightly from how sanctioning is conceptualized in this book. Byman defines passive support as follows: "Passive support has the following characteristics: the regime in question itself does not provide assistance but knowingly allows other actors in the country to aid a terrorist group; the regime has the capacity to stop this assistance or has chosen not to develop this capacity; and often passive support is given by political parties, wealthy merchants or other actors in society that have no formal affiliation with the government." Byman, "Passive Sponsors of Terrorism," 118.

160. This definition builds on Byman, "Passive Sponsors of Terrorism."

161. Ibid., 132.

162. "What Is 'Islamic State'?", *BBC News*, December 2, 2015, www.bbc.com/news/world-middle-east-29052144.

163. Byman, "Passive Sponsors of Terrorism," 133.

164. Tal Becker, *Terrorism and the State: Rethinking the Rules of State Responsibility* (Portland, OR: Hart Publishing, 2006), 5; "Tal Becker," Shalom Hartman Institute, https://hartman.org.il/Faculty_View.asp?faculty_id=162.

165. Michael Schmitt, "In Defense of Due Diligence in Cyberspace," *Yale Law Journal Forum* 125 (2015).

166. Byman and Kreps, "Agents of Destruction?", 15.

167. Byman points to Steven David's 1991 *Choosing Sides* as an articulation of this argument. Steven R. David, *Choosing Sides: Alignment and Realignment in the Third World* (Baltimore, MD: Johns Hopkins University Press, 1991).

168. Jon Abbink has observed in the context of conflicts in Africa that "armed proxy groups . . . if not pushed back on the battlefield, were increasingly reined in by their patrons (for example, the Eritrean opposition groups by the Ethiopians),

because they were not allowed to interfere with the new process of diplomacy." Abbink, "Ethiopia–Eritrea: Proxy Wars and Prospects of Peace," 416.

3 CYBER POWER: GEOPOLITICS AND HUMAN RIGHTS

1. "North Korea Complains to UN About Film Starring Rogen, Franco," Reuters, July 9, 2014, http://uk.reuters.com/article/uk-northkorea-un-film-id UKKBN0FE21B20140709.
2. Peter Elkind, "Inside the Hack of the Century," *Fortune*, July 1, 2015, http://fortune.com/sony-hack-part-1/; Amanda Hess, "Inside the Sony Hack," *Slate*, November 22, 2015, http://www.slate.com/articles/technology/users/2015/11/sony_employees_on_the_hack_one_year_later.html.
3. Dominic Rushe, "Hackers Who Targeted Sony Invoke 9/11 Attacks in Warning to Moviegoers," *The Guardian*, December 17, 2014, www.theguardian.com/film/2014/dec/16/employees-sue-failure-guard-personal-data-leaked-hackers.
4. "North Korea Threatens War on US Over Kim Jong-un Movie," *BBC News*, June 26, 2014, www.bbc.com/news/world-asia-28014069.
5. While a spokesman of the North Korean foreign ministry stated that the movie's release would be considered an "act of war," President Obama described the Sony hack as an "act of cybervandalism" (although other prominent politicians, such as Senator John McCain, did declare it warfare). "North Korea Threatens War"; Eric Bradner, "Obama: North Korea's Hack Not War, but 'Cybervandalism,'" *CNN*, December 24, 2014, http://www.cnn.com/2014/12/21/politics/obama-north-koreas-hack-not-war-but-cyber-vandalism/; Kate Sheppard, "McCain Calls Sony Hack an 'Act of War,'" *Huffington Post*, December 21, 2014, www.huffingtonpost.com/2014/12/21/sony-north-korea-war_n_6362454.html.
6. Richards J. Heuer, *The Psychology of Intelligence Analysis* (Center for the Study of Intelligence, 1999), 70.
7. Klint Finley, "What Exactly Is GitHub Anyway?" *TechCrunch*, July 12, 2014, http://techcrunch.com/2012/07/14/what-exactly-is-github-anyway/.
8. Cade Metz, "How GitHub Conquered Google, Microsoft, and Everyone Else," *Wired*, March 12, 2015, http://www.wired.com/2015/03/github-conquered-google-microsoft-everyone-else/.
9. Dan Goodin, "Massive Denial-of-Service Attack on GitHub Tied to Chinese Government," *Ars Technica*, March 31, 2015, http://arstechnica.com/security/2015/03/massive-denial-of-service-attack-on-github-tied-to-chinese-government/.
10. Bill Marczak et al., "China's Great Cannon," Citizen Lab, University of Toronto Munk School of Global Affairs, April 10, 2015, https://citizenlab.org/2015/04/chinas-great-cannon/.
11. Robert Hackett, "GitHub Triumphant Over Its 'Largest Ever' Cyber Pummeling," *Fortune*, April 3, 2015, http://fortune.com/2015/04/03/github-ddos-china/.

12. It is worth noting that this research report also points to a potential involvement of the National Computer Network Emergency Response Technical Team/ Coordination Center of China (CNCERT/CC). A few weeks after the GitHub DDoS attack, in July 2015, the Chinese government agreed to a new norm outlined in the UNGGE report that "[a] State should not use authorized emergency response teams to engage in malicious international activity."

13. Marczak et al., "China's Great Cannon."

14. James M. Markham, "TV Brings Western Culture to East Germany," *New York Times*, February 13, 1984, www.nytimes.com/1984/02/13/arts/tv-brings-western-culture-to-east-germany.html; Marlis Schaum, "West German TV: The Class Enemy in the Front Room," *Deutsche Welle*, January 7, 2009, www.dw.com/en/west-german-tv-the-class-enemy-in-the-front-room/a-3804892.

15. Monroe Price, *Free Expression, Globalism and the New Strategic Communication* (New York: Cambridge University Press, 2015), 218.

16. Ibid., 203.

17. H.R. 570, 114th Congress, 1st Session (2015), www.govtrack.us/congress/bills/114/hr570/text.

18. Simeon Paterson, "Korean Loudspeakers: What Are the North and South Shouting About?", *BBC News*, January 12, 2016, www.bbc.com/news/world-asia-35278451.

19. "Internet Freedom," HumanRights.gov, www.state.gov/e/eb/cip/netfreedom/index.htm.

    Lorenzo Franceschi-Bicchierai, "Why the US Government Is Investing Millions in Internet Freedom Technologies," Motherboard, *Vice*, September 29, 2015, http://motherboard.vice.com/read/why-the-us-government-is-investing-millions-in-internet-freedom-technologies.

20. US law prohibits such actions targeting Americans domestically, but the law was developed at a time when communication was largely bound by geography. The Internet has undermined the law's geography-based boundaries, which is why US Central Command and the US government are now trying to comply with the law by using other variables such as language or targeting speech websites instead. See also Nick Fielding and Ian Cobain, "Revealed: US Spy Operation That Manipulates Social Media," *The Guardian*, March 17, 2011, www.theguardian.com/technology/2011/mar/17/us-spy-operation-social-networks.

21. Fielding and Cobain, "Revealed: US Spy Operation."

22. Adrian Chen, "The Agency," *New York Times*, June 2, 2015, www.nytimes.com/2015/06/07/magazine/the-agency.html.

23. Adam Segal, *The Hacked World Order* (New York: PublicAffairs, 2016), 184.

24. Price, *Free Expression, Globalism and the New Strategic Communication*, 97.

25. Price, *Free Expression, Globalism and the New Strategic Communication*, 99.

26. Though, admittedly, Prussia and France were at war at the time. See Edmund Ollier, *Cassell's History of the War Between France and Germany, 1870–1871* (London: Cassell, Petter & Galpin, 1873), 350–351.

27. Price, *Free Expression, Globalism and the New Strategic Communication*, 122–123.
28. Office of the Director of National Intelligence, *Background to "Assessing Russian Activities and Intentions in Recent US Elections": The Analytic Process and Cyber Incident Attribution* (McLean, VA: Office of the Director of National Intelligence, January 2017), ii.
29. Ibid., 1.
30. Ibid.
31. Evan Osnos, David Remnick, and Joshua Yaffa, "Trump, Putin, and the New Cold War," *New Yorker*, March 6, 2017, www.newyorker.com/magazine/2017/03/06/trump-putin-and-the-new-cold-war.
32. See, for example, "ISO/IEC 27000:2012(en)," ISO, http://www.iso.org/obp/ui/#iso:std:iso-iec:27000:ed-2:v1:en.
33. "Rogachev," Speakers, EastWest Institute 2015 Global Cyberspace Cooperation Summit, www.cybersummit.info/2015/speakers/rogachev/.
34. Sarah McKune, "An Analysis of the International Code of Conduct for Information Security," https://openeffect.ca/code-conduct/.
35. Cybersecurity" is also difficult to translate into other languages, including Russian and Mandarin, but it is increasingly being adopted as a neologism in other languages. Meanwhile, the term "cybersecurity" has been contested by actors within the United States as well, but for different reasons. As Ed Felten, professor of computer science and public affairs at Princeton University, observed in 2008, before becoming Deputy US Chief Technology Officer at the White House in 2015, "[i]t's now becoming standard Washington parlance to say 'cyber' as a shorthand for what many of us would call 'information security.' I won't fault Obama for using the terminology spoken by the usual Washington experts. Still, it's interesting to consider how Washington has developed its own terminology, and what that terminology reveals about the inside-the-beltway view of the information security problem." Felten points out that outside government, most technical experts use the term "information security," and large companies have chief information security officers. Jennifer Granick at Stanford University, even further removed from Washington than Felten at Princeton, goes a step further, arguing, "When I hear 'cyber' I hear shorthand for military domination of the Internet, as General Michael Hayden, former NSA and CIA head, has said – ensuring U.S. access and denying access to our enemies. Security for me, but not for thee." The explanation for these different terminologies and tensions is rooted in the difference between national-level and international-level discussions. Scholars focusing on domestic policy are sometimes unaware that the term "information security" has developed a life of its own at the international level beyond its original technical definition and meaning. The UK government has been among the most explicit in drawing attention to this issue. In a submission to the UN, the UK acknowledged that many businesses and standards organizations use the term "information security." But the document also highlighted the "potential confusion in using the term 'information security,' which is also

used by some countries and organizations as part of a doctrine that regards information itself as a threat against which additional protection is needed." As the document outlines, "the United Kingdom does not recognize the validity of the term 'information security' when used in this context, since it could be employed in attempts to legitimize further controls on freedom of expression beyond those agreed in the Universal Declaration of Human Rights and the International Covenant on Civil and Political Rights." Ed Felten, "What's the Cyber in Cyber-Security?", Freedom to Tinker, Princeton Center for Information Technology Policy, July 24, 2008, https://freedom-to-tinker.com/blog/felten/whats-cyber-cyber-security/; Jennifer Stisa Granick, "The End of the Internet Dream," *Backchannel*, August 17, 2015, https://backchannel.com/the-end-of-the-internet-dream-ba060b17da61; Tim Maurer and Robert Morgus, "'Cybersecurity' and Why Definitions Are Risky," CSS Blog Network, ETH Zurich Center for Security Studies, November 10, 2014, http://isnblog.ethz.ch/intelligence/cybersecurity-and-the-problem-of-definitions; Timothy Thomas, *Russian Military Strategy: Impacting 21st Century Reform and Geopolitics* (Fort Leavenworth, KS: Foreign Military Studies Office, 2015), 295; Thomas, "Nation-State Cyber Strategies," 466; Cai Cuihong, "Cybersecurity in the Chinese Context: Changing Concepts, Vital Interests, and Prospects for Cooperation," *China Quarterly of International Strategic Studies* 1(3) (2015): 3–4.

36. Martin C. Libicki, "Cyberspace Is Not a Warfighting Domain," *I/S: A Journal of Law and Policy* 8(2) (2012): 336.

37. Robert Belk and Matthew Noyes, *On the Use of Offensive Cyber Capabilities: A Policy Analysis on Offensive US Cyber Policy* (Cambridge, MA: Harvard University Belfer Center for Science and International Affairs, 2012), 14.

38. Marco Roscini, *Cyber Operations and the Use of Force in International Law* (New York: Oxford University Press, 2014), 12.

39. Antonia Chayes, *Borderless Wars: Civil Military Disorder and Legal Uncertainty* (New York: Cambridge University Press, 2015), 139.

40. Roscini also considers cyber attacks to include propaganda or deception including website defacement: Roscini, *Cyber Operations and the Use of Force*, 17.

41. Mary Louise Kelly, "Rules for Cyberwarfare Still Unclear, Even As U.S. Engages in It," *NPR*, April 22, 2016, www.opb.org/news/article/npr-rules-for-cyberwarfare-still-unclear-even-as-us-engages-in-it/.

42. Chayes, *Borderless Wars*, 139; Roscini, *Cyber Operations and the Use of Force*, 15.

43. Gary D. Brown and Andrew O. Metcalf, "Easier Said Than Done: Legal Reviews of Cyber Weapons," *Journal of National Security Law & Policy* 7 (2014): 116–118.

44. Senate Committee on Foreign Relations, *International Cybersecurity Strategy: Deterring Foreign Threats and Building Global Cyber Norms*, 114th Congress, 2nd session, May 25, 2016, www.foreign.senate.gov/hearings/international-cyber

security-strategy-deterring-foreign-threats-and-building-global-cyber-norms-052516.

45. Michael D. Shear and Scott Shane, "White House Weighs Sanctions After Second Breach of a Computer System," *New York Times*, June 12, 2015, www.nytimes.com/2015/06/13/us/white-house-weighs-sanctions-after-second-breach-of-a-computer-system.html.

46. Ellen Nakashima, "U.S. Decides Against Publicly Blaming China for Data Hack," *Washington Post*, July 21, 2015, www.washingtonpost.com/world/national-security/us-avoids-blaming-china-in-data-theft-seen-as-fair-game-in-espionage/2015/07/21/03779096-2eee-11e5-8353-1215475949f4_story.html.

47. Barack Obama, "Presidential Policy Directive 41," Office of the Press Secretary, the White House, July 26, 2016, https://web.archive.org/web/20160729134917/https://www.whitehouse.gov/sites/whitehouse.gov/files/documents/Cyber%2BIncident%2BSeverity%2BSchema.pdf.

48. Roscini, *Cyber Operations and the Use of Force in International Law*, 108–109.

49. "NATO Welcomes Opening of European Centre for Countering Hybrid Threats," North Atlantic Treaty Organization, April 17, 2017, www.nato.int/cps/en/natohq/news_143143.html; Franklin D. Kramer and Larry K. Wentz, "Cyber Influence and International Security," in Cyber Power *and National Security*, ed. Franklin D. Kramer, Stuart H. Starr, and Larry K. Wentz (Dulles, VA: Potomac Books, 2009), 350.

50. P. W. Singer and Allan Friedman, *Cybersecurity and Cyberwar: What Everyone Needs to Know* (New York: Oxford University Press, 2014), 81.

51. Thomas, "Nation-State Cyber Strategies," 476.

52. Thomas, "Chapter Two: China and Information Deterrence."

53. D. Tyurin, "Russia and the West Expand Cyberspace Security Dialogue," *International Affairs* 62(4) (2016) 183–186. The opening presentation of the 2016 conference hosted by Moscow State University's Information Security Institute in Garmisch-Partenkirchen included a very similar comparison and a video of a mushroom cloud explosion in its presentation of the potential consequences of information threats.

54. Nigel Inkster, *China's Cyber Power* (New York: Routledge, 2016), 124; Timothy Thomas, "Chapter Eleven: Comparing Chinese and Russian Cyber Concepts," in *Three Faces of the Cyber Dragon: Cyber Peace Activist, Spook, Attacker*, by Timothy Thomas (Fort Leavenworth, KS: Foreign Military Studies Office, 2012).

55. Thomas, "Nation-State Cyber Strategies," 486.

56. Ibid., 481–482.

57. Jeffrey Carr et al., *Project Grey Goose: Phase I Report: Russia/Georgia Cyber War – Findings and Analysis* (October 17, 2008), 7.

58. Andrei Soldatov and Irina Borogan, *The Red Web: The Struggle Between Russia's Digital Dictators and the New Online Revolutionaries* (New York: PublicAffairs, 2015), 163.

59. Ibid., 11.

60. Ibid., 88–89.

61. Ibid., 109.
62. Ibid., 113.
63. Ibid., 113–115.
64. Ibid., 124–125.
65. Ibid., 149.
66. Ibid., 166–167.
67. Vadim Shtepa, "Russia's Draft Information Security Doctrine at Odds with Realities of Modern Information Environment," *Eurasia Daily Monitor* 13(128) (2016).
68. Soldatov and Borogan, *The Red Web*, 259–260.
69. Shtepa, "Russia's Draft Information Security Doctrine."
70. Soldatov and Borogan, *The Red Web*, 313–314.
71. Segal, *The Hacked World Order*, 70.
72. Thomas, *Russian Military Strategy*, 281.
73. Segal, *The Hacked World Order*, 93.
74. Evan Osnos, David Remnick, and Joshua Yaffa, "Trump, Putin, and the New Cold War," *New Yorker*, March 6, 2017, www.newyorker.com/magazine/2017/03/06/trump-putin-and-the-new-cold-war.
75. Soldatov and Borogan, *The Red Web*, 282.
76. Ibid., 284.
77. Orysia Lutsevych, *Agents of the Russian World: Proxy Groups in the Contested Neighbourhood* (London: Chatham House, 2016), 2.
78. Kevin Pollpeter, "Chinese Writings on Cyberwarfare and Coercion," in *China and Cybersecurity: Espionage, Strategy, and Politics in the Digital Domain*, ed. Jon R. Lindsay et al. (New York: Oxford University Press, 2015), 154.
79. Jon R. Lindsay, "China and Cybersecurity: Controversy and Context," in *China and Cybersecurity: Espionage, Strategy, and Politics in the Digital Domain*, ed. Jon R. Lindsay et al. (New York: Oxford University Press, 2015), 11.
80. Teng Jianqun and Xu Longdi, *Cyber War Preparedness, Cyberspace Arms Control and the United States* (Beijing: China Institute of International Studies, 2014), 48.
81. Nigel Inkster, "Chinese Intelligence in the Cyber Age," *Survival* 55(1) (2013): 46.
82. Ibid., 48.
83. Eric Heginbotham, *The U.S.-China Military Scorecard: Forces, Geography, and the Evolving Balance of Power 1996–2017* (Santa Monica, CA: RAND Corporation, 2015), 283; Jon R. Lindsay, "The Impact of China on Cybersecurity: Fiction and Friction," *International Security* 39(3) (Winter 2014/15): 22; James C. Mulvenon, "Chinese Cyber Espionage," Testimony before the Congressional-Executive Commission on China, June 25, 2013.
84. Inkster, "Chinese Intelligence in the Cyber Age," 58.
85. Jon R. Lindsay, "The Impact of China on Cybersecurity: Fiction and Friction," *International Security* 39(3) (Winter 2014/15): 18–19.
86. Ibid., 28.
87. Segal, *The Hacked World Order*, 136.

88. Ibid., 43.

89. Cai Cuihong, "Cybersecurity in the Chinese Context: Changing Concepts, Vital Interests, and Prospects for Cooperation," *China Quarterly of International Strategic Studies* 1(3) (2015): 12–13.

90. James Mulvenon, "PLA Computer Network Operations: Scenarios, Doctrine, Organizations, and Capability," in *Beyond the Strait: PLA Missions Other Than Taiwan*, ed. Roy Kamphausen et al. (Carlisle, PA: Strategic Studies Institute, 2009), 254.

91. General Dai Qingmin, former head of the PLA General Staff's Fourth Department, is credited with this outcome in China. In his 2008 publication *New Perspectives on War*, Dai described "battlefield network warfare," which focused on computer network attacks and electronic warfare combining signals and electromagnetic capabilities. Dai also promoted the integration of military and civilian forces (further described in Chapter 8). Mulvenon, "PLA Computer Network Operations," 261; Inkster, "Chinese Intelligence in the Cyber Age," 57, 99; Timothy L. Thomas, *Dragon Bytes: Chinese Information-War Theory and Practice* (Ft. Leavenworth, KS: Foreign Military Studies Office, 2004), 55; Thomas, "Nation-State Cyber Strategies," 471.

92. Patrick Boehler, "Hackers Attack http://GreatFire.org, a Workaround for Websites Censored in China," *Sinosphere* (blog), *New York Times*, March 20, 2015, http://sinosphere.blogs.nytimes.com/2015/03/20/hackers-attack-great fire-org-a-workaround-for-websites-censored-in-china/.

93. Bill Marczak et al., "China's Great Cannon," Citizen Lab, University of Toronto Munk School of Global Affairs, April 10, 2015, https://citizenlab.org/2015/04/chinas-great-cannon/.

94. Marczak et al., "China's Great Cannon"; Sebastian Anthony, "GitHub Battles 'Largest DDoS' in Site's History, Targeted at Anti-censorship Tools," *Ars Technica*, March 30, 2015, http://arstechnica.com/security/2015/03/github-bat tles-largest-ddos-in-sites-history-targeted-at-anti-censorship-tools/; Marianna Mao, "China Blocks NY Times After Wen Jiabao Article," *Herdict Blog*, October 29, 2012, www.herdict.org/blog/2012/10/29/china-blocks-ny-times-after-wen-jiabao-article/.

95. Inkster, *China's Cyber Power*, 76.

96. Full disclosure: I was a nonresident fellow of the Citizen Lab but not involved in the research report.

97. Marczak et al., "China's Great Cannon."

98. Dan Goodin, "DDoS Attacks That Crippled GitHub Linked to Great Firewall of China," *Ars Technica*, April 2, 2015, http://arstechnica.com/security/2015/04/ddos-attacks-that-crippled-github-linked-to-great-firewall-of-china/.

99. Kim Zetter, "Inside the Cunning, Unprecedented Hack of Ukraine's Power Grid," *Wired*, March 3, 2016, www.wired.com/2016/03/inside-cunning-unpre cedented-hack-ukraines-power-grid/.

100. Marczak et al., "China's Great Cannon."

101. Timothy Thomas, *Russian Military Strategy: Impacting 21st Century Reform and Geopolitics* (Fort Leavenworth, KS: Foreign Military Studies Office, 2015), 291–292.
102. Full disclosure: I worked at New America's Open Technology Institute from 2012 to 2015.
103. Saeed Kamali Dehghan, "Iran Tightens Online Censorship to Counter US 'Shadow Internet,'" *The Guardian*, July 13, 2011, www.theguardian.com/world/2011/jul/13/iran-tightens-online-censorship.
104. James Glanz and John Markoff, "US Underwrites Internet Detour Around Censors," *New York Times*, June 12, 2011, www.nytimes.com/2011/06/12/world/12internet.html; Kamali Dehghan, "Iran Tightens Online Censorship."
105. Kamali Dehghan, "Iran Tightens Online Censorship."
106. "Iran reacts to New American Initiative 'Internet in a Suitcase,'" *Lenz Iran*, July 14, 2011, http://lenziran.com/2011/06/14/iran-react-to-new-american-initiative-internet-in-a-suitcase/.
107. Price, *Free Expression, Globalism and the New Strategic Communication*, 137–138.
108. Ibid., 141–149.
109. Kayla Ruble, "Iranian Hackers Use a Fake News Organization to Target Thousands," *Vice*, May 29, 2014, https://news.vice.com/article/iranian-hackers-use-a-fake-news-organization-to-target-thousands.
110. Christopher Bronk and Eneken Tikk-Ringas, "The Cyber Attack on Saudi Aramco," *Survival* 55(2) (2013), www.tandfonline.com/doi/abs/10.1080/00396338.2013.784468.
111. James A. Lewis, "Cybersecurity and Stability in the Gulf," Center for Strategic and International Studies, January 2014, https://csis-prod.s3.amazonaws.com/s3fs-public/legacy_files/files/publication/140106_Lewis_GulfCybersecurity_Web_0.pdf.
112. In-person interview with former senior Israeli government official, who requested anonymity, in Tel Aviv on June 25, 2015.
113. "A Report to the National Security Council - NSC 68," National Security Council, White House, April 12, 1950, www.trumanlibrary.org/whistlestop/study_collections/coldwar/documents/pdf/10-1.pdf.
114. Thomas Carothers, *Aiding Democracy Abroad: The Learning Curve* (Washington, DC: Carnegie Endowment for International Peace, 1999), 25.
115. United Nations, "Report of the Group of Governmental Experts on Developments in the Field of Information and Telecommunications in the Context of International Security," July 22, 2015, UN Doc. A/70/174.
116. Roscini, *Cyber Operations and the Use of Force in International Law*, 240–241.

4 CYBER PROXIES ON A TIGHT LEASH: THE UNITED STATES

1. Aliya Sternstein, "$460M CYBERCOM Contract Will Create Digital Munitions," *Defense One*, October 5, 2015, http://www.defenseone.com/technology/2015/10/460m-cybercom-contract-will-create-digital-munitions/122556/; United States

Cyber Command (USCYBERCOM) Omnibus Contract, Solicitation No. HC1028-15- R-0026 (2015), 14.

2. United States Cyber Command (USCYBERCOM) Omnibus Contract, Solicitation No. HC1028-15- R-0026 (2015), 18.

3. Adam Segal, *The Hacked World Order: How Nations Fight, Trade, Maneuver, and Manipulate in the Digital Age* (New York: PublicAffairs, 2016), 91.

4. Allison Stanger, *One Nation Under Contract: The Outsourcing of American Power and the Future of Foreign Policy* (New Haven, CT: Yale University Press, 2009).

5. Kevin R. Kosar, *The Quasi Government: Hybrid Organizations with Both Government and Private Sector Legal Characteristics* (Washington, DC: Congressional Research Service, 2011), 5.

6. Željko Branović, *The Privatisation of Security in Failing States: A quantitative Assessment* (Geneva Centre for the Democratic Control of Armed Forces, 2011), 3.

7. Juan Carlos Zarate, "The Emergence of a New Dog of War: Private International Security Companies, International Law, and the New World Disorder," *Stanford Journal of International Law* 34 (1998): 75.

8. Peter Singer, *Corporate Warriors: The Rise of the Privatized Military Industry* (Ithaca, NY: Cornell University Press, 2003), 93.

9. Branović, *The Privatisation of Security*, 4.

10. Sarah Percy, *Mercenaries: The History of a Norm in International Relations* (Oxford University Press, 2007), 224–225.

11. Ibid., 232–235.

12. Tim Shorrock, *Spies for Hire: The Secret World of Intelligence Outsourcing* (New York: Simon and Schuster, 2009), 191.

13. Office of the Director of National Intelligence, *Key Facts About Contractors* (Washington, DC: Office of the Director of National Intelligence, 2010).

14. Stanger, *One Nation Under Contract*, 84.

15. Office of the Director of National Intelligence, *Key Facts About Contractors*.

16. Ibid.

17. Nicole Perlroth, "The Chinese Hackers in the Back Office," *New York Times*, June 11, 2016, www.nytimes.com/2016/06/12/technology/the-chinese-hackers-in-the-back-office.html.

18. Shorrock, *Spies for Hire*, 264.

19. Ibid., 188.

20. Lachow uses the term "cyber military and security contractors" for these companies in Irving Lachow, "The Private Sector Role in Offensive Cyber Operations: Benefits, Issues and Challenges" (June 15, 2016), http://papers.ssrn.com/abstract=2836201.

21. Singer, *Corporate Warriors*, 63.

22. "Army Awards $125 Million Contract for Cyber Operations," *Defense Systems*, October 15, 2014, https://defensesystems.com/articles/2014/10/15/army-netcom-nci-contract-cyber-operations.aspx.

23. Shorrock, *Spies for Hire*, 134.

24. "ManTech Awarded $250 Million Contract to Prepare the Next Generation of Cyber Warfighters for the Department of Defense," ManTech International Corporation, October 7, 2015, http://investor.mantech.com/releasedetail.cfm?ReleaseID=935519.

25. One of the first acquistions dates to 1998 when CACI acquired QuesTech Inc. for USD 42 million. In 2012, HBHary was bought by ManTech International, and in 2014, a US private firm acquired the Israeli company NSO Group Technologies for USD 120 million. See Shorrock, *Spies for Hire*, 277; Gabriella Coleman, *Hacker, Hoaxer, Whistleblower, Spy: The Many Faces of Anonymous* (New York: Verso, 2014), 210, 233; Orr Hirschauge, "Overseas Buyers Snap up Two More Israeli Cyber Security Firms," *Haaretz*, March 19, 2014, www.haaretz.com/israel-news/business/.premium-1.580721.

26. "ManTech Acquires Oceans Edge Cyber Unit to Expand Advanced Cybersecurity Capabilities," ManTech International Corporation, June 13, 2016, http://investor.mantech.com/releasedetail.cfm?ReleaseID=975559.

27. Chelsey Dulaney, "Raytheon Acquires Blackbird Technologies for $420 million," *Wall Street Journal*, November 5, 2014, www.wsj.com/articles/raytheon-acquires-blackbird-techologies-for-420-million-1415193568; Irving Lachow, "The Private Sector Role in Offensive Cyber Operations: Benefits, Issues and Challenges" (June 15, 2016), http://papers.ssrn.com/abstract=2836201, 9.

28. Shorrock, *Spies for Hire*, 211.

29. "Capabilities," Cybersecurity, ManTech International Corporation, www.mantech.com/solutions/Cyber%20Security/Pages/cybersecurity_capabilities.aspx.

30. "Cyberpatriots," Northrop Grumman, www.northropgrumman.com/Careers/StudentsAndNewGrads/Pages/Cyberpatriot.aspx.

31. In-person expert interview with an employee of a major defense contractor, who requested anonymity, in September 2015.

32. Nicole Perlroth and David E. Sanger, "Nations Buying as Hackers Sell Flaws in Computer Code," *New York Times*, July 13, 2013, www.nytimes.com/2013/07/14/world/europe/nations-buying-as-hackers-sell-computer-flaws.html.

33. "Exclusive Exploits for LEAs," Vupen Security, www.vupen.com/english/services/lea-index.php.

34. "Penetration Testing," Immunity Inc., https://immunityinc.com/services/penetration-testing.html.

35. "Who We Are," Immunity Inc., www.immunitysec.com/company/.

36. "How to buy information," GLEG, http://gleg.net/prices.shtml.

37. "Immunity's Canvas," GLEG, http://gleg.net/canvas.shtml.

38. Shane Harris, *@War: The Rise of the Military-Internet Complex* (New York: Eamon Dolan, 2014), 105.

39. Ibid., 105–107.

40. Lachow, "The Private Sector Role in Offensive Cyber Operations."

41. Aliya Sternstein, "In a First, NSA Advertises Opportunities on http://Monster.com of Federal Contracting," *Nextgov*, December 31, 2016, www.nextgov

.com/security/2015/12/first-nsa-advertises-opportunities-monstercom-federal-contracting/124799/.

42. United States Cyber Command (USCYBERCOM) Omnibus Contract, 16.

43. General Services Administration (GSA) Federal Acquisition Office, "Notification of Award," May 20, 2016, www.fbo.gov/utils/view?id=3bf881d697991a360899ac049665de65.

44. Shorrock, *Spies for Hire*, 271.

45. Jill R. Aitoro, "The SI Organization Is No More. Meet Vencore," *Washington Business Journal*, July 23, 2014, www.bizjournals.com/washington/blog/fedbiz_daily/2014/07/the-si-organization-is-no-more-meet-vencore.html.

46. *Introducing Vencore: Mission Centered. Innovation Driven.* (Chantilly, VA: Vencore, 2016), http://static1.squarespace.com/static/53c80813e4b09390905d8 f2f/t/55d5fedde4b07fd45aed258d/1440087773537/VENCORE+Overview.pdf.

47. Lachow, "The Private Sector Role in Offensive Cyber Operations."

48. "Capabilities," Cyber Security, CACI, www.caci.com/cyber_security/capabilities.shtml.

49. "Cyberspace Joint Operational Planner II Job," SAIC, July 11, 2017, https://jobs.saic.com/job/Fort-Meade-Cyberspace-Joint-Operational-Planner-II-Job-MD-20755/396853400/.

50. Companies also offer training – for example, Exodus Intelligence, a small firm in Austin, Texas – but training is beyond the scope of this research. Nevertheless, given the relationship between defensive and offensive cyber capabilities and the fact that if somebody is good at defense – e.g., a reverse engineer and penetration tester – he or she also knows about offense, this is an area certainly worth studying further.

51. United States Cyber Command (USCYBERCOM) Omnibus Contract, 45–46.

52. Juan Carlos Zarate, "The Emergence of a New Dog of War: Private International Security Companies, International Law, and the New World Disorder," *Stanford Journal of International Law* 34 (1998): 75.

53. Perlroth and Sanger, "Nations Buying as Hackers Sell Flaws."

54. United States Cyber Command (USCYBERCOM) Omnibus Contract, 27.

55. Patrick Malone, "Pentagon Farmed Out Its Coding to Russia," *Daily Beast*, November 4, 2015, www.thedailybeast.com/articles/2015/11/04/pentagon-farmed-out-its-coding-to-russia.html.

56. Jo Becker, Adam Goldman, Michael S. Schmidt, and Matt Apuzzo, "N.S.A. Contractor Arrested in Possible New Theft of Secrets," *New York Times*, October 5, 2016, www.nytimes.com/2016/10/06/us/nsa-leak-booz-allen-hamilton.html.

57. Ellen Nakashima and Ashkan Soltani, "Italian Spyware Firm Relies on U.S. Internet Servers," *Washington Post*, March 3, 2014, www.washingtonpost.com/world/national-security/italian-spyware-firm-relies-on-us-internet-servers/2014/03/03/25f94f12-9f00-11e3-b8d8-94577ff66b28_story.html.

58. Cora Currier and Morgan Marquis-Boire, "Leaked Documents Show FBI, DEA and U.S. Army Buying Italian Spyware," *The Intercept*, July 6, 2015, https://theintercept.com/2015/07/06/hacking-team-spyware-fbi/.

59. Shawn Musgrave, "Hacking Team Had Ties to Local Police Departments Across the US," Motherboard, *Vice*, July 24, 2015, http://motherboard.vice.com/read/hacking-team-had-ties-to-local-police-departments-across-the-us.

60. Bill Marczak, "What We Know About the South Korea NIS's Use of Hacking Team's RCS," Citizen Lab, August 9, 2015, https://citizenlab.org/2015/08/what-we-know-about-the-south-korea-niss-use-of-hacking-teams-rcs/.

61. Alex Hern, "Hacking Team Hacked: Firm Sold Spying Tools to Repressive Regimes, Documents Claim," *The Guardian*, July 6, 2015, www.theguardian.com/technology/2015/jul/06/hacking-team-hacked-firm-sold-spying-tools-to-repressive-regimes-documents-claim.

62. Nicole Perlroth, "Governments Turn to Commercial Spyware to Intimidate Dissidents," *New York Times*, May 29, 2016, www.nytimes.com/2016/05/30/technology/governments-turn-to-commercial-spyware-to-intimidate-dissidents.html.

63. Ibid.

64. Kim Zetter, "Hacking Team Leak Shows How Secretive Zero-Days Exploit Sales Work," *Wired*, July 24, 2015, www.wired.com/2015/07/hacking-team-leak-shows-secretive-zero-day-exploit-sales-work/.

65. Tim Maurer, "Exporting the Right to Privacy," Future Tense, *Slate*, May 15, 2014, www.slate.com/articles/technology/future_tense/2014/05/wassenaar_arrangement_u_s_export_control_reform_keeping_surveillance_tech.html.

66. Sean McFate, *The Modern Mercenary: Private Armies and What They Mean for World Order* (New York: Oxford University Press, 2014), 96.

67. Lachow, "The Private Sector Role in Offensive Cyber Operations," 12.

68. Ibid.

69. Ibid.

70. See, for example, Jason Gewirtz, *Israel's Edge: The Story of the IDF's Most Elite Unit – Talpiot* (Springfield, NJ: Gefen Publishing House, 2015).

71. "Brendan Conlon," crunchbase, www.crunchbase.com/person/brendan-conlon.

72. "Jeff Tang / Chief Scientist," Vahna, www.vahna.com/company/jeff-tang/.

73. Cory Bennet, "NSA Staffers Rake in Silicon Valley Cash," *The Hill*, February 24, 2015, http://thehill.com/policy/cybersecurity/233740-nsa-staffers-rake-in-silicon-valley-cash.

74. Lachow, "The Private Sector Role in Offensive Cyber Operations," 16.

5 CYBER PROXIES ON A LOOSE LEASH: IRAN AND SYRIA

1. Hossein Bastani, "Structure of Iran's Cyber Warfare," Institut français d'analyse stratégique, December 13, 2012, www.strato-analyse.org/fr/spip.php?article223.

2. "Iran's Supreme Leader Tells Students to Prepare for Cyber War," *Russia Today*, February 23, 2014, www.rt.com/news/iran-israel-cyber-war-899/.

3. Bastani, "Structure of Iran's Cyber Warfare.

4. Ibid.

5. Collin Anderson, "Dimming the Internet: Detecting Throttling as a Mechanism of Censorship in Iran" (2013), https://arxiv.org/abs/1306.4361; "First Evidence of Iranian Internet Throttling as a Form of Censorship," MIT Technology Review, June 24, 2013, www.technologyreview.com/s/516361/first-evidence-of-iranian-internet-throttling-as-a-form-of-censorship/.

6. Adam Segal, *The Hacked World Order: How Nations Fight, Trade, Maneuver, and Manipulate in the Digital Age* (New York: PublicAffairs, 2016), 6.

7. James A. Lewis, *Cybersecurity and Stability in the Gulf* (Washington, DC: Center for Strategic and International Studies, 2014), 3; Jim Finkle, "Exclusive: Iran Hackers May Target U.S. Energy, Defense Firms, FBI Warns," Reuters, December 13, 2014, www.reuters.com/article/us-cybersecurity-iran-fbi-idUSKBN0JQ28Z20141213.

8. Jason P. Petterson and Matthew N. Smith, "Developing a Reliable Methodology for Assessing the Computer Network Operations Threat of Iran," master's thesis, Naval Postgraduate School, September 2005, https://fas.org/irp/eprint/cno-iran.pdf, 36.

9. Ibid., 37.

10. Nart Villeneuve et al., *FireEye, Operation Saffron Rose* (2013), 3.

11. CrowdStrike, *CrowdStrike Global Threat Intel Report – 2014* (January 2015), 67.

12. Jeffrey Carr, "Iran's Paramilitary Militia Is Recruiting Hackers," *Forbes*, January 12, 2011, www.forbes.com/sites/jeffreycarr/2011/01/12/irans-paramilitary-militia-is-recruiting-hackers/#351a003472b9. See also "Basij of the Islamic World Has Become Operational," OE Watch, Foreign Military Studies Office, http://fmso.leavenworth.army.mil/OEWatch/201412/MiddleEast_02.html, translated from original at "Janshin-e Sazman-e Basij-e Mostaz'afin: Tashkil-e Basij-e Jahan-e Islam 'Amaliyat-e Shodeh Ast" (The Organization for Mobilization of the Oppressed: The Newly-Formed Basij of the Islamic World Has Become Operational), *Islamic Republic News Agency*, November 7, 2014, http://irna.ir/fa/News/81376959/.

13. Bastani, "Structure of Iran's Cyber Warfare.

14. Ibid.

15. Villeneuve et al., *FireEye:,Operation Saffron Rose*, 3.

16. Heather Adkins, "An Update on Attempted Man-in-the-Middle Attacks," Google Security Blog, August 29, 2011, https://security.googleblog.com/2011/08/update-on-attempted-man-in-middle.html. Even as DigiNotar crumbled and eventually went bankrupt following the hack, a hacker known as the Comodohacker (after the victim of a previous hack) also calling himself "Ich Sun" took credit for the intrusion. The hacker has given interviews describing himself as a 21-year-old Iranian student. Just as students in 1979 created their own name – the Muslim Student Followers of the Imam's Line – to signal their political alignment, the malware used against Comodo included a Persian signature reading *janam fada-ye rahbar*, which means, "I sacrifice my life for the Leader [Ayatollah Khamenei]."

Robert McMillan, "Comodo Hacker Claims Another Certificate Authority," *Computerworld*, March 30, 2011, www.computerworld.com/article/2507509/securityo/comodo-hacker-claims-another-certificate-authority.html; Jeremy Kirk, "Comodo Hacker Claims Credit for DigiNotar Attack," *Computerworld*, September 6, 2011, http://www.computerworld.com/article/2510954/cybercrime-hacking/comodo-hacker-claims-credit-for-diginotar-attack.html; Bastani, "Structure of Iran's Cyber Warfare."

17. Nicole Perlroth, "Google Warns of New State-Sponsored Cyberattack Targets," Bits (blog), *New York Times*, October 2, 2012, http://bits.blogs.nytimes.com/2012/10/02/google-warns-new-state-sponsored-cyberattack-targets/.

18. Nicole Perlroth, "Google Says It Has Uncovered Iranian Spy Campaign," Bits (blog), *New York Times*, June 12, 2013, http://bits.blogs.nytimes.com/2013/06/12/google-says-it-has-uncovered-iranian-spy-campaign/.

19. Cylance, *Operation Cleaver* (2015), https://cdn2.hubspot.net/hubfs/270968/2015_cylance_website/images/cleaver_page/Cylance_Operation_Cleaver_Report.pdf?t=1475096805700, 5.

20. Ibid., 18.

21. Ibid., 30.

22. Ibid., 14. Again, a connection to Ashiyane was found through at least one of the actors involved in Operation Cleaver via the pseudonym "hussein1362."

23. Pierluigi Paganini, "The Cleaver Group Is Once Again in the Headlines Managing a Well-Developed Network of Fake LinkedIn Profiles for Cyber Espionage Purpose," Security Affairs (blog), October 8, 2015, http://securityaffairs.co/wordpress/40828/cyber-crime/iranian-cleaver-hackers-linkedin.html.

24. John Scott-Railton et al., "Group5: Syria and the Iranian Connection," Citizen Lab, August 2, 2016, https://citizenlab.org/2016/08/group5-syria/.

25. The indictment against three members of the Syrian Electronic Army that was unsealed two days earlier on March 22, 2016, explicitly refrains, unlike in the case of the Iranian hackers, from referring to the three as having been "state-sponsored." Meanwhile, the five Chinese mentioned in the 2014 indictment were not proxy actors but officers of the PLA and therefore direct agents of the Chinese military and state.

26. "Manhattan U.S. Attorney Announces Charges Against Seven Iranians for Conducting Coordinated Campaign of Cyber Attacks Against U.S. Financial Sector on Behalf of Islamic Revolutionary Guard Corps-Sponsored Entities," Department of Justice press release (March 24, 2016), www.justice.gov/usao-sdny/pr/manhattan-us-attorney-announces-charges-against-seven-iranians-conducting-coordinated.

27. Scott Macleod, "Radicals Reborn," *Time*, November 15, 1999, http://content.time.com/time/magazine/article/0,9171,992548,00.html.

28. Mark Bowden, *Guests of the Ayatollah* (New York: Grove Press, 2006), 8–9.

29. Ibid., 12.

30. Ibid., 8–9.

31. Ibid., 13.

32. *Case Concerning United States Diplomatic and Consular Staff in Tehran (United States of America v. Iran)*, Order, 12 V 81, International Court of Justice (ICJ), May 12, 1981, www.worldlii.org/int/cases/ICJ/1980/1.html, 29.
33. Ibid., 6.
34. Ibid., 10–12.
35. Bowden, *Guests of the Ayatollah*, 93; *Case Concerning United States Diplomatic and Consular Staff in Tehran*, 15.
36. Ibid., 33.
37. Ibid., 35.
38. Macleod, "Radicals Reborn."
39. *Case Concerning United States Diplomatic and Consular Staff in Tehran*, 35.
40. Bowden, *Guests of the Ayatollah*, 127–128.
41. Macleod, "Radicals Reborn."
42. "Manhattan U.S. Attorney Announces Charges Against Seven Iranians."
43. "Seven Iranians Working for Islamic Revolutionary Guard Corps-Affiliated Entities Charged for Conducting Coordinated Campaign of Cyber Attacks Against U.S. Financial Sector," Department of Justice press release (March 24, 2016), www.justice.gov/opa/pr/seven-iranians-working-islamic-revolution ary-guard-corps-affiliated-entities-charged.
44. Indictment at 4, *United States v. Fathi* (S.D.N.Y. filed March 24, 2016), www .justice.gov/opa/file/834996/download.
45. David E. Sanger and Nicole Perlroth, "Iran Is Raising Sophistication and Frequency of Cyberattacks, Study Says," *New York Times*, April 15, 2015, www .nytimes.com/2015/04/16/world/middleeast/iran-is-raising-sophistication-and-frequency-of-cyberattacks-study-says.html.
46. See Jason P. Petterson and Matthew N. Smith, "Developing a Reliable Methodology for Assessing the Computer Network Operations Threat of Iran," master's thesis, Naval Postgraduate School, September 2005, https://fas .org/irp/eprint/cno-iran.pdf.
47. ".:: Square Root::.," Square Root Education Consultancy, http://squareroot .edu.np/index.php?linkID=85.
48. Iftach Ian Amit, "Cyber[Crime|War]," paper presented at DefCon 18, Las Vegas, NV, July 20–August 1, 2010.
49. Petterson and Smith, "Developing a Reliable Methodology," 41.
50. A separate question is whether the seven Iranians mentioned in the US government's indictment were the only group targeting US financial institutions or if others did so as well. A 2012 *New York Times* article on the DDoS attacks against US banks stated that "[a] hacker group, which calls itself the Izz ad-Din al-Qassam Cyber Fighters, took credit for the attacks in online posts. They enlisted volunteers for the attacks with messages on various sites. On one blog, they called on volunteers to visit two Web addresses that would cause their computers to instantly start flooding targets – including the New York Stock Exchange, Nasdaq and Bank of America – with hundreds of data requests each second." Nicole Perlroth, "Hackers May Have Had Help With Attacks on U.S. Banks, Researchers Say," Bits (blog), *New York Times*, September 27, 2012, http://bits

.blogs.nytimes.com/2012/09/27/hackers-may-have-had-help-with-attacks-on-u-s-banks-researchers-say/.

51. Kevin Fernandez, "Zone-H Celebrates Its 10 Years!", Zone-H, March 9, 2012, www.zone-h.org/news/id/4742?zh=1; "Hackers Warn High Street Chains," *BBC News*, April 25, 2008, http://news.bbc.co.uk/2/hi/technology/7366995.stm.

52. "Sun Army," Zone-H, http://zone-h.org/archive/notifier=Sun%20Army/page=34.

53. Mirror of Armstrong Products UK, Zone-H, March 10, 2012, http://zone-h.org/mirror/id/17210269.

54. Mirror of NASA Langley Research Center home page, Zone-H, April 23, 2010, http://zone-h.org/mirror/id/10598254; the defaced website of the NASA Langley Research Center is no longer active but can be found at http://web.archive.org/web/20090615000000*/http://oea.larc.nasa.gov.

55. CrowdStrike, *CrowdStrike Global Threat Intel Report*, 67.

56. Nicole Perlroth and Quentin Hardy, "Bank Hacking Was the Work of Iranians, Officials Say," *New York Times*, January 8, 2013, www.nytimes.com/2013/01/09/technology/online-banking-attacks-were-work-of-iran-us-officials-say.html.

57. "Manhattan U.S. Attorney Announces Charges Against Seven Iranians."

58. Indictment at 9, *United States v. Fathi* (S.D.N.Y. filed March 24, 2016), www.justice.gov/opa/file/834996/download.

59. Perlroth and Hardy, "Bank Hacking Was the Work of Iranians."

60. Indictment at 5–6, *United States v. Fathi* (S.D.N.Y. filed March 24, 2016), www.justice.gov/opa/file/834996/download.

61. Ibid.

62. "Manhattan U.S. Attorney Announces Charges Against Seven Iranians."

63. Ibid.

64. Christopher M. Matthews, "Google Search Technique Aided N.Y. Dam Hacker in Iran," *Wall Street Journal*, March 27, 2016, www.wsj.com/articles/google-search-technique-aided-n-y-dam-hacker-in-iran-1459122543.

65. Joseph Berger, "A Dam, Small and Unsung, is Caught Up in an Iranian Hacking Case," *New York Times*, March 25, 2016, www.nytimes.com/2016/03/26/nyregion/rye-brook-dam-caught-in-computer-hacking-case.html.

66. Indictment at 11, *United States v. Fathi* (S.D.N.Y. filed March 24, 2016), www.justice.gov/opa/file/834996/download.

67. Nart Villeneuve et al., *FireEye: Operation Saffron Rose* (2013), 2; James Scott and Drew Spaniel, *Know Your Enemies 2.0: The Encyclopedia of the Most Prominent Hacktivists, Nation State and Mercenary Hackers* (Washington, DC: Institute for Critical Infrastructure Technology, February 8, 2016), http://icitech.org/know-your-enemies-2-0/, 23.

68. Scott and Spaniel, *Know Your Enemies 2.0*, 23.

69. Ibid.

70. CrowdStrike, *CrowdStrike Global Threat Intel Report*, 19.

71. "Computer Hacking Conspiracy Charges Unsealed Against Members of Syrian Electronic Army," US Department of Justice, March 22, 2016, www.justice.gov/

opa/pr/computer-hacking-conspiracy-charges-unsealed-against-members-syr ian-electronic-army.

72. Helmi Noman, "The Emergence of Open and Organized Pro-Government Cyber Attacks in the Middle East: The Case of the Syrian Electronic Army," OpenNet Initiative, https://opennet.net/emergence-open-and-organized-pro- government-cyber-attacks-middle-east-case-syrian-electronic-army; CrowdStrike, *CrowdStrike Global Threat Report – 2013 Year in Review* (January 2014), 8; Nicole Perlroth, "The Syrian Electronic Army Is at It Again," Bits (blog), *New York Times*, http://bits.blogs.nytimes.com/2013/12/24/the-syrian-elec tronic-army-is-at-it-again/.

73. Sarah Fowler, "Who Is the Syrian Electronic Army?" *BBC News*, April 25, 2013, www.bbc.com/news/world-middle-east-22287326.

74. Jennifer Preston, "Syria Restores Access to Facebook and YouTube," *New York Times*, February 9, 2011, www.nytimes.com/2011/02/10/world/middleeast/ 10syria.html.

75. Helmi Noman, "The Emergence of Open and Organized Pro-Government Cyber Attacks in the Middle East: The Case of the Syrian Electronic Army," OpenNet Initiative, https://opennet.net/emergence-open-and-organized-pro- government-cyber-attacks-middle-east-case-syrian-electronic-army.

76. Edwin Grohe, "The Cyber Dimensions of the Syrian Civil War: Implications for Future Conflict," *Comparative Strategy* 34(2) (2015): 135–137.

77. Nicole Perlroth, "Hunting for Syrian Hackers' Chain of Command," *New York Times*, May 17, 2013, www.nytimes.com/2013/05/18/technology/financial-times- site-is-hacked.html.

78. Robert Windrem, "Syrian Electronic Army Seen as 'Nuisance,' Not a Serious Cyberthreat," *NBC News*, August 30, 2013, www.nbcnews.com/ news/other/syrian-electronic-army-seen-nuisance-not-serious-cyberthreat- f8C11042663.

79. Perlroth, "Hunting for Syrian Hackers' Chain of Command."

80. CrowdStrike, *CrowdStrike Global Threat Report – 2013 Year in Review* (January 2014), 26–27; Windrem, "Syrian Electronic Army Seen as 'Nuisance.'"

81. Lee Ferran, "Interview with Alleged Member of Syrian Electronic Army," *ABC News*, August 29, 2013, http://abcnews.go.com/blogs/headlines/2013/08/inter view-with-alleged-member-of-syrian-electronic-army/.

82. Perlroth, "The Syrian Electronic Army Is at It Again."

83. Grohe, "The Cyber Dimensions of the Syrian Civil War," 135.

84. Ibid.

85. Andrea Peterson and Ellen Nakashima, "U.S. Charges Three Suspected Syrian Electronic Army Hackers," *Washington Post*, March 22, 2016, www .washingtonpost.com/news/the-switch/wp/2016/03/22/u-s-charges-three-sus pected-syrian-electronic-army-hackers/.

86. Ellen Nakashima, "Syrian Hacker Extradited to the United States from Germany," *Washington Post*, May 9, 2016, www.washingtonpost.com/world/ national-security/syrian-hacker-extradited-to-the-united-states-from-germany/ 2016/05/09/eb855654-15fa-11e6-aa55-670cabef46e0_story.html.

87. These details are known because the US government was able to obtain the records after issuing a search warrant. "Computer Hacking Conspiracy Charges Unsealed," US Department of Justice.

88. Affidavit in Support of Criminal Complaint and Arrest Warrants at 8, *United States v. Romar*, No. 1:15-MJ-498 (E.D. Va. filed September 29, 2015).

89. Ibid.

90. "Computer Hacking Conspiracy Charges Unsealed," US Department of Justice.

91. Jared Keller, "A Fake AP Tweet Sinks the Dow for an Instant," *Bloomberg Businessweek*, April 24, 2013, www.bloomberg.com/news/articles/2013–04-23/a-fake-ap-tweet-sinks-the-dow-for-an-instant.

92. "Computer Hacking Conspiracy Charges Unsealed."

93. David E. Sanger and Eric Schmitt, "Hackers Use Old Lure on Web to Help Syrian Government," *New York Times*, February 1, 2015, www.nytimes.com/2015/02/02/world/middleeast/hackers-use-old-web-lure-to-aid-assad.html.

94. Ibid.

95. IntelCrawler, *Syrian Electronic Army: Hacktivision to Cyber Espionage?* (March 20, 2014), 22.

96. "Behind the Syrian Conflict's Digital Frontlines," FireEye Threat Intelligence Blog, February 2, 2015, www.fireeye.com/blog/threat-research/2015/02/behind_the_syrianco.html, 17.

97. Grohe, "The Cyber Dimensions of the Syrian Civil War," 137.

98. "Behind the Syrian Conflict's Digital Frontlines."

99. *Case Concerning United States Diplomatic and Consular Staff in Tehran (United States of America v. Iran)*, Order, 12 V 81, International Court of Justice (ICJ), May 12, 1981, www.worldlii.org/int/cases/ICJ/1980/1.html, 31–32.

100. Ibid., 29–30.

101. Email correspondence with Collin Anderson dated March 26, 2016.

102. "Computer Hacking Conspiracy Charges Unsealed."

103. Ellen Nakashima and Matt Zapotosky, "U.S. Charges Iran-Linked Hackers with Targeting Banks, N.Y. Dam," *Washington Post*, March 24, www.washingtonpost.com/world/national-security/justice-department-to-unseal-indictment-against-hackers-linked-to-iranian-goverment/2016/03/24/9b3797d2-f17b-11e5-a61f-e9c95c06edca_story.html.

104. Alastair Stevenson, "Iran and North Korea Sign Technology Treaty to Combat Hostile Malware," V3, September 3, 2012, www.v3.co.uk/v3-uk/news/2202493/iran-and-north-korea-sign-technology-treaty-to-combat-hostile-malware; Petterson and Smith, "Developing a Reliable Methodology for Assessing the Computer Network Operations Threat of Iran," 37.

6 CYBER PROXIES ON THE LOOSE: THE FORMER SOVIET UNION

1. Boris N. Mironov, "The Development of Literacy in Russia and the USSR from the Tenth to the Twentieth Centuries," *History of Education Quarterly* 31(2) (1991).

2. Ruth Alvey, "Russian Hackers for Hire: The Rise of the Emercenary," *Janes Intelligence Review* 13(7) (2001): 52–53.

3. "Nearshoring: Top 20 Largest In-House R&D Offices in Ukraine," GoalEurope, October 4, 2013, http://goaleurope.com/2013/10/04/nearshore-out sourcing-top-20-largest-rd-offices-in-ukraine/.

4. Alissa de Carbonnel, "Hackers for Hire: Ex-Soviet Tech Geeks Play Outsized Role in Global Cyber Crime," *NBC News*, August 22, 2013, www.nbcnews.com /technology/hackers-hire-ex-soviet-tech-geeks-play-outsized-role-global-6C10981346.

5. Alvey, "Russian Hackers for Hire," 52–53.

6. de Carbonnel, "Hackers for Hire."

7. Nicole Perlroth, "After Arrest of Accused Hacker, Russia Accuses U.S. of Kidnapping," Bits (blog), *New York Times*, July 8, 2014, http://bits.blogs .nytimes.com/2014/07/08/after-arrest-of-accused-hacker-russia-accuses-u-s-of-kidnapping/.

8. Brian Krebs, "Story-Driven Résumé: My Best Work 2005–2009," Krebs on Security (blog), December 29, 2009, https://krebsonsecurity.com/2009/12/story-driven-resume-my-best-work-2005–2009-3/.

9. Matthew Goldstein and Nicole Perlroth, "Authorities Closing in on Hackers Who Stole Data from JPMorgan Chase," Dealbook, *New York Times*, March 15, 2015, www.nytimes.com/2015/03/16/business/dealbook/authorities-closing-in-on-hackers-who-stole-data-from-jpmorgan-chase.html.

10. de Carbonnel, "Hackers for Hire."

11. Timothy Thomas, *Russian Military Strategy: Impacting 21st Century Reform and Geopolitics* (Fort Leavenworth, KS: Foreign Military Studies Office, 2015), 267.

12. Krebs, "Story-Driven Résumé."

13. Brian Krebs, "When Cyber Criminals Eat Their Own," Security Fix (blog), *Washington Post*, January 26, 2009, http://voices.washingtonpost.com/security fix/2009/01/does_profit_trump_nationalism.html.

14. Brian Krebs, "A Busy Week for Cybercrime Justice," Krebs on Security (blog), March 26, 2012, https://krebsonsecurity.com/2012/03/a-busy-week-for-cyber crime-justice/.

15. Brian Krebs, "The Curious Case of Dmitry Golubov," Security Fix (blog), *Washington Post*, March 28, 2008, http://voices.washingtonpost.com/security fix/2008/03/the_curious_case_of_dmitry_gol.html.

16. Ibid.

17. Brian Krebs, "Ukrainian Cyber Crime Boss Leads Political Party," Security Fix (blog), *Washington Post*, March 13, 2008, http://voices.washingtonpost.com /securityfix/2008/03/ukranian_cybercrime_boss_leads.html.

18. Perlroth, "After Arrest of Accused Hacker."

19. Martha Bellisle, "Russian Convicted in Masterminding Global Online Theft Ring," Associated Press, August 25, 2016, http://bigstory.ap.org/article/ 98b473bd91c543559a87c61ed455c355/jury-gets-case-russian-man-charged-hacking.

20. Perlroth, "After Arrest of Accused Hacker."
21. "Russian Rage over Finland Extradition to US," *BBC News*, January 8, 2016, www.bbc.com/news/world-europe-35267306.
22. Perlroth, "After Arrest of Accused Hacker."
23. "Press release on the upcoming visit of US Secretary of State John Kerry," Ministry of Foreign Affairs of the Russian Federation, December 11, 2015, www.mid.ru/en/foreign_policy/news/-/asset_publisher/cKNonkJEo2Bw/content/id/1977897.
24. Alvey, "Russian Hackers for Hire," 52–53.
25. Alexander Klimburg and Heli Tirmaa-Klaar, "Cybersecurity and Cyberpower: Concepts, Conditions and Capabilities for Cooperation for Action Within the EU," *European Parliament* (2011): 60.
26. Ibid.
27. Eneken Tikk, Kadri Kaska, and Liis Vihul, *International Cyber Incidents: Legal Considerations* (Tallinn: Cooperative Cyber Defence Centre of Excellence, 2010), 15–16.
28. Ibid., 18–19.
29. Ibid., 23–24.
30. Andrei Soldatov and Irina Borogan, *The Red Web: The Struggle Between Russia's Digital Dictators and the New Online Revolutionaries* (New York: PublicAffairs, 2015), 116–117.
31. Ibid., 151–152. The revelation of Nashi's involvement in the attack confirmed the conclusions of a secret 2009 NSA study, according to Adam Segal at the Council on Foreign Relations in New York. Adam Segal, *The Hacked World Order: How Nations Fight, Trade, Maneuver, and Manipulate in the Digital Age* (New York: PublicAffairs, 2016), 65.
32. Tikk et al., *International Cyber Incidents*, 28.
33. I thank the Cooperative Cyber Defence Centre of Excellence for granting permission to include material in this section from Tim Maurer, "Cyber Proxies and the Crisis in Ukraine," in *Cyber War in Perspective: Russian Aggression Against Ukraine*, ed. Kenneth Geers (Tallinn: NATO CCD COE Publications, 2015), https://ccdcoe.org/multimedia/cyber-war-perspective-russian-aggression-against-ukraine.html.
34. "Vladimir Putin Admits for First Time Russian Troops Took over Crimea, Refuses to Rule out Intervention in Donetsk," *National Post*, April 17, 2014, http://news.nationalpost.com/news/world/vladimir-putin-admits-for-first-time-russian-troops-took-over-crimea-refuses-to-rule-out-intervention-in-donetsk.
35. "Feb. 28 Updates on the Crisis in Ukraine," *New York Times News Blog*, February 28, 2014, http://thelede.blogs.nytimes.com/2014/02/28/latest-updates-tensions-in-ukraine/?_r=0.
36. "Kremlin Website Hit by 'Powerful' Cyber Attack," *Reuters*, March 14, 2014, http://www.reuters.com/article/2014/03/14/us-russia-kremlin-cybercrime-idUSBREA2D16T20140314.

37. "'Cyber-Attack' Cripples Ukraine's Electronic Election System Ahead of Presidential Vote," *Russia Today*, 24 May, 2014, http://www.rt.com/news/161332-ukraine-president-election-virus/.

38. "Ukraine Election Narrowly Avoided 'Wanton Destruction' from Hackers (+video)," *Christian Science Monitor*, June 17, 2015, www.csmonitor.com/World/Passcode/2014/0617/Ukraine-election-narrowly-avoided-wanton-destruc tion-from-hackers-video.

39. "Cyber Warrior Steps up Effort to Help in War with Russia," *KyivPost*, February 10, 2015, www.kyivpost.com/content/kyiv-post-plus/cyber-warrior-steps-up-effort-to-help-in-war-with-russia-380184.html.

40. "Ukraine's Lonely Cyberwarrior vs. Russia," *Daily Beast*, February 18, 2015, www.thedailybeast.com/articles/2015/02/18/ukraine-s-lonely-cyber-warrior.html.

41. Soldatov and Borogan, *The Red Web*, 280.

42. Falcon Bjorn, "Cyberwar Special Forces – Ukrainian Hackers vs Russian Occupiers," *Inform Napalm*, June 14, 2016, https://informnapalm.org/en/cyber war-special-forces/.

43. CrowdStrike, *CrowdStrike Global Threat Intel Report – 2014* (January 2015), 27.

44. Jeff Stone, "Meet CyberBerkut, The Pro-Russian Hackers Waging Anonymous-Style Cyberwarfare Against Ukraine," *International Business Times*, December 17, 2015, www.ibtimes.com/meet-cyberberkut-pro-russian-hackers-waging-anon ymous-style-cyberwarfare-against-2228902.

45. Nadiya Kostyuk and Yuri M. Zhukov, online appendix to "Invisible Digital Front: Physical Violence and Cyber Warfare in Ukraine," unpublished paper dated March 15, 2016, 13–14.

46. CrowdStrike, *CrowdStrike Global Threat Intel Report*, 27.

47. Ibid., 26.

48. Kim Zetter, "Inside the Cunning, Unprecedented Hack of Ukraine's Power Grid," *Wired*, March 3, 2016, www.wired.com/2016/03/inside-cunning-unprece dented-hack-ukraines-power-grid/; "Analysis of the Cyber Attack on the Ukrainian Power Grid," E-ISAC and SANS, March 18, 2016, https://ics.sans.org/media/E-ISAC_SANS_Ukraine_DUC_5.pdf.

49. In 2015, the UN Group of Governmental Experts agreed to a voluntary norm to apply in peacetime, stating that "A State should not conduct or knowingly support ICT activitiy contrary to its obligations under international law that intentionally damages critical infrastructure or otherwise impairs the use and operation of critical infrastructure to provide services to the public." After the cyber attack on Ukraine's electrical grid, experts debated whether this would constitute a violation of the norm if the Russian government was responsible and the norm considered binding. Two lines of argument have since emerged why this attack might not constitute a violation. First, the US government considers the conflict between Ukraine and Russia to be an international armed conflict. The peacetime norm would therefore not apply. Second, even if it were not an international armed conflict, one could argue that the cyber attack was not a first strike but retaliation for the previous kinetic attack cutting power to Crimea and therefore arguably not

a violation of the norm were it conceived as a no-first-use regime. "Crimea Power Cut: Ukraine Police Investigate 'Explosion,'" *BBC News,* December 31, 2015, www.bbc.com/news/world-europe-35204304; Ivan Nechepurenko, "Crimea to Face Power Shortages for Months, Officials Say," *New York Times,* January 8, 2016, www.nytimes.com/2016/01/09/world/europe/crimea-power-ukraine-russia .html; "Russian Energy Minister: New Crimean Blackout Prevented," *Moscow Times,* May 20, 2016, https://themoscowtimes.com/news/russian-energy-minister-new-crimean-blackout-prevented-52957; United Nations, "Report of the Group of Governmental Experts on Developments in the Field of Information and Telecommunications in the Context of International Security," July 22, 2015, UN Doc. A/70/174.

50. Chris Demchak, *Wars of Disruption and Resilience: Cybered Conflict, Power, and National Security* (Athens, GA: University of Georgia Press, 2011).

51. Petro Zamakis, "Cyber Wars: The Invisible Front," Ukraine Investigation, April 24, 2014, http://ukraineinvestigation.com/cyber-wars-invisible-front/.

52. Bjorn, "Cyberwar Special Forces."

53. Dmitry Gorenburg, "Russia and Ukraine: Not the Military Balance You Think," *War on the Rocks,* November 10, 2015, http://warontherocks.com/ 2014/11/russia-and-ukraine-not-the-military-balance-you-think/.

54. Heather Harrison Dinniss, "Participants in Conflict: Cyber Warriors, Patriotic Hackers and the Laws of War" in Dan Saxon, ed. *International Humanitarian Law and the Changing Technology of War* (Boston: Martinus Nijhoff Publishers, 2013), 251.

55. Teng Jianqun and Xu Longdi, *Cyber War Preparedness, Cyberspace Arms Control and the United States* (Beijing: China Institute of International Studies, 2014), 13.

56. Ronald J. Deibert, Rafal Rohozinski, and Masashi Crete-Nishihata, "Cyclones in Cyberspace: Information Shaping and Denial in the 2008 Russia–Georgia War," *Security Dialogue* 43(1) (2012): 12.

57. Ibid., 7–8.

58. Ibid., 4.

59. Eneken Tikk, Kadri Kaska, and Liis Vihul, *International Cyber Incidents: Legal Considerations* (Tallinn: Cooperative Cyber Defence Centre of Excellence, 2010), 74–76.

60. John Bumgarner, *Overview by the US-CCU of the Cyber Campaign Against Georgia in August of 2008* (August 2009), 2–3.

61. Deibert et al., "Cyclones in Cyberspace," 14–15.

62. Ibid., 10–11; Tikk et al., *International Cyber Incidents,* 76.

63. Segal, *The Hacked World Order,* 68.

64. Deibert et al., "Cyclones in Cyberspace," 13.

65. Ibid., 17; Jeffrey Carr et al., *Project Grey Goose: Phase I Report: Russia/Georgia Cyber War – Findings and Analysis* (October 17, 2008), 3.

66. Deibert et al., "Cyclones in Cyberspace," 16–18.

67. Krebs, "When Cyber Criminals Eat Their Own."

68. P. W. Singer and Allan Friedman, *Cybersecurity and Cyberwar: What Everyone Needs to Know* (New York: Oxford University Press, 2014), 112.

69. Timothy Newark, *The Mafia at War: Allied Collusion with the Mob* (London: Greenhill Books, 2007), 82.

70. Ibid., 70.

71. Ibid., 109.

72. Ibid.

73. Ibid., 108.

74. "U.S. Charges Russian FSB Officers and Their Criminal Conspirators for Hacking Yahoo and Millions of Email Accounts," Department of Justice press release (March 15, 2017), www.justice.gov/opa/pr/us-charges-russian-fsb-officers-and-their-criminal-conspirators-hacking-yahoo-and-millions.

75. Indictment at 3, 12, *United States* v. *Dokuchaev et al.*, No. 17-cr-00103 (N.D. Ca. filed February 28, 2017), available at www.justice.gov/opa/press-release/file/948201/download; "U.S. Charges Russian FSB Officers and Their Criminal Conspirators."

76. Ibid.

77. Ibid.

78. Indictment at 4, *United States* v. *Dokuchaev et al.*, No. 17-cr-00103 (N.D. Ca. filed February 28, 2017), www.justice.gov/opa/press-release/file/948201/download.

79. "U.S. Charges Russian FSB Officers and Their Criminal Conspirators."

80. Ibid.

81. Ibid.

82. Indictment at 3, *United States* v. *Dokuchaev et al.*, No. 17-cr-00103 (N.D. Ca. filed February 28, 2017), www.justice.gov/opa/press-release/file/948201/download.

83. Indictment at 16, *United States* v. *Dokuchaev et al.*, No. 17-cr-00103 (N.D. Ca. filed February 28, 2017), http://www.justice.gov/opa/press-release/file/948201/download.

84. "U.S. Charges Russian FSB Officers and Their Criminal Conspirators."

85. Indictment at 6, 13, *United States* v. *Dokuchaev et al.*, No. 17-cr-00103 (N.D. Ca. filed February 28, 2017), www.justice.gov/opa/press-release/file/948201/download.

86. Seth Fiegerman, "Verizon Cuts Yahoo Deal by $350 Million," *CNN*, February 21, 2017, http://money.cnn.com/2017/02/21/technology/yahoo-verizon-deal/.

87. Indictment at 10, *United States* v. *Dokuchaev et al.*, No. 17-cr-00103 (N.D. Ca. filed February 28, 2017), www.justice.gov/opa/press-release/file/948201/download.

88. "U.S. Charges Russian FSB Officers and Their Criminal Conspirators."

7 CHANGE OVER TIME: CHINA'S EVOLVING RELATIONSHIPS WITH CYBER PROXIES

1. Bill Gertz, "Chinese Spy Who Defected Tells All," *Washington Times*, March 19, 2009, www.washingtontimes.com/news/2009/mar/19/exclusive-chinese-spy-who-defected-tells-all/.
2. Nicole Perlroth, "Case Based in China Puts a Face on Persistent Hacking," *New York Times*, March 29, 2012, www.nytimes.com/2012/03/30/technology/hacking-in-asia-is-linked-to-chinese-ex-graduate-student.html.
3. We owe the detailed information about the first generation of Chinese hackers and assessments of their relationship with the government to Scott Henderson, who, after spending two decades working in the US intelligence community as a Chinese linguist, retired from the US Army in 2004 and joined a private intelligence contractor in Fort Leavenworth, Kansas. In fact, he became such an authority on Chinese hacktivists that his blog was read by the Chinese hackers themselves, with one emailing him to complain at one point because the blog had been censored. When Henderson started his open source research into the Chinese hacking community, he found hundreds of websites and hacker forums. Based on what he saw there, he concluded that the hackers at that time had no connection to the government. According to him, "If this was some secret government-run organization, it was the most horribly run secret government organization in the universe." Scott Henderson, "Beijing's Rising Hacker Stars ... How Does Mother China React?", *IO Sphere* (Fall 2008): 30; Mara Hvistendahl, "Hackers: The China Syndrome," *Popular Science*, April 23, 2009, www.popsci.com/scitech/article/2009–04/hackers-china-syndrome.
4. Henderson, "Beijing's Rising Hacker," 25.
5. Email correspondence with Nigel Inkster dated March 22, 2017.
6. Elsa B. Kania, "A Force for Cyber Anarchy or Cyber Order? – PLA Perspectives on 'Cyber Rules,'" *China Brief* 16(11) (2016), https://jamestown.org/wp-content/uploads/2016/07/CB_16_11_2.pdf, 19.
7. I thank Adam Segal for pointing out that the documents focus primarily on the defense industrial base. See also Robert Sheldon and Joe McReynolds, "Civil-Military Integration and Cybersecurity: A Study of Chinese Information Warfare Militias," in *China and Cybersecurity: Espionage, Strategy, and Politics in the Digital Domain*, ed. Jon R. Lindsay et al. (New York: Oxford University Press, 2015), 189.
8. Ibid., 192.
9. Bryan Krekel et al. quoted in Sheldon and McReynolds, "Civil-Military Integration and Cybersecurity," 194.
10. Nigel Inkster, *China's Cyber Power* (New York: Routledge, 2016), 104.
11. Scott J. Henderson, *The Dark Visitor: Inside the World of Chinese Hackers* (Fort Leavenworth, KS: Foreign Military Studies Office, 2007), 6.
12. Inkster, *China's Cyber Power*, 32.
13. Henderson, *The Dark Visitor*, 18–19.

14. Elisabeth Rosenthal, "Beijing Students and Women, Defying Ban, Protest Anti-Chinese Violence in Indonesia," *New York Times*, August 18, 1998, www .nytimes.com/1998/08/18/world/beijing-students-women-defying-ban-protest-anti-chinese-violence-indonesia.html.
15. Henderson, *The Dark Visitor*, 16–17.
16. The term "Honker" comes from *hóngkè* (紅 客) or "red guest" – suggesting that these are patriotic actors as opposed to traditional (criminal) hackers, who are called *hēikè* (黑客) or "black guest."
17. John Leyden, "Hidden Dragon: The Chinese Cyber Menace," *The Register*, December 24, 2011, www.theregister.co.uk/2011/12/24/china_cyber crime_under ground_analysis/.
18. Owen Fletcher, "Patriotic Chinese Hacking Group Reboots," *Wall Street Journal*, October 5, 2011, http://blogs.wsj.com/chinarealtime/2011/10/05/patrio tic-chinese-hacking-group-reboots/.
19. Henderson, *The Dark Visitor*, 32.
20. Ibid., 36; email correspondence with Nigel Inkster dated March 22, 2017.
21. Henderson, *The Dark Visitor*, 21–22.
22. James Mulvenon, "PLA Computer Network Operations: Scenarios, Doctrine, Organizations, and Capability," in *Beyond the Strait: PLA Missions Other Than Taiwan*, ed. Roy Kamphausen et al. (Carlisle, PA: Strategic Studies Institute, 2009), 277–279.
23. Henderson, *The Dark Visitor*, 111–112.
24. Timothy L. Thomas, *Dragon Bytes: Chinese Information-War Theory and Practice* (Ft. Leavenworth, KS: Foreign Military Studies Office, 2004), 28.
25. Henderson, *The Dark Visitor*, 118.
26. Mulvenon, "PLA Computer Network Operations, 277–279.
27. Henderson, *The Dark Visitor*, 10.
28. Scott Henderson, "Beijing's Rising Hacker Stars . . . How Does Mother China React?", *IO Sphere* (Fall 2008): 30.
29. Ibid., 29.
30. Thomas, *Dragon Bytes*, 59.
31. Timothy Thomas, *The Dragon's Quantum Leap: Transforming from a Mechanized to an Informatized Force* (Fort Leavenworth, KS: Foreign Military Studies Office, 2009), 223–224.
32. Henderson, "Beijing's Rising Hacker Stars," 27.
33. Thomas, *Dragon Bytes*, 10.
34. Ibid., 75.
35. Ibid., 137.
36. Robert Sheldon and Joe McReynolds, "Civil-Military Integration and Cybersecurity: A Study of Chinese Information Warfare Militias," in *China and Cybersecurity: Espionage, Strategy, and Politics in the Digital Domain*, ed. Jon R. Lindsay et al. (New York: Oxford University Press, 2015), 195.
37. Sheldon and McReynolds, "Civil-Military Integration and Cybersecurity," 204.
38. Bryan Krekel, Patton Adams, and George Bakos, "Occupying the Information High Ground: Chinese Capabilities for Computer Network

Operations and Cyber Espionage," report prepared for the U.S.-China Economic and Security Review Commission by Northrop Grumman Corp., March 7, 2012, http://nsarchive.gwu.edu/NSAEBB/NSAEBB424/docs/Cyber-066.pdf, 53–54.

39. Henderson, *The Dark Visitor*, 112–113.
40. The various efforts by the state to recruit hackers from universities, etc., are excluded because they are not about state sponsorship but about these actors becoming part of the state, as others have convincingly argued; see Sheldon and McReynolds, "Civil-Military Integration and Cybersecurity," 192.
41. Krekel et al., "Occupying the Information High Ground", 60–61.
42. Ibid., 60.
43. Henderson, *The Dark Visitor*, 105.
44. Inkster, *China's Cyber Power*, 77.
45. Mulvenon, "PLA Computer Network Operations," 277–279; Henderson, *The Dark Visitor*, 102; Mara Hvistendahl, "China's Hacker Army," *Foreign Policy*, March 3, 2010, http://foreignpolicy.com/2010/03/03/chinas-hacker-army/.
46. Henderson, *The Dark Visitor*, 60–61.
47. Mara Hvistendahl, "Hackers: The China Syndrome," *Popular Science*, April 23, 2009, www.popsci.com/scitech/article/2009-04/hackers-china-syndrome.
48. Sheldon and McReynolds, "Civil-Military Integration and Cybersecurity," 2015), 195.
49. Inkster, *China's Cyber Power*, 98.
50. Ibid., 68–69.
51. Dawn S. Onley and Patience Wait, "Red Storm Rising," GCN, August 17, 2006, https://gcn.com/articles/2006/08/17/red-storm-rising.aspx; Henderson, *The Dark Visitor*, 67.
52. Henderson, *The Dark Visitor*, 111.
53. Ibid.
54. Thomas, *The Dragon's Quantum Leap*, 185.
55. Simon Elegant, "Enemies at the Firewall," *Time*, December 6, 2007.
56. Ken Dunham and Jim Melnick, "'Wicked Rose' and the NCPH Hacking Group," http://krebsonsecurity.com/wp-content/uploads/2012/11/WickedRose_andNCPH.pdf.
57. Elegant, "Enemies at the Firewall."
58. Kathrin Hille, "Chinese Military Mobilises Cybermilitias," *Financial Times*, October 12, 2011, www.ft.com/content/33dc83e4-c800-11e0-9501-00144feabdc0.
59. Ibid.
60. Robin Wauters, "McAfee Calls Operation Aurora A 'Watershed Moment in Cybersecurity', Offers Guidance," *Washington Post*, January 17, 2010, www.washingtonpost.com/wp-dyn/content/article/2010/01/17/AR2010011700562.html.
61. James Scott and Drew Spaniel, *China's Espionage Dynasty: Economic Death by a Thousand Cuts* (Washington, DC: Institute for Critical Infrastructure Technology, July 28, 2016), 20.

62. "Hacker Academy," *Week in China*, September 26, 2014, http://www.weekin china.com/2014/09/hacker-academy/.

63. Josephine Wolff, "Can Campus Networks Ever Be Secure?", *The Atlantic*, October 11, 2015, www.theatlantic.com/technology/archive/2015/10/can-cam pus-networks-ever-be-secure/409813/.

64. Inkster, *China's Cyber Power*, 39.

65. Thomas, *The Dragon's Quantum Leap*, 225.

66. Ibid.

67. Scott Henderson, "Withered Rose ... Law Done Come and Got Him," The Dark Visitor (blog), April 9, 2009, www.thedarkvisitor.com/tag/withered-rose/.

68. Jon R. Lindsay, "The Impact of China on Cybersecurity: Fiction and Friction," *International Security* 39(3) (Winter 2014/15): 18.

69. Inkster, *China's Cyber Power*, 40.

70. Eric Heginbotham, *The U.S.-China Military Scorecard: Forces, Geography, and the Evolving Balance of Power 1996–2017* (Santa Monica, CA: RAND Corporation, 2015), 275.

71. Loretta Chao and Brian Spegele, "Beijing Tightens Cyber Controls," *Wall Street Journal*, December 17, 2011, www.wsj.com/articles/SB1000142405 2970204643804577101522579231922; Inkster, *China's Cyber Power*, 42.

72. "Chinese Communist Party: Communiqué on the Current State of the Ideological Sphere," Council on Foreign Relations, September 1, 2013, www .cfr.org/non-state-actors-and-nongovernmental-organizations/chinese-commu nist-party-communique-current-state-ideological-sphere/p36592.

73. Inkster, *China's Cyber Power*, 42.

74. Nigel Inkster, "The Chinese Intelligence Agencies: Evolution and Empowerment in Cyberspace," in *China and Cybersecurity: Espionage, Strategy, and Politics in the Digital Domain*, ed. Jon R. Lindsay et al. (New York: Oxford University Press, 2015), 45.

75. Ibid., 30–31.

76. Ellen Nakashima and Adam Goldman, "In a First, Chinese Hackers Are Arrested at the Behest of the U.S. Government," *Washington Post*, October 9, 2015, www.washingtonpost.com/world/national-security/in-a-first-chinese-hack ers-are-arrested-at-the-behest-of-the-us-government/2015/10/09/0a7b0e46-6778- 11e5-8325-a42b5a459b1e_story.html.

77. Ibid.

78. "First China-U.S. Cyber Security Ministerial Dialogue Yields Positive Outcomes," *Xinhua*, December 2, 2015, http://news.xinhuanet.com/english/ 2015–12/02/c_134874733.html.

79. Jen Weedon, Testimony before the US-China Economic and Security Review Commission, Hearing on Commercial Cyber Espionage and Barriers to Digital Trade in China, June 15, 2015, www.uscc.gov/sites/default/files/Weedon% 20Testimony.pdf. See also Ellen Nakashima, "Chinese Government Has Arrested Hackers It Says Breached OPM Database," *Washington Post*, December 2, 2015, www.washingtonpost.com/world/national-security/chinese- government-has-arrested-hackers-suspected-of-breaching-opm-database/2015/

12/02/0295b918-990c-11e5-8917-653b65c809eb_story.html?
utm_term=.832ab9981d7b.

80. See Nakashima, "Chinese Government Has Arrested Hackers."

81. As the BBC pointed out, the "[p]iracy of goods, brands and copyrighted
materials is so rife in China that there is a word for the results – Shan Zhai, a
term originally used to describe a bandit stronghold outside government control." "Anish Kapoor Accuses China of Copying 'Bean' Sculpture," *BBC News*,
August 12, 2015, www.bbc.com/news/entertainment-arts-33886678.

82. Mara Hvistendahl, "The Decline in Chinese Cyberattacks: The Story Behind
the Numbers," *MIT Technology Review*, October 25, 2016, www.technologyre
view.com/s/602705/the-decline-in-chinese-cyberattacks-the-story-behind-the-
numbers/.

83. Nakashima and Goldman, "In a First, Chinese Hackers Are Arrested."

84. Chris Buckley, "Xi Jinping Announces Overhaul of China's Military Forces,"
New York Times, November 26, 2015, www.nytimes.com/2015/11/27/world/asia/
xi-jinping-china-military-peoples-liberation-army.html.

85. Ying Yu Lin, "The Secrets of China's Strategic Support Force," *The Diplomat*,
August 31, 2016, http://thediplomat.com/2016/09/the-secrets-of-chinas-strategic-
support-force/.

86. Sheldon and McReynolds, "Civil-Military Integration and Cybersecurity," 193.

87. Ibid., 200.

88. Ibid., 207–208.

89. Ibid., 193.

90. Ibid., 202–203.

91. Henderson, *The Dark Visitor*, 117.

92. Inkster, *China's Cyber Power*, 104.

93. Sheldon and McReynolds, "Civil-Military Integration and Cybersecurity,"
200–201; Krekel et al., "Occupying the Information High Ground," 53–54.

94. Justin V. Hastings, "Understanding Maritime Piracy Syndicate Operations,"
Security Studies 21(4) (2012): 689.

95. "Fact Sheet: President Xi Jinping's State Visit to the United States," Office of
the Press Secretary, the White House, September 25, 2015; David J. Lynch and
Geoff Dyer, "Chinese Hacking of US Companies Declines," *Financial Times*,
April 13, 2016, www.ft.com/content/d81e30de-00e4-11e6-99cb-83242733f755.

96. Lynch and Dyer, "Chinese Hacking of US Companies Declines."

97. Inkster, *China's Cyber Power*, 134.

98. Kevin Pollpeter, "Chinese Writings on Cyberwarfare and Coercion," in *China
and Cybersecurity: Espionage, Strategy, and Politics in the Digital Domain*, ed.
Jon R. Lindsay et al. (New York: Oxford University Press, 2015), 147.

99. Inkster, "Chinese Intelligence in the Cyber Age," 54.

8 THE THEORY: STATE RESPONSIBILITY AND CYBER PROXIES

1. United Nations, "Report of the Group of Governmental Experts on Developments in the Field of Information and Telecommunications in the Context of International Security," June 24, 2013, UN Doc. A/68/98.
2. Email correspondence with Dirk Roland Haupt dated January 5, 2016.
3. "Co-Chairs' Summary Report" (ARF Workshop on Proxy Actors in Cyberspace, Hoi An City, March 14–15, 2012), www.mofa.go.jp/files/000016404.pdf.
4. Harold Hongju Koh, "International Law in Cyberspace" (USCYBERCOM Inter-Agency Legal Conference, Fort Meade, MD, September 18, 2012), www .state.gov/s/l/releases/remarks/197924.html.
5. I thank Duncan Hollis for this observation. It also implies that it excludes essentially all actors that fall under Mumford's definition of proxies as discussed in the previous section.
6. Some legal scholars have argued that states have the right to use force even against non-state actors carrying out an armed attack when the state where these non-state actors operate from is "unwilling or unable" to stop their activity. The US government's actions targeting the Islamic State in Syria seem to support this position, yet it remains highly controversial. This debate differs from previous debates about a state being "unwilling or unable" in the context of humanitarian interventions in that the objective of the interventions differs. See Ashley Deeks, "'Unwilling or Unable': Toward a Normative Framework for Extra-Territorial Self-Defense," *Virginia Journal of International Law* 52(3) (2012); Kevin Jon Heller, "The Absence of Practice Supporting the 'Unwilling or Unable' Test," Opinio Juris (blog), February 17, 2015, http://opiniojuris.org/2015/02/17/unable-unwilling-test-unstoppable-scho larly-imagination/; footnote 1 in Monica Hakimi, "Defensive Force Against Non-State Actors: The State of Play," *International Law Studies* 91 (2015), 2.
7. While this section draws heavily on international law, it is important to highlight that the various tests and logical distinctions originate in various bodies of international law and institutions. International lawyers have developed different, sometimes competing standards based on highly fact-dependent circumstances, ranging from the International Court of Justice (ICJ) to the International Criminal Tribunal for the former Yugoslavia (ICTY), and applying only under specific conditions. Table 8.1 focuses on the logical distinctions made in these various standards describing different degrees of separation between a state and the non-state actor. Table 8.1 therefore integrates the different bodies of law and combines them for the purpose of developing a comprehensive framework detailing the logical differentiations of a state's relationship with a non-state actor without regard for the legal consequences of different categorizations – e.g., the legal availability of countermeasures, etc. It is limited to scenarios where the state is aware of the proxy's activities.
8. J. Brierly, "The Theory of Implied State Complicity in International Claims," *British Yearbook of International Law* 9 (1928). Brierly prefers to call it the latter, and this article uses "condonation" for the non-punishment of an activity, while referring to "implied complicity" in case of non-prevention to maintain a logical distinction between the two omissions. Another relevant international law concept

in this context is denial of justice and "By what artifice might a state owe a duty to the world at large to maintain an adequate system for the administration of justice?" Jan Paulsson, *Denial of Justice in International Law* (New York: Cambridge University Press, 2005), 1; I thank Duncan Hollis for this addition; other relevant works on denial of justice include Alwyn Freeman, *The International Responsibility of States for Denial of Justice* (London/New York: Longmans, Green and Company, 1938), 758.

9. Jason Healey, "The Spectrum of National Responsibility for Cyber Attacks," *Brown Journal of World Affairs* 18(1) (2011).

10. References with * build on the following literature: UN International Law Commission, "Draft Articles on the Responsibility of States for Internationally Wrongful Acts, with commentaries," 2001, UN Doc. A/56/10; Michael Schmitt and Liis Vihul, "Proxy Wars in Cyber Space: The Evolving International Law of Attribution," *Fletcher Security Review* I(II) (2014). References with ** build on Daniel Byman, "Passive Sponsors of Terrorism," *Survival* 47(4) (2005); Byman illustrates this type of relationship in describing the US relationship regarding the IRA, Saudi Arabia's approach to Al Qaeda, and Pakistan's approach to Al Qaeda. References with *** are based on *Prosecutor v. Dusko Tadic (Appeal Judgement)*, IT-94-1-A, International Criminal Tribunal for the former Yugoslavia (ICTY), July 15, 1999.

11. *Military and Paramilitary Activities in and Against Nicaragua (Nicaragua v. US)* [1986] ICJ Rep 14.

12. J. Brierly, "The Theory of Implied State Complicity in International Claims," *British Yearbook of International Law* 9 (1928).

13. Derek Jinks, "State Responsibility for the Acts of Private Armed Groups," *Chicago Journal of International Law* 4(1) (2003).

14. For a discussion and recommendation on how to distinguish and use "adoption" vs. "endorsement" or "approval," see UN International Law Commission, "Draft Articles on the Responsibility of States for Internationally Wrongful Acts, with commentaries," 2001, UN Doc. A/56/10, art. 6.

15. Brierly, "The Theory of Implied State Complicity," 48–49.

16. It is noteworthy that linguistic challenges are not limited to the term "proxy." For example, article 17(7) of the *Draft Articles on the Responsibility of States for Internationally Wrongful Acts* mentions, "[t]he choice of the expression, common in English, 'direction and control', raised some problems in other languages, owing in particular to the ambiguity of the term 'direction' which may imply, as is the case in French, complete power, whereas it does not have this implication in English."

17. Michael Schmitt and Liis Vihul, "Proxy Wars in Cyber Space: The Evolving International Law of Attribution," *Fletcher Security Review* I(II) (2014): 71.

18. Byman, "Passive Sponsors of Terrorism," 140.

19. For a good illustration, see Derek Jinks on how the response to 9/11 expanded state responsibility to include "harboring," in Derek Jinks, "State Responsibility for the Acts of Private Armed Groups," *Chicago Journal of International Law* 4 (1) (2003).

20. Jason Healey, "The Spectrum of National Responsibility for Cyber Attacks," *Brown Journal of World Affairs* 18(1) (2011).

21. Khushbu Shah and Polo Sandoval, "Texas Inmate Who Didn't Kill Anyone Gets Stay of Execution," *CNN*, August 19, 2016, www.cnn.com/2016/08/19/us/texas-execution-jeff-wood/;Tex. Penal Code Ann. § 7, available at http://www.statutes.legis.state.tx.us/Docs/PE/html/PE.7.html.

22. Michael Schmitt, "In Defense of Due Diligence in Cyberspace," *Yale Law Journal Forum* 125 (2015); Duncan Hollis, "An e-SOS for Cyberspace," *Harvard International Law Journal* 52(2) (2011); Healey, "The Spectrum of National Responsibility for Cyber Attacks."

23. International Law Association Study Group on Due Diligence in International Law, "First Report," March 7, 2014, www.ila-hq.org/en/committees/study_groups.cfm/cid/1045.

24. SS *Lotus (France v Turkey)* 1927 PCIJ (Ser. A) No 10.

25. Schmitt, "In Defense of Due Diligence in Cyberspace," 72.

26. *Trail Smelter Arbitration* (United States *v.* Canada), Arbitrational Tribunal, March 11, 1941.

27. An interesting analogy to this issue is the discussion in the humanitarian community about the provision of humanitarian assistance and the 1991 UN General Assembly resolution 46/182 shifting the language from a state having to "request" such assistance to its being provided "with the consent of the affected country." See United Nations, "Strengthening of the coordination of humanitarian emergency assistance of the United Nations," December 19, 1991, UN Doc. A/RES/46/182.

28. Email correspondence with Dirk Roland Haupt dated January 5, 2016.

29. Michael N. Schmitt and Sean Watts, "Beyond State-Centrism: International Law and Non-state Actors in Cyberspace," *Journal of Conflict & Security Law* (published online, August 13, 2016): 8.

30. Marco Roscini, *Cyber Operations and the Use of Force in International Law* (New York: Oxford University Press, 2014), 87.

31. Nicole Perlroth, "The Chinese Hackers in the Back Office," *New York Times*, June 11, 2016, www.nytimes.com/2016/06/12/technology/the-chinese-hackers-in-the-back-office.html.

32. For US scholars in favor of due diligence, see Oren Gross, "Legal Obligations of States Directly Affected by Cyber-Incidents," *Cornell International Law Journal* 48 (2015); Schmitt, "In Defense of Due Diligence in Cyberspace."

33. Edwin M. Borchard, *The Diplomatic Protection of Citizens Abroad or the Law of International Claims* (New York: Banks Law Publishing Co., 1915): 217–218.

34. Healey, "The Spectrum of National Responsibility for Cyber Attacks."

35. Mark Clayton, "In Cyberarms Race, North Korea Emerging as a Power, not a Pushover," *Christian Science Monitor*, October 19, 2013, www.csmonitor.com/World/Security-Watch/2013/1019/In-cyberarms-race-North-Korea-emerging-as-a-power-not-a-pushover/.

36. Jordan Robertson, Dune Lawrence, and Chris Strohm, "Sony's Breach Stretched From Thai Hotel to Hollywood," *Bloomberg*, December 7, 2014,

www.bloomberg.com/news/articles/2014–12–07/sony-s-darkseoul-breach-stretched-from-thai-hotel-to-hollywood.

37. Daniel Schearf, "North Korea's 'World Class' Cyber Attacks Coming from China," *Voice of America*, November 21, 2013, www.voanews.com/a/north-kor eas-world-class-cyber-attacks-coming-from-china/1795349.html.

38. Jeff Goldman, "Swiss Bank Hacker Arrested in Thailand," e-Security Planet, May 8, 2014, www.esecurityplanet.com/hackers/swiss-bank-hacker-arrested-in-thailand.html.

39. "Lesotho Man Hacked Pattaya Hotel's Email to Defraud Foreigners: Police," *The Nation*, May 16, 2015, www.nationmultimedia.com/national/Lesotho-man-hacked-Pattaya-hotels-email-to-defraud-30260229.html.

40. "Vietnam Jails Russian Fraudsters for ATM Theft," Agence France Presse, September 2, 2016, www.taipeitimes.com/News/biz/archives/2016/09/02/2003654322.

41. "Police in Vietnam Arrested Chinese Credit Card Hacker for Stealing $4.9 Million," *Doy News*, July 17, 2015, www.doynews.com/article/police-vietnam-arrested-chinese-credit-card-hacker-stealing-49-million.

42. Jen Wheedon, Testimony before the US-China Economic and Security Review Commission, Hearing on Commercial Cyber Espionage and Barriers to Digital Trade in China, June 15, 2015, www.uscc.gov/sites/default/files/Weedon%20Testimony.pdf.

43. Roscini, *Cyber Operations and the Use of Force*, 214.

44. Derek Jinks, "State Responsibility for the Acts of Private Armed Groups," *Chicago Journal of International Law* 4 (2003).

45. Peter Singer, *Corporate Warriors: The Rise of the Privatized Military Industry* (Ithaca, NY: Cornell University Press, 2003), 31.

46. Graham Cluley, "Are DDoS (Distributed Denial-of-Service) Attacks Against the Law?", Naked Security, Sophos, December 9, 2010, https://nakedsecurity .sophos.com/2010/12/09/are-ddos-distributed-denial-of-service-attacks-against-the-law/.

47. Andrew Marszal, "Uzbek Receptionist at Luxury Thai Resort Accused by FBI of Aiding £22m Hack," The *Telegraph*, August 2, 2016, http://www.telegraph.co .uk/news/2016/08/02/uzbek-receptionist-at-luxury-thai-resort-accused-by-fbi-of-aidin/.

48. CrowdStrike, *CrowdStrike Global Threat Intel Report – 2014* (January 2015), 65.

49. "76 Chinese 'Hackers' Stole Sh1.5Bn, Says Embassy," *Nairobi News*, January 16, 2015, http://nairobinews.nation.co.ke/news/76-chinese-hackers-stole-sh1-5bn-says-embassy/.

50. "Taiwan Says Kenyan Police Used Tear Gas to Put Taiwanese on Plane to Mainland China," Reuters, April 12, 2016, http://af.reuters.com/article/topNews/idAFKCN0X90G1.

51. Cyrus Ombati, "77 Chinese Held Over Alleged Plot to Hack Communication Systems in the Country," *Standard Digital*, December 4, 2014, www.standard media.co.ke/article/2000143513/77-chinese-held-over-alleged-plot-to-hack-com munication-systems-in-the-country?pageNo=1.

52. Lily Kuo, "The Strange Case of 77 Blue-Collar Chinese Migrants That Kenya Is Calling 'Cyber-Hackers,'" *Quartz*, November 20, 2015, http://qz.com/530427/a-new-wave-chinese-immigrants-seeking-opportunity-in-africa-are-finding-misery-and-struggle-instead/.
53. www.amcharts.com/visited_countries/#AL,AT,BE,BA,BG,HR,CY,CZ,DK,EE, FI,FR,DE,GI,GR,HU,IS,IE,IM,IT,XK,LV,LI,LT,LU,MK,MT,MC,ME,NL, NO,PL,PT,RO,SM,RS,SK,SI,ES,SE,CH,TR,GB,AI,AG,BS,BB,BZ,BM,VG, CA,KY,CR,CU,DM,DO,SV,GD,GT,HT,HN,JM,MX,MS,NI,PA,KN,LC,VC, TT,TC,US,AR,BO,BR,CL,CO,EC,FK,GY,PY,PE,SR,UY,VE,EG,GM,GH, KE,LS,LR,MW,MU,NG,CG,SH,SC,SL,ZA,SZ,TZ,ZM,ZW,HK,IN,IQ,IL,JP, JO,MY,MM,PK,PH,SG,KR,LK,TH,AU,FJ,KI,NR,NZ,PG,SB,TO,TV.
54. www.amcharts.com/visited_countries/#AT,BE,BG,HR,CY,CZ,DK,EE,FI,FR, DE,GI,GR,HU,IE,IM,IT,LV,LI,LT,LU,MT,NL,PL,PT,RO,RU,SK,SI,ES, SE,CH,TR,UA,GB,AG,BS,BB,BZ,BM,VG,CA,DM,GD,JM,MX,PA,KN,LC, VC,TT,US,AR,BR,FK,UY,VE,EG,MA,NG,ZA,CN,HK,IN,IL,JP,MY,PH,KR, TH,AU.
55. For a similar view, see Oren Gross, "Legal Obligations of States Directly Affected by Cyber-Incidents," *Cornell International Law Journal* 48 (2015).
56. Schmitt, "In Defense of Due Diligence in Cyberspace," 78–79; for an interesting discussion of potential options for responses in the counterterrorism context, see Byman, "Passive Sponsors of Terrorism."

9 THE PRACTICE: SHAPING CYBER PROXY RELATIONSHIPS

1. Daniel Byman, "Passive Sponsors of Terrorism," *Survival* 47(4) (2005): 135.
2. For a related discussion, see Martha Finnemore and Duncan B. Hollis, "Constructing Norms for Global Cybersecurity," *American Journal of International Law* 110(3) (July 2016): 450–452.
3. G20 Leaders' Communiqué, Antalya Summit, November 15–16, 2015.
4. Department of State, *Report to Congress: Department of State International Cyberspace Policy Strategy* (Washington, DC. 2016), www.state.gov/documents/organization/255732.pdf.
5. Christopher Painter, "Beyond the Box Office: Real World Efforts to Raise Cyber Awareness and Capacity Worldwide," DipNote (blog), US Department of State, https://blogs.state.gov/stories/2016/10/31/beyond-box-office-real-world-efforts-raise-cyber-awareness-and-capacity-worldwide.
6. "WSIS and Building a Global Culture of Cybersecurity," International Telecommunication Union, www.itu.int/osg/csd/cybersecurity/WSIS/.
7. Caitríona Heinl, "Regional Cybersecurity: Moving Toward a Resilient ASEAN Cybersecurity Regime," *Asia Policy* 18 (2014): 151.
8. "Merkel's China Visit Marred by Hacking Allegations," *Der Spiegel*, August 27, 2007, www.spiegel.de/international/world/espionage-report-merkel-s-china-visit-marred-by-hacking-allegations-a-502169.html; Mark Landler, "Clinton Urges Global Response to Internet Attacks," *New York Times*, January 21, 2010, www.nytimes.com/2010/01/22/world/asia/22diplo.html; Siobhan Gorman, "U.S. Eyes

Pushback on China Hacking, *Wall Street Journal*, April 22, 2013, www.wsj
.com/articles/SB10001424127887324345804578424741315433114.

9. According to the cybersecurity expert Richard Bejtlich, "The United States Air
    Force coined the phrase advanced persistent threat in 2006 because teams
    working within the service needed a way to communicate with counterparts
    in the unclassified public world. . . APT refers to specific threat actors. . . The
    term is most frequently applied to distinct groups operating from the Asia-
    Pacific region." See Richard Bejtlich, "What APT Is (and What It Isn't),"
    Information Security (July/August 2010).

10. Adam Segal, *The Hacked World Order: How Nations Fight, Trade, Maneuver,
    and Manipulate in the Digital Age* (New York: PublicAffairs, 2016), 131–132.

11. Mandiant, *APT1: Exposing One of China's Cyber Espionage Units* (2013), www
    .fireeye.com/content/dam/fireeye-www/services/pdfs/mandiant-apt1-report.pdf,
    2–6.

12. Nigel Inkster, "Chinese Intelligence in the Cyber Age," *Survival* 55(1) (2013):
    59–60.

13. Alex S. Wilner, "Apocalypse Soon? Deterring Nuclear Iran and Its Terrorist
    Proxies," *Comparative Strategy* 31(1) (2012): 32.

14. Daniel Byman and Sarah Kreps, "Agents of Destruction? Applying Principal–
    Agent Analysis to State-Sponsored Terrorism," *International Studies
    Perspectives* 11(1) (2010): 2.

15. Ora Szekely, "A Friend in Need: The Impact of the Syrian Civil War on Syria's
    Clients (A Principal–Agent Approach)," *Foreign Policy Analysis* 12 (2016): 455.

16. Byman and Kreps, "Agents of Destruction?", 14.

17. For a comparable effort in the context of maritime piracy, see Justin V.
    Hastings, "Understanding Maritime Piracy Syndicate Operations," *Security
    Studies* 21(4) (2012): 712.

18. Byman and Kreps, "Agents of Destruction?", 14.

19. Gabriella Coleman, *Hacker, Hoaxer, Whistleblower, Spy: The Many Faces of
    Anonymous* (New York: Verso, 2014), 194, 303.

20. "AP: U.S. Military Launches Aggressive Cyberwar on ISIS," *CBS News*, February
    26, 2016, www.cbsnews.com/news/isis-targeted-us-military-cyberwar/.

21. Jonathan Lusthaus, "Trust in the World of Cyber Crime," *Global Crime* 13(2)
    (2012); Jonathan Lusthaus, "How Organised Is Organised Cyber Crime?",
    Global Crime 14(1) (2013).

22. Barack Obama, "Executive Order – Blocking the Property of Certain Persons
    Engaging in Significant Malicious Cyber-Enabled Activities," Office of the
    Press Secretary, the White House, April 1, 2015, www.whitehouse.gov/the-
    press-office/2015/04/01/executive-order-blocking-property-certain-persons-enga
    ging-significant-m.

23. Targeted Financial Sanctions Project at Brown University's Watson Institute for
    International Studies, "Background Paper on Targeted Sanctions," prepared at
    Workshop on United Nations Sanctions July 16–17, 2004, www
    .watsoninstitute.org/pub/Background_Paper_Targeted_Sanctions.pdf.

24. Robin Wauters, "China Blocks Access to Twitter, Facebook After Riots," *TechCrunch*, July 7, 2009, https://techcrunch.com/2009/07/07/china-blocks-access-to-twitter-facebook-after-riots/.

25. "U.S. Charges Five Chinese Military Hackers for Cyber Espionage Against U.S. Corporations and a Labor Organization for Commercial Advantage," Department of Justice press release (May 19, 2015), www.justice.gov/opa/pr/us-charges-five-chinese-military-hackers-cyber-espionage-against-us-corporations-and-labor.

26. In addition, some limitations imposed by domestic law that prevent a state from taking actions cannot be reasonably expected to change, such as laws to protect minors (which might come into play in the case of a juvenile hacker) or the freedom of speech protections in the United States (which came into play in the context of the IRA sympathizers in the United States. See Byman, "Passive Sponsors of Terrorism," 131).

27. In-person conversation with Arvid Bell in Washington, DC, on November 17, 2016.

28. Kate Manuel, *Definitions of "Inherently Governmental Function" in Federal Procurement Law and Guidance* (Washington, DC: Congressional Research Service, 2014); see also, L. Elaine Halchin, *The Intelligence Community and Its Use of Contractors: Congressional Oversight Issues* (Washington, DC: Congressional Research Service, 2015).

29. Dennis Broeders, *Investigating the Place and Role of the Armed Forces in Dutch Cyber Security Governance* (prepared for the Netherlands Defence Academy, Faculty of Military Sciences NLD MoD, Task Force Cyber) (Erasmus Universiteit Rotterdam, 2015), 42.

30. During the Obama administration, the US government distinguished between three categories of function that are subject to review in contracting decsions: (1) inherently governmental functions, (2) closely associated functions, and (3) critical functions. This third category was created in 2009 following growing concerns such as those by the Senate Select Committee on Intelligence that contractors were "improperly performing inherently governmental functions" in the wake of the wars in Afghanistan and Iraq and the explosion of the market for private security companies. Creating an additional category introduced an additional hurdle to outsourcing within the governmental bureaucracy. The memorandum was implemented in the context of military operations through the Pentagon's instruction DoDI 1100.22, published in April 2010. It also increased the bureaucratic hurdles to prevent contractors from encroaching on the state's monopoly on the legitimate use of force. The instruction highlighted that "risk mitigation shall take precedence over cost savings," and that if inherently governmental and commercial tasks cannot be distinguished, the inherently governmental classification applies. Office of Management and Budget Office of Federal Procurement Policy, "Publication of the Office of Federal Procurement Policy (OFPP) Policy Letter 11–01, Performance of Inherently Governmental and Critical Functions," *Federal* Register 76, no. 176

(September 12, 2011): 56227–56228; Halchin, *The Intelligence Community and Its Use of Contractors*, 4–5; Department of Defense, "Department of Defense Instruction 1100.22 (Policy and Procedures for Determining Workforce Mix)," April 12, 2010, 2, 14.

31. Department of Defense, "Department of Defense Instruction 1100, 19.
32. Oona Hathaway and Rebecca Crootof, "The Law of Cyber-Attack," *California Law Review* 100 (2012): 853.
33. James R. Lisher II, "Outsourcing Cyberwarfare: Drawing the Line for Inherently Governmental Functions in Cyberspace," *Journal of Contract Management* (Summer 2014): 7.
34. Ibid., 9, 17.
35. Ibid., 15.
36. Core contract personnel "are those independent contractors or individuals employed by industrial contractors who augment USG [U.S. government] civilian and military personnel by providing direct technical, managerial, or administrative support to IC elements." They are barred from engaging in inherently governmental activities. See Halchin, *The Intelligence Community and Its Use of Contractors*, 10, 15, 21.
37. Juan C. Zarate, *The Cyber Financial Wars on the Horizon: The Convergence of Financial and Cyber Warfare and the Need for a 21st Century National Security Response* (Washington, DC: FDD Press, 2015), 3.
38. "Black Hat Survey: 36% of Information Security Professionals Have Engaged in Retaliatory Hacking," *Business Wire*, July 26, 2012, www.businesswire.com/news/home/20120726006045/en/Black-Hat-Survey-36-Information-Security-Professionals.
39. Michael Riley and Jordan Robertson, "FBI Probes If Banks Hacked Back As Firms Mull Offensives," *Bloomberg*, December 30, 2014, www.bloomberg.com/news/articles/2014–12-30/fbi-probes-if-banks-hacked-back-as-firms-mull-offensives.
40. Ibid.
41. Shane Harris, *@War: The Rise of the Military-Internet Complex* (New York: Eamon Dolan/Mariner Books, 2014), 119–120.
42. Dawn Chmielewski and Arik Hesseldahl, "Sony Pictures Tries to Disrupt Downloads of Its Stolen Files," *re/code*, December 10, 2104, https://web.archive.org/web/20150102045015/http://recode.net/2014/12/10/sony-pictures-tries-to-disrupt-downloads-of-its-stolen-files/; Charlie Osborne and Zack Whittaker, "Amazon Denies Sony Used AWS for Denial-of-Service Counter-Attack," *ZDNet*, December 11, 2014, http://www.zdnet.com/article/amazon-denies-sony-counterattack/.
43. Riley and Robertson, "FBI Probes If Banks Hacked Back."
44. Matthew Goldstein, "Private Eye May Face Court Over Hacking," DealBook (blog), *New York Times*, February 12, 2015, https://dealbook.nytimes.com/2015/02/12/inquiry-into-hacking-delves-into-private-investigators/.
45. Department of Justice, *Prosecuting Computer Crime* (Columbia, SC: Office of Legal Education, 2015), 180.

46. Riley and Robertson, "FBI Probes If Banks Hacked Back."

47. Ibid.

48. Broeders, *Investigating the Place and Role of the Armed Forces*, 42–43.

49. Andrew Nusca, "Hayden: 'Digital Blackwater' May Be Necessary for Private Sector to Fight Cyber Threats," *ZDNet*, August 1, 2011, www.zdnet.com/blog/btl/hayden-digital-blackwater-may-be-necessary-for-private-sector-to-fight-cyber-threats/53639.

50. Nigel Inkster, *China's Cyber Power* (New York: Routledge, 2016), 34.

51. Barry Posen, "Nationalism, the Mass Army, and Military Power," *International Security* 18(2) (1993), 83.

52. Declan McCullagh to Politech mailing list, "FBI's NIPC on 'Cyber Protests' and Political Hacking," October 30, 2001, www.politechbot.com/p-02727.html.

53. Scott Henderson, "Beijing's Rising Hacker Stars . . . How Does Mother China React?", *IO Sphere* (Fall 2008): 29–30.

54. Scott J. Henderson, *The Dark Visitor: Inside the World of Chinese Hackers* (Fort Leavenworth, KS: Foreign Military Studies Office, 2007), 118.

55. Department of Homeland Security, "Encourages Heightened Cyber Security as Iraq-U.S. Tensions Increase," Advisory 03–002, February 11, 2003.

56. Cory Bennett, "Did the US Take Down North Korea's Internet?", *The Hill*, December 23, 2014, http://thehill.com/policy/cybersecurity/227944-was-the-us-behind-north-koreas-internet-outage.

57. Michael T. Klare, "Subterranean Alliances: America's Global Proxy Network," *Journal of International Affairs* 43(1) (1989): 103.

58. Herman J. Cohen, "US-Africa Policy as Conflict Management," *SAIS Review* 21.1 (2001): 242.

59. McCullagh, "FBI's NIPC on 'Cyber Protests'."

60. Andrei Soldatov and Irina Borogan, *The Red Web: The Struggle Between Russia's Digital Dictators and the New Online Revolutionaries* (New York: PublicAffairs, 2015), 151.

10 CONCLUSION: CYBER PROXIES, THE FUTURE, AND SUGGESTIONS FOR FURTHER RESEARCH

1. John Lewis Gaddis, *The Long Peace: Inquiries into the History of the Cold War* (New York: Oxford University Press, 1989); Nils Petter Gleditsch, "The Liberal Moment Fifteen Years On," *International Studies Quarterly* 52(4) (2008); Kalevi J. Holsti, "The Horsemen of the Apocalypse: At the Gate, Detoured, or Retreating?", *International Studies Quarterly* 30(4) (1986); Robert Jervis, "The Political Effects of Nuclear Weapons: A Comment," *International Security* 13(2) (1988); Steven Pinker, *The Better Angels of Our Nature: Why Violence Has Declined* (New York: Viking, 2011). However, there has been an uptick in an increasing number of internationalized armed conflicts at the beginning of the twenty-first century compared to the decade after the end of the Cold War. Thérése Pettersson and Peter Wallensteen, "Armed Conflicts, 1946–2014," *Journal of Peace Research* 52(4) (2015); Eric Melander, "Organized Violence in

the World 2015: An Assessment by the Uppsala Conflict Data Program," UCDP Paper number 9, http://www.pcr.uu.se/digitalAssets/61/c_61335-l_1-k_ucdp-paper-9.pdf.

2. Marcus Weisgerber, "The Price of an F-35 Was Already Falling. Can Trump Drive it Lower?" *Defense One*, January 27, 2017, www.defenseone.com/busi ness/2017/01/f-35s-price-has-been-falling-can-trump-lower-it-even-more/134919/.

3. Tim Maurer and Robert Morgus, "'Cybersecurity' and Why Definitions Are Risky," CSS Blog Network, ETH Zurich Center for Security Studies, November 10, 2014, http://isnblog.ethz.ch/intelligence/cybersecurity-and-the-problem-of-definitions.

4. Letter dated 12 September 2011 from the Permanent Representatives of China, the Russian Federation, Tajikistan, and Uzbekistan to the United Nations addressed to the Secretary-General, UN Doc. A/66/359, https://ccdcoe.org/sites/default/files/documents/UN-110912-CodeOfConduct_0.pdf.

5. Erica D. Borghard and Shawn W. Lonergan, "Can States Calculate the Risks of Using Cyber Proxies?", *Orbis* 60(3) (2016).

6. Kenneth W. Abbott et al., eds., *International Organizations as Orchestrators* (New York: Cambridge University Press, 2015).

7. Ariel Ahram, *Proxy Warriors: The Rise and Fall of State-Sponsored Militias* (Stanford University Press, 2011).

8. I traveled to Be'er Sheva on June 25, 2015, together with a group of journalists, as part of a visit organized by the Israeli government.

9. Gill Cohen, "Intel Units Due to Start Moving to Southern Israel in 2022," *Haaretz*, August 18, 2016, www.haaretz.com/israel-news/1.737583.

10. Presentation by Rivka Carmi in Be'er Sheva on June 25, 2015.

11. Daniel Byman, "Passive Sponsors of Terrorism," *Survival* 47(4) (2005): 136–139.

12. Timothy Thomas, "Chapter Eleven: Comparing Chinese and Russian Cyber Concepts," in *Three Faces of the Cyber Dragon: Cyber Peace Activist, Spook, Attacker*, by Timothy Thomas (Fort Leavenworth, KS: Foreign Military Studies Office, 2012).

13. Thomas Schelling, *Arms and Influence* (New Haven, CT: Yale University Press, 2008), 260–263.

14. Ibid.

15. Ibid., 66–67.

16. Jan Kallberg and Steven Rowlen, "African Nations as Proxies in Covert Cyber Operations," *African Security Review* 23(3) (2014): 308.

17. "Kenya Breaks 'Chinese-Run Cyber Crime Network,'" *BBC News*, December 4, 2014, www.bbc.com/news/world-africa-30327412.

18. James A. Lewis, "Report of the International Security Cyber Issues Workshop Series," report prepared for the United Nations Institute for Disarmament Research, International Security Cyber Issues Workshop Series "Managing the Spread of Cyber Tools for Malicious Purposes," Geneva, Switzerland, June 15–16, 2016, www.unidir.org/files/publications/pdfs/report-of-the-international-security-cyber-issues-workshop-series-en-656.pdf, 6.

19. Joe Uchill, "Israel Cyber Head: US-Backed Cyber Norms Too Broad," *The Hill*, September 13, 2016, http://thehill.com/policy/cybersecurity/295651-israel-cyber-head-us-supported-cyber-norms-too-broad.

FUTURE RESEARCH

1. Idean Salehyan, "The Delegation of War to Rebel Organizations," *Journal of Conflict Resolution* 54 (2010): 508–509.
2. Daniel Byman and Sarah Kreps, "Agents of Destruction? Applying Principal–Agent Analysis to State-Sponsored Terrorism," *International Studies Perspectives* 11(1) (2010): 14.
3. Robert Axelrod and Rumen Iliev, "Timing of Cyber Conflict," *PNAS* 111(4): 1302.
4. Joji Thomas Philip and Harsimran Singh, "Spy Game: India Readies Cyber Army to Hack into Hostile Nations' Computer Systems," *Economic Times*, August 6, 2010, http://economictimes.indiatimes.com/et-cetera/spy-game-india-readies-cyber-army-to-hack-into-hostile-nations-computer-systems/articleshow/6258977.cms; cf. "Desi Hackers Join Indian Cyber Army!", *Times of India*, August 5, 2010, http://timesofindia.indiatimes.com/tech/jobs/Desi-hackers-join-Indian-cyber-army/articleshow/6260494.cms; see also "India Recruiting Hackers for Elite Cyber Offensive," TechEye, August 6, 2010, www.techeye.net/security/india-recruiting-hackers-for-elite-cyber-offensive.
5. Adam Segal, "The Rise of Asia's Cyber Militias," *The Atlantic*, February 23, 2012, www.theatlantic.com/international/archive/2012/02/the-rise-of-asias-cyber-militias/253487/.
6. In-person interview with Pavan Duggal in New Delhi, India, on October 19, 2015.
7. Surabhi Agarwal, "Cyber Emergency: Teach, Train and Employ Half a Million Ethical Hackers," *Business Standard*, March 6, 2014, www.business-standard.com/article/companies/cyber-emergency-teach-train-and-employ-half-a-million-ethical-hackers-114030501258_1.html.
8. Juan C. Zarate, *The Cyber Financial Wars on the Horizon: The Convergence of Financial and Cyber Warfare and the Need for a 21st Century National Security Response* (Washington, DC: FDD Press, 2015), 6.
9. "The Montreux Document," Federal Department of Foreign Affairs, www.eda.admin.ch/eda/en/fdfa/foreign-policy/international-law/international-humanitarian-law/private-military-security-companies/montreux-document.html.
10. N.R. Kleinfeld and Somini Sengupta, "Hacker, Informant and Party Boy of the Projects," *New York Times*, March 8, 2012, www.nytimes.com/2012/03/09/technology/hacker-informant-and-party-boy-of-the-projects.html.
11. Government's notice of intent to move pursuant to section 5k1.1(A)(1)-(5) of the sentencing guidelines and pursuant to Title 18, United States Code, Section 3553(e) at 11, *United States* v. *Monsegur*, No. 11 Cr. 666 (LAP) (S.D.N.Y. filed August 5, 2011).

12. According to a statement by the hacker Jeremy Hammond during his sentencing hearing in November 2014, "After Stratfor, I continued to break into other targets, using a powerful 'zero day exploit' allowing me administrator access to systems... Sabu continued to supply me with lists of vulnerable targets. I broke into numerous websites he supplied, uploaded the stolen email accounts and databases onto Sabu's FBI server, and handed over passwords and backdoors that enabled Sabu (and, by extension, his FBI handlers) to control these targets. These intrusions, all of which were suggested by Sabu while cooperating with the FBI, affected thousands of domain names and consisted largely of foreign government websites, including Brazil, Turkey, Syria." He added that "[a]ll of this happened under the control and supervision of the FBI and can be easily confirmed by chat logs the government provided to use pursuant to the government's discovery obligations in the case against me." See Gabriella Coleman, *Hacker, Hoaxer, Whistleblower, Spy: The Many Faces of Anonymous* (New York: Verso, 2014), 358–359; Mark Mazzetti, "F.B.I. Informant Is Tied to Cyberattacks Abroad," *New York Times*, April 23, 2014, www.nytimes.com/2014/04/24/world/fbi-informant-is-tied-to-cyberattacks-abroad.html; Benjamin Weiser and Mark Mazzetti, "Hacker Helped Disrupt 300 Web Attacks, Prosecutors Say," *New York Times*, May 24, 2014, www.nytimes.com/2014/05/25/nyregion/hacker-helped-disrupt-attacks-prosecutors-say.html; "FBI Informant Led Cyber Attacks on Turkey Govt," *Sky News*, August 11, 2014.http://news.sky.com/story/1316635/fbi-informant-led-cyber-attacks-on-turkey-govt.
13. Nazli Choucri, *Cyberpolitics in International Relations* (Cambridge, MA: MIT Press, 2012), 14.
14. Samuel Issacharoff and Richard H. Pildes, "Targeted Warfare: Individuating Enemy Responsibility," *New York University Law Review* 88(5) (2013): 2.
15. Togzhan Kassenova, "Implementing Nonproliferation Programs: The Cooperative Threat Reduction Process in the Former Soviet Union," in *International Cooperation on WMD Nonproliferation*, ed. Jeffrey W. Knopf (Athens, GA: University of Georgia Press, 2016), 88.
16. Ibid.
17. In-person research interview in Kiev, Ukraine, on July 24, 2015.
18. CrowdStrike, *CrowdStrike Global Threat Report – 2013 Year in Review* (January 2014), 29.
19. F-Secure, *The Convergence of Crimeware and APT Attacks* (2014), www.f-secure.com/documents/996508/1030745/blackenergy_whitepaper.pdf, 11; Trey Herr, *PrEP: A Framework for Malware and Cyber Weapons* (Washington, DC: George Washington University Cyber Security Policy and Research Institute, 2014); see also Trey Herr and Ryan Ellis, "Disrupting Malware Markets," in *Cyber Insecurity: Navigating the Perils of the Next Information Age*, ed. Richard Harrison and Trey Herr (Lanham, MD: Rowman & Littlefield, 2016), 105–121.
20. F-Secure, *The Convergence of Crimeware and APT* Ibid., 2.
21. Ibid.

22. Andrey Nikishin, "ICS Threats. A Kaspersky Lab View, Predictions and Reality," presentation at RSA Conference, Moscone Center, San Francisco, CA, February 29 – March 4, 2016.

23. Idan Aharoni, "SCADA Systems Offered for Sale in the Underground Economy," *Infosec Island*, June 22, 2015, www.infosecisland.com/blogview/24608-SCADA-Systems-Offered-for-Sale-in-the-Underground-Economy.html.

24. John Leyden, "Water Treatment Plant Hacked, Chemical Mix Changed for Tap Supplies," *The Register*, March 24, 2016, www.theregister.co.uk/2016/03/24/water_utility_hacked/.

25. Aliya Sternstein, "The Pentagon Wants to 'Fingerprint' the World's Hackers," *Defense One*, May 4, 2016, www.defenseone.com/technology/2016/05/pentagon-wants-fingerprint-worlds-hackers/128024/.

26. Scott Charney et al., *From Articulation to Implementation: Enabling Progress on Cybersecurity Norms* (Microsoft, June 2016), https://mscorpmedia.azureedge.net/mscorpmedia/2016/06/Microsoft-Cybersecurity-Norms_vFinal.pdf.

27. Nicole Perlroth, "Intelligence Start-Up Goes Behind Enemy Lines to Get Ahead of Hackers," *New York Times*, September 13, 2015, www.nytimes.com/2015/09/14/technology/intelligence-start-up-goes-behind-enemy-lines-to-get-ahead-of-hackers.html.

28. "Sepulveda, Daniel Alejandro," Biographies, Bureau of Public Affairs, US Department of State, www.state.gov/r/pa/ei/biog/bureau/209063.html.

29. Jordan Robertson, Michael Riley, and Andrew Willis, "How to Hack an Election," *Bloomberg Businessweek*, March 31, 2016, www.bloomberg.com/features/2016-how-to-hack-an-election/.

30. David P. Fidler, *Overview of International Legal Issues and Cyber Terrorism* (Bloomington, IN: International Law Association Study Group on Cybersecurity, Terrorism, and International Law, 2015); Maura Conway, "What Is Cyberterrorism?" *Current History* 101(659) (2002): 436–342.

31. P. W. Singer and Allan Friedman, *Cybersecurity and Cyberwar: What Everyone Needs to Know* (New York: Oxford University Press, 2014), 96–97.

32. Alex Kingsbury, "Documents Reveal Al Qaeda Cyberattacks," *U.S. News*, April 14, 2010, www.usnews.com/news/articles/2010/04/14/documents-reveal-al-qaeda-cyberattacks.

33. Jose Pagliery, "ISIS Is Attacking the U.S. Energy Grid (and Failing)," *CNN*, October 16, 2015, http://money.cnn.com/2015/10/15/technology/isis-energy-grid/.

34. "ISIL-Linked Hacker Arrested in Malaysia on U.S. Charges," Department of Justice press release (October 15, 2015), www.justice.gov/opa/pr/isil-linked-hacker-arrested-malaysia-us-charges.

35. According to the US Department of Justice, Ferizi, who used the pseudonym "Th3 Dir3ctorY," was the leader of the Kosova Hacker's Security hacktivist group, which participated in operations by Anonymous. Ellen Nakashima, "U.S. Accuses Hacker of Stealing Military Members' Data and Giving It to ISIS," *Washington Post*, October 16, 2015, www.washingtonpost.com/world/

national-security/in-a-first-us-charges-a-suspect-with-terrorism-and-hacking/ 2015/10/15/463447a8-738b-11e5-8248-98e0f5a2e830_story.html; "ISIL-Linked Hacker Arrested in Malaysia on U.S. Charges," Department of Justice press release (October 15, 2015), www.justice.gov/opa/pr/isil-linked-hacker-arrested-malaysia-us-charges; Jay Turla, "Getting to Know Kosova Hacker's Security Crew plus an Exclusive Interview with Th3 Dir3ctorY," InfoSec Institute, June 11, 2013, http://resources.infosecinstitute.com/getting-to-know-kosova-hackers-security-crew-plus-an-exclusive-interview-with-th3-dir3ctory/.

36. Margaret Coker, Danny Yadron, and Damian Paletta, "Hacker Killed by Drone Was Islamic State's 'Secret Weapon,'" *Wall Street Journal*, August 27, 2015, www.wsj.com/articles/hacker-killed-by-drone-was-secret-weapon-1440718560; Lorenzo Franceschi-Bicchierai, "How a Teenage Hacker Became the Target of a US Drone Strike," Motherboard, *Vice*, August 28, 2015, http://motherboard.vice.com/read/junaid-hussain-isis-hacker-drone.

Index

Abbott, Kenneth 45
Abu Nidal Organization 141
aircraft
　Airbus crash in Spain 9
　avionics, remote access to 9
　MH17, downing of 44
Al Qaeda 132
　"franchises" 34
　support for 47–8
Alabama Claims Arbitration (1872) 130
Anonymous (hacktivist group) x, xv, 17, 58, 89, 141
ASEAN (Association of South-East Asian Nations) 124, 139
Assad, Bashar al-, President 89, 90, 92
attribution problem 22–5, 129
　attributing actions of a proxy to a state, challenge of 22–3, 24–5
　attributing responsibility for malicious actions, difficulty of 16, 22–3
　attribution capabilities, improvement in 23
　concealing identity or activity 25
　false flag operations, effects of 23–4
　increased commoditization, difficulties caused by 23
　and Internet's technical characteristics 39–40
　states' asymmetric capabilities 24
　time required for attribution 23, 24

backdoors 13
"BadB" (Vladislav Horohorin) 25, 102, 152
Baxley nuclear plant 30
beneficiaries
　ability to mobilize or stop a proxy 36, 41–2
　beneficiary's benefit 36, 38–41
　　casualties, desire to avoid 39
　　direct conflict, desire to avoid 39
　　hacktivists, preventing 40
　　keeping actors focused on foreign targets 41

　need for capabilities 38–9
　plausible deniability, enabling 39–40
　shortage of skilled labour 38–9
　proxy relationships 31–2
　changes in nature of beneficiary-proxy relationship 35–6
　main types of see delegation; orchestration; sanctioning
Bobbit, Philip 40, 154
Booz Allen Hamilton 77, 78
Borogan, Irina 59–60
Brierly, J. L. 129
Browns Ferry nuclear plant 30

CACI 74, 77
CarderPlanet 41, 102
Carlin, John 90, 92
Carnegie Endowment for International Peace 159
cars, hacking into 9, 10
Charter of the United Nations 3
China 3, 6
　Academy of Military Sciences 108
　Baidu search engine, attack on 82
　China Institute for Contemporary International Relations 18
　China Institute for International Studies 14, 82
　content as information security threat 6
　cyber proxies, changing relationships with 43, 107–19
　creation of militia units/move towards orchestration 112–15
　external and internal dimensions of cybersecurity 107–8
　hacktivists' rise/government's passive support for 108–12
　links between state and private, blurred nature of 107–8
　military, role of 108

Made in the USA
Monee, IL
13 January 2020